# Hollywood Lights
# Nashville Nights

"The *Hee Haw* Honeys were the best; they always stole the show."

– Jett Williams
Daughter of country music legend Hank Williams
Grammy Nominee
Author of *Ain't Nothin' as Sweet as My Baby*

"When I was a little girl, my dream was to grow up to be a *Hee Haw* Honey."

– Georgette Jones
Recording Artist
Daughter of country music legends Tammy Wynette
and George Jones
Author of *The Three of Us: Life with George and Tammy*

"*Hee Haw* and the Grand Ole Opry shared a building, so I'd be over there all the time just hanging with the *Hee Haw* gang and my old friend Buck. I always wanted to look like the *Hee Haw* girls."

– Jan Howard
*Grand Ole Opry* Star
Author of *Sunshine and Shadow*

"You think Dean Martin had some good-looking gals – those Goldiggers on his TV show? Let me tell you, the *Hee Haw* Girls were the best – ever!"

– T.G. Sheppard
Recording Artist

"*Hee Haw's* got a wonderful place in my heart. I started watching it when I was a kid and fell in love with the *Hee Haw* Girls. So, when I grew up and actually got to be on the show, well that was very, very, *very* cool."

– T. Graham Brown
Recording Artist

Victoria Hallman
& Diana Goodman
as told to Victoria Hallman

# Hollywood Lights Nashville Nights

## Two Hee Haw Honeys Dish Life, Love, Elvis, Buck & Good Times in the Kornfield

BearManor Media

2018

*Hollywood Lights, Nashville Nights: Two* Hee Haw *Honeys Dish Life, Love, Elvis, Buck, and Good Times In the Kornfield*

© 2018 Victoria Hallman and Diana Goodman

Events, locales and conversations in this book were recreated from the co-authors' personal memories. Some names and details have been changed to protect the privacy of individuals. This book was written by co-author Victoria Hallman in its entirety, including Part I Diana and Part III Diana, which were written by Victoria Hallman, based on recorded interviews with co-author Diana Goodman. Uncredited photographs were provided by the co-authors from their personal collections.

Photo editing: Kohlphoto

Cover photos: Victoria Hallman and Buck Owens, courtesy of Becky Scott

Elvis Presley and Diana Goodman, © Ron Galella/Ron Galella, Ltd.

For information, address:

BearManor Media
P. O. Box 71426
Albany, GA 31708

bearmanormedia.com

Typesetting and layoutby John Teehan

Published in the USA by BearManor Media

ISBN — 978-1-62933-331-1

*Thanks to Bruce Phillips, Esq.*

# Part I
# Diana

Diana Goodman (1970s)

Joe Esposito, Elvis Presley, Diana Goodman Elvis Tour (1975).
© Ron Galella/Ron Galella, Ltd.

# Chapter 1

DIANA
*Summer 1975*

**I'M THE ONLY PERSON** I know who could start out for the mall and wind up in Elvis Presley's living room. I had never paid enough attention to Elvis to even know he lived in Memphis, and I sure had no thought of wasting my afternoon sweating in the hot sun with a bunch of tourists, but the cab driver insisted I could not leave town without seeing Graceland, so there I was standing in the broiling heat, my brand-new denim mini-dress sticking to my thighs.

Ten minutes was as much of that fun as I could stand. I had just about decided to hunt down that cab driver, when a little old man appeared from a booth on the other side of the gates, waving his arms at me. *What now?* I walked over and stood across from him. "Hi."

He pressed his nose to the fence. "Would you like to come inside?"

"Oh, is Elvis home?"

"Shh!" His eyes shot to the tourists. "No, Elvis is not home."

Somehow that didn't strike me right. It didn't seem good manners to visit a person's house if they weren't home, but a golf cart was already pulling up, and just like that, a guy with a brown mustache hopped out to help me onto the passenger seat, and away we went, breezing up the driveway.

The golf cart chauffeur introduced himself as Dave, one of Elvis's bodyguards, and I told him I was Miss Georgia, visiting Memphis on a PR trip for the pageant. After that, I didn't hear much of what he said, because my mind was occupied trying to figure out why I'd be invited to Elvis's house if Elvis wasn't home. I suspected the old man had lied to me about that. No problem. Right about then, Dave almost drove us into a flowerbed, trying to steer while looking at my sweat-slick thighs. He'd tell me anything I wanted to know.

Dave gave me the same story as that lying little old man.

They must have thought I was stupid or something. If Elvis wasn't home, why were all these Cadillacs parked in front? I was at least smart enough to figure out that whoever could afford that many expensive cars was probably the same person who could afford such an expensive house. I'm not sure what kind of place I expected Elvis Presley to have, but this old-south white-columned mansion wasn't it. My only experience of Elvis had been the time my aunt took me to a drive-in to see *Blue Hawaii*, so maybe I thought he'd live in something Polynesian. And wouldn't you expect somebody like Elvis to keep his doors locked? Guess not. We walked in as pretty as you please.

Now this was more like it. Everybody's always saying how tacky Graceland is, but I thought all that red velvet and shag carpet was pretty cool.

Dave said I could wait in the jungle room. I had no idea what a jungle room might be, so what a surprise when I saw it was Polynesian, *Blue Hawaii,* exactly as I'd imagined. And would you look at that? A cascade of water was spilling down a rock wall, just like in the movie. There was even a real, live, parrot in a cage. My aunt would have a fit when she heard.

Dave instructed me to sit on the couch until he got back, so I was sitting there looking at all the exotic plants and fake animal skins, listening to the bird squawk, when out of nowhere, a little girl came tearing in on a Big-Wheel, blonde hair flying, knocking into that expensive tiki furniture like she was playing bumper cars. My mama would have torn me up.

Thinking of my sweet mama, I remembered the gossip that went around when Elvis married his girlfriend. Everybody said he had to marry her because she was pregnant. Come to think of it, hadn't I heard he was recently separated? Hey, wait a minute, if his wife didn't live here anymore, who was that little girl visiting? Daddy, of course. Elvis was in this house.

Graceland has a lot of rooms, and men kept coming and going, checking me out. I'd be able to sweet-talk at least one of them into telling me the truth.

Wrong again, Diana.

Okay, if that was how they wanted to play, I'd just have to take a look around and see for myself. As soon as the little girl big-wheeled out of the room, I got up from the sofa and twisted my head in every direction. A buttery smell was coming from back *there*. Maybe Elvis was the kind to hang out in the kitchen. I followed my nose and peeped in.

It was a homey room with wooden cabinets, a harvest-gold refrigerator, and Tiffany-style light fixtures. Beside the sink lay a bunch of bananas. Suddenly I recognized the buttery smell. Somebody had just fried a banana sandwich. Somebody like one of those three women standing in a huddle around a cookbook.

One of the women looked up and smiled. "Come on in, dahlin.'"

Glory hallelujah! In the Deep South of those days, you could lay money that black ladies of a certain age were pillars of their church. I had stumbled into the only three people at Graceland I could absolutely count on to tell me the truth.

At least they didn't lie to me. When I asked Elvis's whereabouts, they simply folded their arms, poked out their lips, and went deaf and dumb. No doubt the Holy Spirit would restore their power of speech as soon as I was out of earshot, so I left with a "Nice to meet y'all" and eased on down the hallway, stopping at every corner to look and listen before taking a giant step across. One hallway after another, I poked my head into this room and that, until finally I wound up back in the foyer, and crept to the curving staircase, looking up. The stairs ended at a closed door.

For longer than was safe, I stood staring up at that door, gathering my nerve and straining my ears for the sound of footsteps. Then when I was sure nobody was near, I shot one last glance left-right, and set the toe of my sandal on the first riser.

A deep voice behind me said, "What are you doing?"

*Where in the name of good grief did he come from?* I pasted on my pageant-winning smile and turned to face him. "Thinking I might like to see the second floor."

Dave, the bodyguard, shook his head. "Elvis is taking a nap up there."

"Okeydokey." I escaped to my designated spot on the couch in the jungle room and collapsed. My legs were shaking like a shimmy dancer, and I needed time alone to hatch a plan. I may not have made it up those stairs yet, but I had moved way ahead in this game. Not only did I now know that Elvis was in the house, I knew his exact location and exactly what he was doing. That was a lot of knowing for somebody who, less than an hour before, didn't even know she was in the same city as Elvis. Now he was lying in bed one floor above me.

An image of a sleeping Elvis popped into my head. Would he have on PJs, or did he nap in the nude? Uh-oh, the sleeping Elvis in my head was now a naked sleeping Elvis. What if I snuck into his bedroom and slipped under the covers? *Diana!* Now the picture in my mind was a naked Diana rubbing her bare skin against naked sleeping Elvis. *Your skin won't be fit to rub after your mama tans your hide.* What would happen if they caught me sneaking up those stairs? Surely a girl couldn't get arrested for accidentally wandering into a man's bedroom. Unless there was some kind of special law about Elvis. I'd lose the Miss Georgia crown if I got arrested, but who'd be worrying about any old rhinestone tiara while she was lying naked next to Elvis Presley? *What are you thinking, girl?* Thinking I'll hide someplace, watch until nobody's around, and then –

Dave walked in. "Want to go get some coffee? We need to drop you at your hotel."

I didn't like coffee, but I'd learn to like it for another shot at that staircase.

*　*　*

Cream to the brim and four packs of sugar turned the bitter black stuff into something I could sip. The longer I kept Dave sitting in that pie-shop chair across the table from me, the better my chances for getting back to Graceland. So, I was sipping coffee and fantasizing what lay beyond that staircase door to Elvis's bedroom, when I heard, "Elvis wants to know if you'd like to go to a movie with him tomorrow night."

No telling how long it took me to realize Dave was waiting for an answer. I jerked the plastic water glass to my mouth and threw my head back, draining it till crushed ice fell on my nose. "Ahem." I brushed at my nose and cleared my throat. "You mean – did you say, 'with Elvis'?"

Dave nodded. "Yeah. Not that I wouldn't want to take you myself, but Elvis likes you."

Under normal circumstances, I might have wondered how Elvis knew he liked me, but as Junior Samples would say, this Elvis "sitchays-hun" was a "rat fur piece" from normal. It was several more months before I learned about the closed-circuit TV's at Graceland.

*　*　*

Back in my motel room, I stared at the two items hanging in the closet. Any other beauty queen on a trip to Memphis would know enough to toss an extra something in her suitcase, on the chance that Elvis Presley asked her for a date. To tell the truth, I was a little miffed that the pageant people had not prepared me for this eventuality. My entire weekend wardrobe consisted of pedal pushers and blouse, the sweat-soaked denim outfit I'd worn to Graceland, and a backless polka-dot dress that I called my Daisy Mae because when I wore it, people told me I looked like L'il Abner's girlfriend. The dress was more for a cocktail party than a movie, but at least the cinch belt showed off my figure.

I sighed and took Daisy Mae out of the closet.

The hours I spent beautifying myself to win Miss Georgia didn't compare with the time I took getting dolled up for my date with Elvis. The limo arrived at 9 p.m. Dave sat facing me, and every time I glanced at the empty seat to my right, my heart pounded so hard my breasts jiggled. I trailed my hand across the velour upholstery where Elvis would soon be sitting, and imagined him greeting me with a soft kiss. As little as I knew about Elvis, I did remember he had soft-looking lips.

At Graceland, the driveway was even more crowded with Cadillacs than before. Elvis's movie parties always began with an entourage of his friends leaving in a convoy that would have looked like a funeral procession if a hearse had led the way. Tonight, the lead car would be this very limo. Dave told me that no one was allowed to leave ahead of Elvis. So, we waited. And waited.

Then just when I thought I couldn't stand it one more second, the doors of Graceland flew open, a flash of royal-blue polyester leaped onto the portico, and there stood Elvis in a Superman pose, feet wide, hands on hips. Once we'd all had time to get a good look, he flung a lock of hair off his forehead – except his hair was sprayed too stiff to fling – and did the famous curled lip while he straightened the Dracula collar of his costume.

*Oh, a costume party. Good thing I dressed as Daisy Mae.* Then why did Dave have on plain old jeans and a knit shirt? Actually, once my eyes adjusted, Elvis's gull-wing collar didn't seem all that unusual. But those bell-bottoms that looked like he was wearing hoop skirts on his legs? And check out those mag-wheel sunglasses. Wouldn't dark glasses this time of night make it hard to see? No getting around it, his behavior was unusual. I mean, leaping onto his own front porch and posing like it was Vegas?

I slapped my forehead. *Elvis wouldn't put on a grand entrance like that for these pals he sees every week. That performance was for you, Diana. Oh Lordy, here he comes.*

A few yards from the car, he lifted one side of his sunglasses and winked at me. My heart pounded till my breasts were jiggling like Jell-O having a fit. Step-by-step, he closed the distance. I scrabbled in my purse for a breath mint, but time was up, Elvis was at the car door.

He made a military pivot, walked straight to the limo behind us and got in.

I twisted my head around in a one-eighty like that *Exorcist* girl, expecting to look out the rear window and see him coming back. Then the driver behind us started his engine and drove around to the front of the line. *Nobody leaves ahead of Elvis.*

"Why is Elvis in that other car?" I asked.

"He's going to the movie." Dave said this with a straight face.

"I thought I was supposed to be with Elvis."

"You are."

My instincts told me not to press so I turned my attention to craning my neck for a better view inside the lead limo. *Was that a girl I saw?* Oh, well, she must be with one of the other men. She couldn't be with Elvis, because every time we stopped at a red light, his car pulled alongside, and he lifted his sunglasses to give me another wink. *All-righty then.*

My face fell when we rounded a corner and the Memphian Theater came into view. I expected a grand old movie palace like the Fox in Atlanta. The Memphian wasn't any bigger than our picture show back home, but it was old all right. It even still had one of those 1930s neon marquees. Where were the searchlights and popping flash bulbs? Elvis was arriving! And I was arriving with him. At that, a shiver went up my spine and my heart resumed its breast-jiggling pace. *Silly girl, you don't need bright lights to make a grand entrance with Elvis Presley.* I smiled and picked up my shiny new purse to get out of the car.

Dave's hand gripped my arm. "Not yet."

I braced for something I didn't want to hear, something like Elvis had changed his mind.

"Elvis will be going in ahead of us," Dave said.

I swallowed dry spit. "But I am with Elvis?"

Dave explained that even though I was with Elvis, instead of sitting next to Elvis, I was to sit one row behind and one seat to his right. Sitting that way would let Elvis see me better when he turned around to talk.

"So, whoever is with Elvis, that's where she's supposed to sit?"

"Yep."

The movie was a Kung Fu thing. Peter Sellers was in it, I think. I sat where Dave instructed: second row, Elvis in front of me one seat to my left, half a row of guys to his right, half a row of girls to his left. I watched the girls as much as I watched Elvis, especially the one sitting next to him.

What a chatterbox. She giggled and gabbed with her girlfriends non-stop and every ten minutes they all hopped up and ran to the lobby. Mostly they went to the concession stand. I've never seen anyone eat more chocolate than that girl. Then while she was opening yet another box of Junior Mints or Milk Duds, she'd be complaining about getting fat. She didn't look fat to me; she looked downright slinky. Especially her long legs in the denim hot pants she was wearing, and her waist looked about eighteen inches in that ruffled midriff top. She was pretty enough, if you like long dark wavy hair and vampire-red lipstick. Somebody who liked that type might even consider her beautiful.

I wasn't too concerned about her. She and Elvis weren't paying much attention to each other. Not that he ignored her, exactly. She'd lean over and make a comment, and he'd tilt his head to hers and answer. They seemed easy together, but not lovey-dovey at all, more the way I acted with my brother, or the way my parents were with each other after all these years. Wait a minute, could that be Priscilla? I was pretty sure Priscilla had long dark hair, and it would explain the little girl on the big wheel.

Priscilla or whoever, I was glad she was a chocoholic, because every time she made a Milk Dud run, Elvis turned and talked to me. I have no idea what he said, and I may not have known at the time, because as soon as I looked in those eyes I was gone. I mean *gone*. There was something supernatural about Elvis. It was like everything had disappeared except us. I could almost see our souls flowing into each other on the connection between his eyes and mine. He felt it, too. I could feel him feeling it.

With that kind of magic happening, conversation was beside the point, but I do remember the first thing he said to me. The very first time the girls ran to the lobby, he turned sideways with his arm on the back of his seat, looked me up and down and said, "That sure is a pretty dress."

How about that, he liked my Daisy Mae. Wouldn't you know it? The only time I get anything right is when I think I'm getting it wrong.

So, the night went on that way, the girls going to get candy, Elvis and me talking about nothing, our souls saying it all. Then the fellow sitting in the seat directly in front of me stood up headed for the lobby, and at almost the same instant, the girl sitting next to Elvis got up. Only this time, her friends did not get up with her. I snapped my fingers. Why hadn't I realized? It wasn't that she had been sitting next to Elvis, it was that Elvis had been sitting between them. She was leaving with the guy who had just vacated his seat. They were a couple.

But instead of following the guy up the aisle, when she got to his empty chair in front of me, she knelt in the seat, facing backwards, staring me straight in the face.

"I hear you're Miss Georgia." She tilted her head and smiled. "I'm Linda Thompson, Miss Tennessee.

Diana (1970s)

# Chapter 2

SOMETHING WAS VERY WRONG HERE. This girl Linda Thompson was not Miss Tennessee. At least she was not the Miss Tennessee I knew, which made it even odder that she was looking at me as if my polite hello when she introduced herself was not enough to suit her. Heaven knew, the last thing I wanted to do was insult an acquaintance of Elvis, but as much as I tried to place her, she didn't strike me at all familiar, and although there had to be millions of girls named Linda Thompson, I couldn't recall ever hearing that name in my life.

Thank goodness it didn't seem to make her mad. After a few seconds, when she didn't get whatever response she wanted from me, she started babbling away, smiling and twisting her hair around her finger, as if we were best of friends. I didn't catch everything she was saying, because I found the whole situation too confusing, and the harder I tried to figure out what was going on, the more tongue-tied I got, so I just sat there smiling, watching her lips move, until finally I caught a name I recognized. "Harold Glasser? I know him!" My voice sounded shrill to my ears, but I was proud to be able to say something at last. I let out a deep breath. Harold Glasser was a pageant official for Miss USA, and a mutual acquaintance of mine and Linda's, so now some of what she'd been saying made sense. I found out that although she was not the reigning Miss Tennessee, she was indeed Miss Tennessee 1972. What a relief to know that this friendly girl was not looking me straight in the eye, lying through her pearly little teeth – and who knew? – she might even be an ally for me with Elvis. Then just as I was about to inquire how she was acquainted with him, one of the girls she'd been sitting with bounced over and said, "I smell fresh popcorn. Let's go to the concession stand."

Linda smiled at me. "Want to go get some popcorn with us?"

*Popcorn?* Me sitting there with kernels stuck in my teeth and Elvis six inches from my face, no thanks. I took a sip from my giant cup of diet Tab cola, and said. "I'm happy with my drink, but it's nice of you to ask."

Linda wiggled her fingers bye-bye, and disappeared up the aisle. Never in a million years would I have imagined that the next time we met, Elvis would be dead. In the light from the screen, his skin glowed, everything about him godlike perfection. Except for one small blemish. His thumbnail was bruised to a bloody pulp. I wondered how his bodyguards had allowed such an injury to happen, but on the other hand, bodyguards couldn't protect him from everything, and that bruise was proof that Elvis was not the god he seemed.

As if to make certain I realized it, at one point in the movie, he turned around, and offered his hand, "I think I forgot to introduce myself. I'm Elvis Presley," and during the first movie, the comedy with Peter Sellers, whenever something funny happened, he would turn around to make sure I was enjoying the joke. Then in the next movie, there was a horribly violent scene, where a car kept running over babies. Elvis turned to me and said in a grave voice, "Those are not real babies," like a child shooing away monsters in the dark.

We watched a triple-feature, but it went by too fast, and I began feeling anxious, wondering what would happen when the final film was over. What I wanted to happen was for Elvis to usher me up the aisle and into his car, but when THE END came on the screen, Elvis stood up and stretched, then thanked me for coming, and said he hoped to see me again.

*Oh, no,* I thought, *He didn't even ask for my number.* Now he was heading up the aisle and out the door, out of my life. Elvis had left the building. Yet again, Dave offered a coffee stop before dropping me at my hotel, and yet again I accepted. If I kept getting stuck with Dave, I might learn to like coffee. I might even learn to like Dave, but for the moment, he was nothing more to me than my last desperate link to Elvis. He placed his hand behind my back, guiding me into the lobby, and when he opened the door onto the street, sunshine rushed in. I hadn't calculated leaving the theater just as the Memphis shopkeepers were opening up. If my Daisy Mae dress had seemed doubtful the night before, it seemed downright shameful in broad daylight, but it probably wasn't the first time the waitress in the Waffle House had seen a girl in a cocktail dress straggle in on the morning after. I hoped she'd hear Dave and me talking about Elvis, so she'd understand that I wasn't just any old party girl. I was a girl who knew Elvis Presley. I'd had a *date* with Elvis Presley, and as long as I lived, nobody could take that away from me.

Dave and I didn't have much to say, and neither of us wanted anything to eat, so we sipped our coffee in silence. I wondered why he'd even bothered asking me to come. I would have liked to think that Elvis told him to get me some breakfast, but I'd never know for sure. Then Dave pulled a notebook and pen out of his pocket and slid them across the table. "I need your contact info."

I must have hesitated, because he added, "It's not for me. Elvis asked me to get your phone number for him."

The flight to Atlanta was the longest trip of my life. Getting off the plane, I wove in and out of dawdling passengers, getting to the head of the line as fast as I could, until finally, I set foot in the airport and spotted my brother's dark bushy head among the throng waiting at the gate.

I threw my arms around his neck. "I've got so much to tell you!"

Ray said he was in a hurry, had to get back to work, which suited me fine. I'd rather tell him about Elvis after we got in the car and I had his full attention. While he got my luggage, I raced ahead and out to the passenger pick-up area, where my chariot awaited. People might have laughed to see Elvis's latest flame, who only yesterday traveled in a chauffeured-limo, now hiking up her pants-leg and climbing into a white panel van with "Ray's Home Repair and Improvement" emblazoned on each side, but the humor was lost of me. My mind was too busy rehearsing the big story I was going to tell my brother.

I shouldn't have bothered. After nearly a whole day of waiting and wishing to share my astonishing news, it spilled out of my mouth so fast I hardly knew what I was saying, but Ray caught the drift.

His mustache crooked up on one side, in a snicker. "Elvis Presley, huh? Yeah, well, when does Elvis get to meet me?" My brother, the comedian. Ha. Ha. Ha. Wouldn't he be surprised when the King himself showed up on Mama and Daddy's doorstep?

My mama would be thrilled to hear all about it, and then she'd make me tell it over and over to all her friends. I ignored Ray, and gazed out the window of the van, re-rehearsing my tale.

Our house wasn't anything fancy, a typical 1950s four-bedroom brick ranch, barely big enough for a couple to raise two sons and three daughters. I left Ray to unload my bags, and ran through the backdoor, into the kitchen. "Mama, wait till you hear!"

People say I look like my mama, and I love hearing it, because to my eyes she was the quintessential natural beauty, and never more so than on that day standing at the kitchen sink in Bermuda shorts and a sleeveless white blouse, sunshine through the window lighting her curly blonde hair. "Hey, darlin. You hungry?" she asked.

"I'll just grab a Tab." I opened the fridge. "Mama, really, I've got something important to tell you."

"Okay," she said, "you can tell me while I unload the dishwasher."

I sat down at the little Formica-topped dinette table and began to tell my story.

Mama didn't even look at me while I talked, just kept unloading dishes. Even when I finished, waiting for her to comment, she went right on working, barely mumbling, "Sounds like you had a good time."

I heaved a sigh and put Mama above Ray on my mental list of people who were going to be very surprised when Elvis and I got married. Till then, I wasn't going to tell them one more thing. They could just wait and see.

Meantime, I would tell my friend Pam. She would go crazy hearing this. I grabbed the yellow wall phone, dialed her number, and stretched the cord to reach my seat at the table. I had barely begun to tell her, when she interrupted me. "Hey, Diana, why don't we all go out to dinner Friday night, and you can tell everybody at the same time." That sounded good to me. I didn't want to keep the phone tied up calling friends when Elvis might be trying to get through. I hung up, grabbed another Tab from the fridge, and sat down, waiting for his call.

I was still sitting there when Mama set the table for dinner, and still there when everybody came in for breakfast the next morning. And the next. The only time I budged was to go to the bathroom, and even then, I kept the door cracked to make sure I'd hear the phone if it rang.

By the time Friday night rolled around, I had lost some of my enthusiasm for storytelling, and Pam had to up the ante to coax me out of the house, by making dinner reservations at the Polaris in Atlanta, a revolving restaurant atop the Hyatt Regency that was my very favorite. I dolled up in my baby blue polyester pantsuit, slipped my feet into the white platform heels that I now called my Elvis shoes – What a show-and-tell for my friends! – made everyone in the house swear to answer the phone on first ring, and off I went with renewed energy to share my big adventure with my pals.

At the end of the evening, I had four more names to add to the list of people who were going to be very surprised when I became Mrs. Presley. They all thought I was making the whole thing up, and who could blame them? I had always been star-struck. My bedroom was wallpapered with rock-star posters and my nose was always stuck in a fan magazine. That's how I learned the truth about Linda Thompson and Elvis. Although I didn't believe it at the time.

Days turned into weeks of keeping vigil by the phone. I didn't eat, didn't sleep. I knew my family was worried, because I could hear them whispering behind my back, but nothing got my attention until one day, my fourteen-year-old sister, Crystal, pointed out that the dishwater roots of my golden hair had widened from a half-inch to half-a-foot. Well now, that wouldn't do. What if Elvis called and wanted to see me right that minute?

I was out the door and off to the drugstore. The clerk was ringing up another customer's purchases, so I placed my box of Miss Clairol Baby Blonde on the counter and walked over to the magazine stand. Smiling at me from the first cover I spotted was none other than Elvis. The girl in the picture with him was Linda Thompson. According to the caption, she was his girlfriend. I turned the magazine around so that the back cover faced forward. Maybe I should inform the drugstore owner that he shouldn't have such lies on his magazine rack. Everybody knew these tabloid rags were nothing but hogwash. Why on earth would Elvis invite me on a date, with his girlfriend sitting right there beside him? He wouldn't. So much for that.

Then I saw them on another cover, and another, until I could no longer deny that she was in fact his girlfriend, and had been for several years. But I also heard that things were rocky between them, and she might be moving out of Graceland. Graceland? She lived there? While those stories gave me hope that she'd soon be gone, they also made me wonder if she had been around on the day I was sneaking through the house trying to get into Elvis's bedroom. What if I had walked in on the two of them in bed? Thank God for saving me from that, but it didn't mean things were over for Elvis and me, it simply explained why he was taking a while getting in touch. Maybe he was having a hard time getting rid of her.

I was a long way from giving up, but I now realized that I couldn't live the rest of my life in my parents' kitchen waiting for the phone to ring. Besides, I'd had an extremely tempting offer not long before I left for Memphis. My friend Paulette called from Hollywood to say she'd moved in with her boyfriend, B.J. Thomas, and they'd like for me to come visit. *B.J. Thomas? Really? The "Raindrops Keep Fallin' On My Head" singer? Wow.* The timing could not have been better. I started packing my bags for L.A.

Paulette said she'd pick me up curbside at LAX, and she was right on time. I spotted her before she spotted me. Paulette's huge smile could be seen a mile away, and with the top down on the silver Mercedes 450SL she was driving, her long hair shimmered like dark water in the California sun. "Heyyy!" She popped the trunk for the sky-cap and hopped out of the car, grabbing me in a best-friend hug. "Welcome to, L.A.!"

Sliding into the passenger seat, I stroked the leather upholstery. "Where did you get this?"

"It's B.J.'s," she winked, "I wanted you to arrive in style."

"I appreciate that," I said, "and I can't wait to meet B.J. Are we far from your house? I've never been here, you know, and I have no idea where I am." We had left the airport area and were on a busy street, bordered by all kinds of stores and restaurants that didn't look like my idea of Hollywood or Beverly Hills or anyplace in the Los Angeles of my dreams.

She raised an eyebrow. "This area is not all that great, is it? But, depending on the traffic, it's only about a twenty-minute drive to our place. Speaking of which, I have a surprise for you."

I smiled. "Just when I thought things couldn't get any better."

"I've found a very special place for you to stay," she beamed.

"I thought I was staying with you," I said.

She nodded. "I know, honey. I was really looking forward to having you with us, but B.J.'s sick, and I think you'll be very happy when you hear my surprise."

I had been happy thinking I was going to stay with my best friend at B.J. Thomas's house. This had better be good. Then it hit me. She wasn't just smiling like this was something good, she was smiling like this was something huge. When I had called to tell Paulette that I was taking her up on her invitation, I had filled her in on my Elvis adventure, to which she replied, "That is amazing. B.J. knows Elvis. This is going to be fun." Recalling the conversation, my heart started pounding so hard I could barely breathe. Elvis had a house in Hollywood. Could it be? Of course, it could, this whole thing was a set-up for the big surprise. The *huge* surprise. My angel-friend Paulette was taking me to Elvis.

"You're going to stay at Harold Robbins's house." Paulette said.

I must have looked as sick as I felt, because she slowed the car. "Diana?"

"I'm sorry." I gulped back my disappointment. "What did you say? Whose house?"

"Harold Robbins. He's a writer."

In my head, I saw a bespectacled old man wearing a moth-eaten cardigan, leading me upstairs to a spare room in an attic lined with musty books.

"Did you read *The Betsy*?" Paulette asked.

"No. I don't read much," I answered.

"He's a movie producer, too. Did you see *The Carpetbaggers*, with George Peppard?"

*Movie producer? George Peppard?* The booklined attic I'd envisioned morphed into a Beverly Hills estate à la Playboy Mansion. I closed my eyes, seeing myself beside a sparkling blue swimming pool, with a butler in a white jacket bringing me a fancy cocktail on a silver tray.

Then the car took a sharp turn and my eyes popped open. Paulette had pulled into a driveway, and the house at the end was not my imagination, it was the house of my dreams. No Playboy Mansion, for sure, and no Graceland. This was better than either. Who'd want one of those old piles when you could live in a modern spread like this? I was so bedazzled, Paulette had to jostle me out of my stupor when we pulled up to the house. "Hey, you coming in?"

We heaved my bags out of the trunk and over to the gate-like double doors, which immediately swung open to reveal a petite uniformed housemaid standing in a massive gleaming hallway that opened into an even more massive living area. In a heavy Spanish accent, she introduced herself as Consuelo.

Before I had time to wonder if this little woman was the one to carry my bags, a man appeared down the hallway, coming towards us. If this was the butler, he certainly didn't look anything like the Mr. French character I remembered from *Family Affair*. This man was tall, tanned, and classically handsome. I recalled that at some point during the drive to the house, while I was imagining all sorts of things, Paulette had been telling me that Harold Robbins was at his other home, in Europe, with a house-sitter taking care of his place here, which would explain this dark-haired dreamboat, who was making his way toward me, and getting more handsome with every step. On closer inspection, his face seemed familiar, and he had the bronzed chiseled features of a typical leading man. Dare I hope that my first Hollywood roommate might also be the first Hollywood star I met?

"I'm Anthony Herrera," he offered his hand.

I didn't recognize the name, but he sure had a movie-star smile.

"Let me show you to your room," he said, gathering my luggage. His tight-fitting black jogging suit left little doubt that he was plenty fit to handle my bags, so I stepped back and beamed admiration as he tucked one suitcase under each bicep and grabbed two more in each hand. Then

Paulette popped a kiss on my cheek, and with a quick excuse about having to get back to B.J., she was out the door and I was following Anthony to my bedroom.

Now it hit me that as handsome and charming as this man was, I did not recognize his face because I'd never laid eyes on him, and here I was, letting him lead me into the bedroom of a house where my only protection was a tiny maid who probably wouldn't understand the word "help", no matter how loud I screamed it. What had I been thinking coming out here on such a whim? I was nothing more than a little country girl fresh off the farm. Might as well call me Ellie Mae Clampett.

"Here we are." Anthony stopped at a door and set my bags inside. "I'll be in the living room where you came in," he said, "so after you catch your breath, come find me, and I'll show you around."

Now I felt ashamed of myself for thinking such terrible thoughts about this kind man. "That's very nice of you," I said, "I'll be there in a few minutes."

He closed the door, and I took a look around the room. Where the entry hall had felt cool and sleek, like stepping into the lobby of a luxury high-rise, the bedroom felt more like coming into a comfortable hotel suite after a long hard trip. It was decorated in soothing earth-tones, and the big bed was already turned down, tempting me to crawl between the crisp sheets that looked like somebody had spent hours starching and ironing them. But with Anthony waiting for me in the living room, there was no time for a nap. At the end of the room was an open doorway. I strolled over and peeked into the en-suite bathroom. Back home, seven of us shared one bath, so for me, this was the ultimate luxury. Especially the deep porcelain soaking tub and separate walk-in shower. Later tonight, I might try out both, but first I'd better find Anthony and let him show me around this palace I'd stumbled into.

I was surprised when Harold Robbins's bedroom was the first stop on the tour, and even more surprised when I learned that he shared it with his wife, Grace. Walking into such a personal space seemed almost an invasion of privacy, but Anthony strolled in like it was nothing, sailed past the huge bed, and to the end of the room, which was a long, mirrored wall of closets. He slid back one mirrored door, and said, "If you ever need something special to wear, you're welcome to anything here."

*What?* I couldn't believe my ears, but neither could I resist a peek, so I joined Anthony at the closet wall for a closer look at the most fabulous wardrobe I'd ever seen. Silks and satins, furs and feathers, rhinestones, sequins, beads, it was too much glamour to take in all at once, so I promised myself a return trip, and moved on.

California sunshine streamed through large windows in the spacious kitchen, where the housekeeper was scrubbing the tile countertops. She gave us a brief nod then continued her work. Anthony said, "Anytime you get hungry, Consuelo will be happy to make you something to eat."

*Anytime?* My own personal cook, wow, this deal got more unbelievable by the minute.

Anthony gestured to the breakfast area, where a table was set for two. "I'll be having dinner a little later, just something light. You're welcome to join me."

"I'd like that very much," I said. "Thank you."

*Could this get any better?* Yes, it could. He ushered me outside to the patio, and I walked straight into my Hollywood-dream lifestyle, complete with swimming pool, lounge chairs, and umbrella tables. There were even floats bobbing on the sparkling water, just waiting for me to tie on my string bikini and while away lazy days doing nothing more strenuous than rubbing baby oil on my body to perfect my California-girl tan. The only thing missing was that English butler I'd imagined bringing me a cocktail on a silver tray. Reality was a Mexican maid wearing a white apron, but from what Anthony had been telling me, the cocktail could remain in the picture.

I was ready to start work on my tan right that minute, but Anthony said, "Guess we'd better go back in and finish the tour."

*Finish?* I couldn't believe there was more to see. We rambled around past this room and that, then stepped into the banquet-size dining room. "The Robbinses like to entertain in style," Anthony commented, which I soon saw was an understatement, when on our final stop of the tour, he threw back a pair of double doors to reveal an atrium that could easily have been the lanai of a Hawaiian resort, from the bistro sets and cocktail sofas encircling the indoor pool, to the long, mirrored bar lined with swivel stools. I felt like Gomer Pyle on his first trip to the big city. *Gohh-ohh-lee!* Even so, why would anybody want to swim inside the house and waste all that California sunshine? I was just starting to calculate whether there might be enough hours of daylight left for me to get a start on my tan that very day, when Anthony said, "I bet you're anxious to get unpacked," and glanced at his watch, "You've got just enough time before dinner, if you still want to join me. How about if I knock on your door when I head to the kitchen?"

So much for the pool. I found my way to my room, wondering if I should change clothes, but decided it would be easier to keep on the jeans and peasant blouse I'd worn on the plane. To think, only that morning, I had put these clothes on at my parents' house in Georgia, now here I was, still wearing the same thing, like I'd been beamed up by Scotty to a whole new world.

Right on time, Anthony knocked at my door, and escorted me to the table in the kitchen's dining nook, where Consuelo set before us plates with chicken breasts and salads that looked like something I might order at the Polaris in Atlanta, which at that time, I thought of as the ultimate fine dining. Anthony offered white wine from a bottle on the table, and I accepted, glad for the relaxation it provided in making conversation.

He asked about my friendship with Paulette, and surprised me by inquiring about Elvis. Of course, I was quite happy to fill him in on that, to the point that I realized I might be hogging the conversation, and should toss the ball his direction. "Are you in show business?" I asked, then realized it may not have been the appropriate thing to say right out of the box.

I was relieved when he smiled and said, "Isn't everyone?" but it wasn't much of an answer.

I took a long swig of wine and stared him in the face. "You look like you could be an actor."

"Unfortunately, I am," he laughed.

"Unfortunately?"

"Just kidding." He refilled his glass from a bottle of light red wine that was on the table next to my bottle of white. I thought a bottle of wine each was a tad too much, but he seemed in a jolly mood, so I wasn't about to complain. "In fact," he said, "I just got a new role."

"Really? That's great. What?"

He shrugged. "Just another soap."

"Soap? You mean a soap opera? Wow. Which one?"

"Are you asking which one I used to be on, or which one I'm on now?"

"Either. Both." Whether from the wine or excitement that I was having dinner with a genuine Hollywood star, my head was feeling a little fuzzy. Probably best to just sit back and let Anthony have the floor. "Please tell me all about yourself," I said. "I really do want to hear."

"Okay, well for too many years to talk about I was James Stenbeck, the bad guy on *As the World Turns*, and now I'm playing a college professor on the *Young and the Restless*."

"That is incredible," I breathed, and from that point on I didn't have to worry about keeping up my end of the conversation. Anthony talked until bedtime, but when I got back to my room, I found myself with three empty hours to kill before my eyes would close.

Fortunately, my room had all the conveniences you'd find in a hotel, even a TV and telephone, but I was still a little miffed at my family and friends about the way they had received my Elvis news, so maybe they didn't deserve to know about my glamorous new Hollywood lifestyle. It sure would be fun to tell them, though, and my sister Rhonda was expecting my first niece or nephew any day, so I really did need to call and check on her.

Rhonda was glad to hear from me, but not as impressed with my news as I'd hoped. She mostly wanted to know what I planned to do next, and I had no idea what to tell her. Like Scarlett O'Hara, I'd think about that tomorrow – by the pool.

You can be sure that as soon as my eyes opened the next morning, I tied on my red-striped bikini and ran to the patio, barely slowing up to grab a banana from the kitchen, on my way. So here I was at last, slathered in iodine and baby oil, drifting on a float in a swimming pool, high above Sunset Boulevard in Beverly Hills, living my Hollywood dream. Except that after a few hours, the dream got a little boring. Back home at the public pool, my sisters and girlfriends were always hanging with me, gabbing, laughing, and flirting with the lifeguards. Anthony didn't seem to be around this morning, so I supposed he was off doing whatever stars did during the day. He might even be filming the *Young and the Restless. Hey!* I sat straight up. *Maybe I can get him to take me along to the TV studio sometime.* Now there was a plan my sister would approve. *See, Rhonda, I told you I'd think of something tomorrow. Well, here's tomorrow and I've already thought of something before I've even had lunch.* I gave myself a slap on the back, *Good day's work, Diana,* and decided to knock off early to go watch some TV. Come to think of it, it was about time for the *Young and the Restless.* What fun to see Anthony on the tube! But as I was walking in, Consuelo came out of the kitchen, jabbering Spanish at me, until finally I caught something that sounded like "phone."

"Oh!" I said. *It might be Elvis.* "Can I take it in my room?"

She nodded, and I jogged down the hall, hurrying to my bedside telephone.

It wasn't Elvis, but I was plenty happy to hear Paulette's voice. My hope was that B.J. would be feeling better tonight and we'd all go out on the town, so I was disappointed when she said he was still in his "funk," whatever that was, but just as with my living quarters, she once again offered a consolation prize. "Have you ever heard of Lance Rentzel?" she asked.

I thought for a few seconds, then said, "Sounds familiar."

"He was the Dallas Cowboys' star wide receiver," she said, "but you probably remember him as Joey Heatherton's ex-husband, and – guess what? – you're going out with him tonight."

I did remember the name Lance Rentzel, and in the back of my mind, something about it made me uneasy.

# Chapter 3

JOEY HEATHERTON WAS EVERY INCH the Hollywood blonde bombshell I'd always dreamed of becoming. There couldn't possibly be anything wrong with her husband. *Ex-husband,* whispered a voice inside my head, but I was in no mood to be bossed around by some pesky little voice that didn't know shoot from Shinola about movie stars and athletes. I should have left that little voice back in Georgia, and if Little Voice didn't shut up I wouldn't take her out on the town with me tonight. I wagged my finger at my image in the bathroom mirror, then looked myself up and down, noting that the baby oil and iodine had burnished my skin to a goddess-like bronze. All that was left to complete the perfection was a short walk down the hall to my personal designer boutique left to me by Grace Robbins.

Standing in front of the long expanse of mirrored doors, I almost expected Monty Hall to appear. *Let's Make a Deal; Door number one, two or three? Or four, five, six, seven, eight, nine, or ten?* With great care, I slid open the door at the far end, swept my eyes down the row of shimmering, flowing garments, and reached for a lilac satin gown that caught my eye. It was the most beautiful dress I'd ever seen. It was also the smallest, unless you counted children's clothes. Was Grace Robbins a midget or was I a giant? I hung the child-size dress back in the closet and went down the long row of mirrors, opening door after door, finding nothing that would have fit me past my tenth birthday. Just to be sure, I put my arms through the straps of one of the gowns, and was aghast to see that Grace Robbins was at least half a foot smaller than me in every direction. Was this how they grew 'em in California? More importantly, was this how they liked 'em? I slumped back to my room, trailing in my wake the visions I'd had of my first night in Hollywood, "dressed the part." After my tantalizing brush with Grace Robbins's dream-duds, I couldn't bear the thought of hitting the scene dressed in a blue-light bargain from K-mart.

Actually, it was from Zayre, but it was baby blue, and standing in front of the full-length mirror in my room, I thought that maybe I didn't look too bad. I had to admit the spaghetti straps showed my tan to advantage, and the color almost perfectly matched my eyes. Sure, it may not have been the finest Italian silk, but in my stiletto heels, the thin tee-shirt fabric skimmed the six-foot length of my body like a second skin, and if that wasn't enough to make anyone forget to check the label, the thigh-high slit surely would. It almost made me glad I was too tall to wear Grace Robbins's tiny clothes. Smiling at my image in the mirror, I applied a final coat of Maybelline Big Lash, dabbed Bonne Bell pink gloss on my lips and cheeks and it was time to go.

Diana and Joey Heatherton Pageant '80!

Waiting for me in the living room were a couple of the best-looking guys I'd ever seen. I hadn't been expecting two, but I sure wasn't complaining. Really, I hadn't known what to expect about anything that evening. I didn't even know where we were going or what we might do, so I was glad to see they were wearing blazers with open-collar shirts, which meant my dress and heels wouldn't be too far off the mark. They both had light hair, between blond and golden brown, and were of similar build, which made me wonder if they might be teammates, as it turned out they were. But my other first impressions couldn't have been more wrong. I had immediately tagged one of them "California Surfer Boy" and the other "Mid-west All-American," when in fact "Surfer Boy" was Lance Rentzel, a native Oklahoman, who became star halfback for the Oklahoma Sooners, and it was the other hunk, the one I'd dubbed "Mid-west All-American," who was the genuine California boy from Los Angeles, and who had played for San Diego State. Each had been early draft picks for the NFL, so by the time they became teammates with the Los Angeles Rams, my two escorts had achieved world-wide fame, and in Lance's case, infamy. But on that night, I knew none of this. They were simply a couple of good-looking football players, who were nice enough to take me out and show me the town. Heaven knows I needed somebody to show me around. I hadn't been in town long enough to even know where I was.

The sprawl of this city was more than I could grasp. I knew it was bigger than Atlanta, but I never could have imagined how much bigger. Viewed from the air, when I was flying in, Los Angeles seemed to begin not long after the pilot announced we were flying over the Grand Canyon. I'd heard that Kansas City was located in two states, so was it possible that Los Angeles stretched all the way from the Grand Canyon to where I was now? I didn't want to think on it too hard, because that would only intimidate me, so it was something of a relief just to let these big strong guys chauffeur me anywhere they pleased, while I watched the landscape roll by the car window. Paulette had said that the Robbins house was in Beverly Hills, so I wondered if going downhill meant we were leaving the area, because I knew from watching the *Beverly Hillbillies* that this was a good address. Why would we want to leave? Weren't there any restaurants or clubs in Beverly Hills?

Lance was in the backseat, and I was up front with Fred. "Where are we going?" I asked him.

"Pips," he said. At least that's what I thought I heard. *Pips? What kind of place would be called Pips?* The only thing I could connect that word to was "pip squeak," which didn't sound glamorous enough for my first night in Hollywood.

"Is it far from here?"

"Not at all," he said. "Aw, wait minute, for a second there I forgot that you just flew into town. If you'd spent any time here, you'd know all about Pips." He gave me a wink. 'Pretty girls like it a lot."

I considered for a moment and decided I didn't mind the wink. "Guess I should take that as a compliment, so thank you, but Pips is a funny name, isn't it?"

"Not for a backgammon club."

*Backgammon club? Who ever heard of such a thing?* In my mind, a backgammon gameboard belonged in the same cupboard as checkers and chess, so once again, here came my imaginary old man in the motheaten sweater, only this time, instead of an author escorting me upstairs to a booklined attic, he was a pipe smoker sitting across from me on the other side of a backgammon board in a dimly-lit men's club called Pips.

"Here we are." Fred turned into the driveway of a mid-century modern building where uniformed parking attendants scurried to-and-fro, opening car doors for middle-aged men who exuded the kind of money it took to afford the Ferraris, Lamborghinis and Rolls Royces they drove, and their dates who looked like supermodels dressed for a Hollywood premier.

Stepping from the car, I ran my hands down my sides, self-consciously smoothing the tee-shirt cotton of my dress, trying to avert my eyes from the woman who had exited the car in front of ours, but I couldn't help catching the flutter of her silk skirt as she entered the club, and the sparkle of her diamond earrings as she nodded to the doorman. I glanced at the turquoise bracelet circling my wrist and considered stashing it in my purse. That bracelet was a souvenir from a friend's trip to New Mexico. How could I have thought this get-up I was wearing would be appropriate for a night out in Beverly Hills? Was it too much to hope that this Pips club would be so dimly lit that nobody could get a good look at my clothes?

Yes, it would be too much to hope. The foyer appeared to be Pips' designated photography studio, complete with the required lighting. As we entered, a group of well-heeled patrons were saying cheese for a photographer with a professional-looking camera. The three women of the group were even more elegantly turned out than the woman I'd noticed before, and it didn't help my feelings that one of their men nudged his buddy, with a nod my direction, and puckered his lips in a silent wolf whistle. Normally, I liked having my picture made, but this was not the night. Over to one side of the foyer was a line of people standing well back, who appeared to be waiting to get in. I took a couple of steps that direction to camouflage myself among them. Then it occurred to me that the lights might be turned up to allow a visual inspection before granting entrance to the club. I thought I'd heard of a disco in New York that did that. *Oh, my.* And here I was, dressed like I was entering a wet tee-shirt contest. I closed my eyes. *Dear God, I don't care what you do with me, just please don't let my cheap dress keep Lance and Fred from getting in.* When I opened my eyes, a dark-haired man in a tuxedo was striding towards us, with great purpose. I tightened my hand around the strap of my white plastic patent-leather purse and prepared to be ejected.

"Good evening!" he greeted Lance and Fred with two-fisted hand-shakes.

Lance said, "Hey, Joe, I want you meet Diana Goodman."

Joe's enthusiastic welcome seemed genuine, and he asked Lance if we were dining this evening, so I figured my wardrobe had at least passed the entrance exam, and I was relieved to hear Lance reply, "We'll just grab a bite in the bar," because I could see the bar area straight ahead, and it looked pretty dark in there.

Rats. We'd only taken a couple of steps before a gray-haired man grabbed Lance's arm to say "hey," then two steps further a man grabbed Fred, and on and on, like we were in some kind of receiving line. In my hurry to go hide in the darkness, it took a while for me to realize that each of these buddies made it a point to compliment me, some politely, some edging toward flirtation, and some teasing Lance and Fred that I was out of their league. In each case, my escorts agreed wholeheartedly, and I even began to detect a glint of proprietary pride in Fred's eyes. Interestingly, I found him the more attractive of the two. *But he's not Elvis, Diana.* No, and neither was anyone else in this place. I thought it odd that in a swanky joint like this, I hadn't spotted one celebrity. Except for the ones I was with. Suddenly it occurred to me that my escorts were the most famous men in the room. That would account for all the back-slapping. Now I noticed that we were turning heads with every step we took. And why not? Hadn't my first impression been *best looking guys I'd ever seen*? And the women in here might be better dressed than I was, but not a one of them could have made it past the first elimination of the Miss Georgia pageant. I lifted my chin, gave my head a little shake to make my blonde mane shimmer, and sailed into the bar area, flanked by the handsomest men in the room.

What a surprise to find that this part of the club was a small disco, complete with mirrored walls, a DJ booth, and above the dancefloor, a spinning disco ball shooting colored lights everywhere. The only difference in this and discos I'd been to, was the volume of the music, which was loud enough to make you want to dance, but not too loud to talk over. I wondered what any of this had to do with backgammon, but as soon as we got settled into a booth at the back of the room, Lance said, "One drink, then we'll show you around," so I figured I'd wait to find out.

I just hoped I didn't have to wait too long because that banana I'd had for breakfast was becoming a distant memory. Surely Lance's idea of showing me around would include something more substantial than the nibbles bowl the waitress brought with our drinks, but meantime, my lime daiquiri was delicious, so I sat back to sip my drink and enjoy the music. The song was "Kung Fu Fighting," which reminded me of the Peter Sellers Kung Fu movie I'd watched with Elvis, and sent me off on a cloud of remembering, until the DJ broke the spell with "Do It 'til You're Satisfied," and dancers flooded the floor. I'd never seen such expensively covered bottoms shaking booty like that, and said so to the guys.

Fred laughed, "Not only are you hilarious, you have a point. There's probably a million bucks in designer duds on that dance floor." He lifted his glass, toasting the dancers. "Here's to a-list booties."

"Really? This is the a-list? What about the man in the tuxedo, the one who greeted us, is he somebody special, the owner or something?"

Fred thought for a second, then he said, "Oh, you mean Joe De Carlo. He's the manager, among other things. He also manages Sonny and Cher."

"What?" I jerked my head back and forth, scanning the room for America's favorite couple. "Are they here?"

"Who's here?" Lance started looking around, too.

"Sonny and Cher," I said.

"They are?" Lance twisted his head this way and that.

Fred said, "You two, you're killing me. No, I haven't seen Sonny and Cher tonight, I think they're in the middle of a divorce." He winked at me. "Keep an eye out, though, because this isn't a bad place for star-spotting. I thought I saw Barbi Benton when we came in, not that she's such a big star. She's probably playing backgammon."

"Barbi Benton comes here?" I said. "I'd love to meet her. My friend Paulette – y'all know Paulette – she's a Playboy Bunny, so Hugh Hefner's her boss. Barbi Benton's his girlfriend."

Fred said, "If Paulette knows Hugh Hefner, she knows the owner of Pips."

The two of them smiled, watching me while I figured it out. "Hugh Hefner owns this place? I'd love to meet him. As I said, my friend Paulette is a Playboy Bunny . . ."

"Whoa, wait a minute," Fred interrupted me, "I misspoke. I should have said Hugh Hefner founded Pips. Nobody owns it. It's a non-profit." Responding to my blank look, he explained, "That means all the money goes to charity."

"How sweet," I said. "I mean, charity's a good thing, but if nobody owns it, and Joe is the manager, what does Hugh Hefner do?"

From behind me, a voice said, "We let him help out in the kitchen."

I swiveled around to see a small gray-haired man smiling at me. "I'm Joe Scott, welcome to Pips."

Fred pointed at Mr. Scott. "This is the manager."

"I thought Joe was the manager," I said.

Joe Scott laughed. "I am."

Lance said, "Forget the title, Joe, right now you're the man who can do a favor for me."

Joe spread his hands. "Name it."

Lance nodded. "This young lady is Diana Goodman, Miss Georgia 1975."

Joe smiled at me. "She sure is."

Lance said, "So I thought you'd like to put her name on the list."

"My pleasure." Joe held out his hand and I gave him mine. "You are welcome anytime. Tell 'em Joe sent you." He gave my hand a squeeze and walked away.

I looked from Lance's face to Fred's. "List? Is that the a-list you were talking about?"

Fred chuckled. "Yep, and now that you're on the a-list, I guess we can show you the rest of the club."

"Oh!" I squealed, and wriggled out of the booth. So that's what they'd been waiting for.

Lance asked the waitress to save our table and he and Fred ushered me from the swirling lights of the disco, into the English-club refinement of the dining room.

The aroma of steaks grilling in the kitchen was so mouthwatering, I had to restrain myself from diving into the middle of someone's dinner, but apparently Lance and Fred had not yet worked up an appetite. After pausing to let me look around the room, Fred asked, "Do you play backgammon?" and when I didn't answer immediately, he said, "If you're going to start coming here, you'd better learn the game, because those people in there are serious," he pointed to a doorway leading to another room, "meaning serious money."

"Well since I have no money at all, I don't have to worry about serious money," I said.

Fred gave me a sidelong look. "Pretty as you are, you won't need any money around here. Let's go see if there's a board available."

But there wasn't, and if Barbi Benton had been there, she was long gone, so we joined a group of regulars watching a hotly contested match between a couple of Lance and Fred's friends, then went back to our table in the disco for another round of drinks.

I couldn't imagine that these two big guys weren't hungry yet, with li'l ol' me ready to gnaw the leather upholstery off the booth we were sitting in, so when Lance got up and left the table, I jumped to the conclusion that he'd gone into the dining room to make our dinner arrangements. What a shock when he stalked back into the disco and without even glancing my way, came over to our booth, leveled a look at Fred and said, "We need to get out of here."

Fred slid out of the booth, with me right behind him, and the three of us beat it for the door. I never heard Lance Rentzel utter another word, but on the way home, the uneasy feeling I'd had earlier came back redoubled. In the ten minutes that Lance had been gone from our table in the disco, something had transformed Dr. Jekyll into Mr. Hyde. I felt sure whatever had caused that transformation was somehow connected to the thing about Lance Rentzel I couldn't quite recall.

When we got to the Robbins house, ever the gentleman, Fred escorted me to the front door. Inviting him in didn't seem an option with Lance brooding in the back seat of the car, so for a few seconds, we stood in awkward silence, glancing at each other and away, then he put his hands on my shoulders, gazing into my eyes.

"I'm sorry about the way tonight ended," he said. "It's not what I wanted or expected. Do you have a pencil or something I can write on?"

He dropped his hands from my shoulders and I opened my purse. "I stole a napkin from Pips," I smiled, "and here's a pen.

He palmed the napkin, wrote on it, and handed it back to me. "I think we deserve another shot at this, don't you? Call me when you're in town again. I hope next time you'll be coming back for good." He kissed my cheek and walked away.

Watching him go, I wanted to run after him, beg him to stay, but that would never do, so I just stood there, watching until the taillights disappeared down the hill. Then I walked slowly into the silent house, back to my room, wondering what I'd done wrong.

I'm not sure exactly when I recalled the snippet of memory that had been nagging me about Lance Rentzel, but it may have been while I was sitting on the side of my bed, agonizing over why he'd ended the night so early, and in such a rude way. Gradually, news reports from a few years earlier surfaced in my brain. I still wasn't completely clear on what it was, but it had something to do with Lance Rentzel exposing himself to a little girl. *Well. No wonder he behaved so strangely. He is strange.*

I reminded myself that Lance's transgressions should be no reflection on Fred, then reached into my purse for the Pips napkin, and sat there staring at his phone number. Would he be home yet? I had no idea where he lived, and anyway, he'd said to call him next time I was in town, not now. With tender care, I folded the napkin into my wallet and dialed Paulette.

Once again, no answer. So, there I sat, the evening still young, all dressed up and nowhere to go. Except that wasn't exactly true. The manager at Pips had promised Lance he would put my name on the list. I could call a cab that would take me right back down that hill and into all the glamour I'd just left. Fred had assured me that a pretty girl like me would never need any money at Pips, so for a few minutes I sat on the edge of the bed, imagining myself sitting at that carved wood bar, surrounded by handsome rich men vying to buy me lime daiquiris. Maybe one of them would even offer to buy me one of those steaks that had smelled so heavenly. But even if I didn't need any money once I got to Pips, how much would it cost me to get there? The car ride to the club hadn't seemed all that long, but I had no idea how much taxi fares might be in Los Angeles. *A lot more than in Atlanta, you can bet.* Then I remembered the line of people at the door of Pips, straightening their collars and checking their makeup in purse mirrors, all hoping they'd pass inspection to be allowed inside. What if I blew all my money on a cab only to wind up waiting with those people? The very thought sent chills down my spine. Rather than risk that shame, I'd put on my baby-doll pj's and get in bed with the latest issue of *Glamour Magazine,* which is exactly what I did.

My third day in L.A. started out exactly like my second day, with another banana breakfast, after which I tied on my string bikini and headed for the pool to work on my tan, but as luxurious as this might sound, it seemed all wrong. Sure, I had planned to spend some time by the pool, but the whole purpose of the trip was to become a movie star, and to accomplish that, Paulette had promised to introduce me to all the right people. *So, where's Paulette? If B.J.'s still sick after this many days, maybe he belongs in a hospital.* My pesky friend Little Voice tapped me on the shoulder. *Diana, wishing ill on others will come back to bite you in the butt.*

I didn't really want B.J. to be sick enough to be in the hospital, I wanted him well enough to let Paulette leave the house. Around noon, I called her again, and again got no answer.

Then, just when it looked like I was facing another do-nothing day of slathering baby oil and iodine on my skin, with no plans for the evening, who should appear but Anthony. Here he came, strolling out to the pool, looking every inch the soap star, wearing sunglasses with a tight-fitting polo shirt and his usual black jogging pants. *Diana, don't be looking at him like that, he's not Elvis.*

When he got to the chaise where I was sunning myself, he lowered his sunglasses and swept his eyes up and down my body. "Nice tan."

"Thanks. Have a seat." I patted the lounge chair beside mine.

"Wish I had time," he said, "but I've got a lot of things to do. We're having a party tonight, how about that? And I want you to be my special guest."

"Ohh." It seemed anytime I started thinking nothing good was ever going to happen to me, something always popped up. *Up pops the devil?* "I'd love to come," I said.

Anthony's face spread into a genuine Hollywood smile. "Glad to hear it. Seven o'clock, by the indoor pool." He turned to go, then came back. "Oh, and I'll be having dinner around six o'clock, if you'd like to join me again."

"I'll be there," I said.

With nothing better to do, I went into the house at 3:30 to dress for my dinner date with Anthony. *Date? Diana, he's not Elvis.*

No, Anthony was not Elvis, which is why it didn't bother me when, at five minutes till six I was still in my pink terry-cloth robe with electric curlers in my hair. With I shrug, I sauntered into the breakfast room and sat down across from Anthony. His only comment was a polite, "Good evening," but he did raise his eyebrows and look pointedly at my headful of curlers.

Still staring at the curlers, he raised a bottle of Chardonnay and asked, "Wine?"

I accepted, and Consuelo placed plates of pasta Alfredo before us, along with a basket of bread exuding a strong aroma of garlic.

Anthony brought the basket to his nose for a long appreciative whiff, before opening the bread cover and offering it to me.

Having skipped dinner the night before, I tucked into my meal with almost as much gusto as Anthony ate his. During our first night's dinner, we had only scratched the surface about my relationship with Elvis, so tonight, Anthony picked up where we left off, and this time he wanted more details. When I assured him that the relationship was brand new, he smiled, "Brand new things are always the most exciting, don't you agree?"

I wasn't sure I did agree, but I smiled and nodded, anyway.

At 6:30, he looked at his watch, then at my bathrobe, and said. "As charming as you look in that, um – ensemble? – I think we should get dressed for our soirée."

I hadn't bothered to ask what to wear to the party, because I'd already chosen the perfect "ensemble," as Anthony had put it. What could possibly be more appropriate for my first Hollywood "soirée" than the dress I had worn with Elvis? Once again, my lucky dress would be the Daisy Mae.

Giving myself a final once over in the mirror, I thought I looked even better than I had on that night at the Memphian theater. The Daisy Mae dress was backless, perfect for showing off my hard-earned tan, and no one could say the red polka dots weren't eye-catching. So off I went, feeling like the special guest Anthony had told me I was.

People were beginning to arrive as I walked in, and although I didn't recognize any Hollywood stars, they all had one thing in common, they all looked rich. There's just something about designer dresses and tailor-made suits, but even in my polyester polka dots, heads turned my direction, and Anthony immediately came over with a warm welcome. *Well, doesn't he look elegant,* I thought. Dressed in a dark sport coat and gray trousers with a silk shirt open at the neck, this was a side of Anthony I hadn't seen before, and I was impressed. Sweeping his arm, he gestured to the tables and chairs circling the pool. "Where would you like to sit, my dear?"

"I think I'll take a seat at the bar, if that's okay," I said, thinking that one of the tall swivel stools would give me a bird's-eye view of the crowd, as well as provide the perfect pedestal to showcase myself in all my bronze and blonde glory. The two bartenders might also come in handy if I didn't find someone to talk to, but I needn't have worried about that. Escorting me to the bar, Anthony introduced me left and right, and I must admit I preened a bit. After all, here I was at a gen-u-*wine* Hollywood party on the arm of a real-live soap-opera star, who seemed plenty proud to show me off, almost treating me like a date, politely helping me onto a barstool, and telling the bartenders to take good care of me until he returned. Which he did very soon, and quite often. I wasn't sure whether he was paying special attention to me because I was the new girl at the party, or whether his drink just needed a lot of refreshing, but it soon became apparent that his frequent trips to the bar were taking their toll. After two or three visits to check on me, the next time he came over, he slung his arm around my shoulder when he asked, "Everything okay?" Then the next time, he pulled me close, with his face inches from mine. "You look beautiful, tonight." Fumes of the garlic bread from dinner mixed with the brown liquor he was drinking wafted into my face. I turned my head and leaned away but there was no escaping his arm clamped around my shoulders; he was not done with me yet.

This time, when his face swooped toward mine, I twisted my head so that he spoke into my ear. "Would you have sex with me while some other people watch?"

I peered into his face to make sure I'd heard right, "Have you lost your mind?"

He answered with a lop-sided grin and a tilt of his head towards the mirror behind the bar. I followed his gaze, not believing what I saw. At first, I thought the wavering shadows from the pool lights were distorting my vision, or that since I wasn't used to drinking, maybe the daiquiris were having an effect, because, on the far side of the pool, I thought I saw a naked man, face down on a chaise, doing pushups, with a woman's legs wrapped around his, waving her feet in the air. And weren't those female hands clawing at his back, or was I the one losing my mind? I glanced away to clear my vision, and my eyes landed on a group of people sitting at a table a few feet from the copulating couple, watching with rapt attention.

I shoved Anthony with all my might and slithered out of his grasp, hitting the floor running, but not quickly enough to avoid catching sight of several other groups enjoying couples' sexhibitions.

Running as hard as I could in my white platform "Elvis" heels, I made it to my room, slammed the door and locked it behind me, then barely able to breathe, I leaned against the doorframe, shivering with an icy cold like I'd never felt. Acting on instinct, I dragged the desk chair to the door, wedged it under the knob, and jumped into bed, clothes and all, curling into a fetal position with the covers over my head.

A few seconds later, Anthony was at the door. "Aw, c'mon, Diana. I'm sorry, I didn't mean to make you mad. Everything's all right. Just a little fun. Open the door, let me apologize." He waited for me to answer, and when I didn't, he rattled the doorknob.

I peeked from beneath the covers, staring at the door, realizing this room I'd thought was a refuge was nothing more than a trap. If I screamed, no one would hear me, and even if they did, who would come? I certainly didn't want it to be any of those party guests I'd fled. I glanced at the phone beside the bed. Police? But what was there to tell? No one had harmed me, at least not physically, but I was harmed all right. Not only was I frightened – who knew what might happen if Anthony broke down my door? – but I felt dirty in a way I could never have imagined. I was no angel by anybody's measure, but this was a loss of innocence, total and complete. I'd been robbed of something that not even the Los Angeles Police Department could recover.

After what seemed an eternity of Anthony's wheedling at the door, I heard him walk away. Headed back to the party, no doubt. He was the host, after all, and things should be in full swing by now. A wave of nausea swept over me, thinking what manner of things might be going on that very second under this same roof. I desperately wanted to take a shower, to stand beneath scalding water to wash away the filth. I had been baptized in church, but right now I felt like I needed an extra-long dip in the river Jordan.

I thought about running a bath; I thought about calling Paulette; I even thought about crawling out the window. But a bathtub wasn't the river Jordan; beyond the window, there was nowhere to run; and I didn't want Paulette to know this had happened. I never wanted anyone to know. Over and over I repeated, "I didn't do anything wrong," until I fell asleep, wearing my lucky Daisy Mae dress that hadn't turned out to be so lucky.

*   *   *

It's never a good sign when you wake up the next morning wearing your cocktail dress. With returning consciousness, the horror of the night before came flooding back. I pulled myself up into a sitting position, and looked around the room, noting that the chair was still beneath the doorknob. I was safe for the moment, but God only knew what lay beyond that door. I sat motionless, listening for any sound from the other side, hearing only silence. I would have preferred the hum of Consuelo's vacuum cleaner.

A bright slice of light beneath the draperies made me want to throw them wide and let in the California sunshine. Instead, I tiptoed over, and barely parted the curtains for a peek outside. The shrubbery looked razor-trimmed, the grass mowed to one-inch precision, and not a single rose wilted on the vine. Lynn Anderson's hit song came into my head, *I beg your pardon, I never promised you a rose garden. No* As eerie as the outdoor perfection was, it gave me courage to open my bedroom door, which I knew I had to do.

Stepping beyond the doorway, I looked this way and that, listening as I continued down the hall, peering into each room I passed, until I came upon Consuelo in the party room, cleaning up last night's mess. *As if that kind of mess could ever be cleaned up.* Giving me her usual fish-eye, she went back to her work, and I went back to my room to decide what to do.

First, I would call my mama. Not that I wanted to tell her what had happened. Nosiree, as far as I was concerned, Mama would go to her grave not knowing about this. I just needed the sound of her voice.

"Hey, honey," she said. "I was just now looking for your phone number out there in California. Some man's been calling here, saying he's Elvis Presley."

# Chapter 4

"MAMA! THAT *IS* ELVIS!" I shot up from the bed, clutching the phone in both hands.

"Why would Elvis Presley be calling our house, Diana?" The way she said my name, it sounded like she was "put out" with me.

I took a deep breath to calm my voice. "Don't you remember? I told you Elvis said he would call."

"Yes, I do remember." She still sounded "put out." "I imagine everybody around here remembers all that Elvis foolishness you were talking when you came back from Memphis, and I'm sure whoever's calling here, is some crazy friend of yours playing a prank on you, and I do not appreciate it one bit. I keep hanging up on him and he keeps calling back."

"It is not a prank, Mama. It's Elvis."

"Well," she said, "Even if it is him – which it is not – what business has Elvis Presley got calling here asking for you? I think he's my age, Diana."

"But, Mama, he's Elvis," I said.

She heaved a sigh. "I don't know what difference that makes, but I tell you what, if you really want some crazy prank caller to get in touch with you, if he calls again, I'll give him the phone number."

"You promise?'

"We'll see," she said.

I collapsed onto the bed, in a state close to catatonic. *Elvis called.* Zooming from last night's depths to this kind of high was like lift-off in a rocket. It took me several minutes to come down to earth, but even after I got my senses back, never once did I consider that Mama could be right about it being a prank call. I did, however, consider myself to be in something of a pickle. Even though this had boosted me out of last night's despair, I still had to face the dilemma of being in the same house with Anthony Herrera. I had called Mama with some idea of telling her I was

Elvis and Diana Elvis Tour (1975). © Ron Galella/Ron Galella, Ltd.

flying back home tonight, to regroup and make a more solid plan, before coming back to L.A. for a longer stay, but this news about Elvis changed everything.

First of all, Elvis was a movie star, who surely had some sort of residence in Hollywood, maybe even Beverly Hills. What if he was right down the street from me this very second? That made me want to race for the door and go running up and down the streets calling his name. On the other hand, if I could get a taxi to take me to the airport soon enough, I might make it back home to be there when he called again. That seemed a pretty good idea, since it also cut the risk of Mama changing her mind about giving my phone number to a "prank caller." But what if Mama did give him my number and he tried to reach me here after I was gone? I repeat, *pickle*.

Scrambling my brain into a rat's nest wasn't helping, and somehow, my most brilliant ideas always seemed to come to me while I was on a pool float. I did the sensible thing. I strapped on my bikini and headed outside.

It couldn't have been more than five minutes after I got settled onto the float when I heard a male voice say, "Good morning, Diana," and opened my eyes to see Anthony standing beside the pool looking down at me.

"Please forgive me for last night," he said, "We'd all had too much to drink, and things got out of hand. I should have realized you weren't used to that kind of party. It's a long way from a small town in Georgia to Hollywood, and I was out of line to expect you to make the leap so fast."

*That's a leap I'll never make*, I thought. When I didn't answer, he said, "You don't need to lock yourself in your room, I won't bother you again, and I'll make sure that no one else does."

I nodded, and he walked back into the house, ending a distasteful situation in a way that allowed me to shelve it in the back of my mind until I was better able to deal with it. For now, I had more important things to think about, but I didn't have long to ponder, because right about the time I began to consider lunch, Consuelo stalked out of the house, and picked up the phone that sat on an umbrella table near the door, pointing the receiver at me."

It took a second for me to realize what she meant. "Oh! Phone call for me?"

She gave me a curt nod and laid the receiver on the table.

*Elvis!* I launched myself off the float, in the direction of the pool ladder, and climbed onto the hot concrete, running for the phone. "Hello?" I bent over, gasping for breath.

"Diana? This is Joe."

"Who?"

"I'm calling for Elvis," he said.

Somebody named Joe wanting to speak to Elvis. Could this be Mama's prank caller?

"Elvis is not here," I said, "Who are you?"

"This is Joe Esposito, Diana, and I know Elvis is not there, because he's right here with me, wanting to talk to you."

The next thing I heard was that velvet voice saying my name, "Diana? Where you been, honey? Didn't you know I was going to call? Why'd you leave town?"

"Well, I waited a long time, and then my friend invited me to come to Hollywood. . ."

He cut me off, "Hey, baby, I want you to go to the show with me tonight."

*Another movie date.* I melted. "Oh, I'd love that."

"Can you be ready in two hours?

"I sure can."

"Good, I'll send the plane for you."

"Did you say plane? Aren't you out here in Hollywood?'

"No, baby, I'm in New York. What did you think I meant? You're coming with me tonight, aren't you?"

"Of course, I am."

"All right then," he said, "I'm putting Joe back on to get your address. Limo will pick you up in two hours."

Now I had to ask Joe to wait while I went inside and hunted down the address. *By now they must be thinking I'm some kind of nut.*

*Whew.* This was almost too much to comprehend. I gave Joe the address then said bye and waded back into the pool for a few more minutes of "float time" to get my thoughts straightened out. As anxious as I was to see Elvis, I was a little relieved that I'd have to fly all the way to the east coast. During those five empty hours in the air, I could set my beauty case on the little tray table at my seat, and do my hair and makeup on the plane, which meant I didn't have to rush right now, I could relax and close my eyes, imagining Elvis greeting me at the airport, giving me that soft, slow kiss I had missed out on in Memphis. *Mm-mm-mmmm,* I wiggled my head, feeling his lips on mine.

The sound of the sliding doors opening woke me from my dream, and here came Consuelo marching over to the phone table. This time, instead of pointing the receiver at me, she jabbed it my direction. I felt like saying, *Isn't answering the phone part of your job?* but satisfied myself with giving her a "look" when I took the receiver from her hand. This was probably my mother calling to tell me that the prankster had called back, and she'd given him my number. Wouldn't she be surprised? Finally, *finally.* If revenge is a dish best served cold, then everybody who had doubted my Elvis story was about to enjoy a gourmet feast of crow on ice.

For good measure, I put a dollop of attitude in my voice when I said, "Hello?"

"Hey, baby, this is Elvis. Can you be ready in *one* hour?"

*What?* "Yes."

He said, "I started thinking about it and realized that you'll need to leave sooner to make it here for the show tonight, so the limo will be there in an hour, okay?"

"AOK." I'd still have a long plane ride to make myself "Elvis-worthy" and I wanted a little more dream-time on the pool float. Once again, I waded into the water, and once again, Consuelo came out of the house, stomped over to the phone, and jabbed the receiver at me. Surely this time it was my mom.

"Hey, it's Elvis. Thinking about it some more, there's no way I can get the plane out there and get you back here in time. I'm sorry."

*Oh, no!*

"I'm going to have to charter a Learjet in L.A. to bring you. It's a fast little jet, and I sure want you to get here to see me perform. I think the show's at the Nassau Coliseum tonight, then we've got some other dates up the east coast. Hope you can stay awhile."

*Perform?* A rash of goosebumps creeped over my body, with the realization that this was no movie date. I was going on tour with Elvis

"Can you be ready in thirty minutes?"

*Thirty minutes?* Frantically, I started wringing chlorine and baby oil from my hair. "Well." I took a deep breath. "I can be ready, but I'm not sure I'll have time to pack everything."

"No," he said, "don't pack anything. There's not enough time. Just bring yourself and we'll take care of whatever you need after you get here."

I packed anyway, if you could call literally throwing things in suitcases packing, then I plugged in the hot curlers, and jumped in and out of the shower, toweling my skin, blowing my hair and brushing my teeth all at the same time, leaving the few spare minutes it took to get the curlers in my hair and put on the same jeans and peasant blouse I'd worn on the flight coming out.

*Ding-dong.* At the door, stood a tall uniformed chauffeur. His eyes flicked up and down, taking in my country-girl clothes and pausing with a slight frown at the curlers in my hair. "I'm here to pick up Dian-*er,*" he said in a thick English accent.

"I'm Dian-er, um Diana," I said.

He gave me a doubtful look, as if I was not at all the dream-girl he'd anticipated taking to Elvis Presley. But he politely gathered my bags and off we went.

The only thing I knew about a Learjet came from the Carly Simon song "You're So Vain," *you flew your Learjet up to Nova Scotia to see the total eclipse of the sun,* which was supposedly about Warren Beatty, so I thought it must be a pretty cool way to travel. Elvis had called it a "fast little jet," but I was still surprised at how small it was, small enough for the pilots and me to communicate conversationally, cockpit-to-cabin, although we didn't do much talking. Once we were in the air, I went ahead and styled my hair and put on my makeup, then thumbed a few pages of a magazine, finally deciding I'd rather daydream about Elvis. I closed my eyes and thought about the evening ahead. I could easily imagine Elvis greeting me at the airport; I'd been dreaming of that moment for over a month, but imagining being with him at his show was harder because I'd never done anything remotely like it. Would I watch from backstage, or would there be a special front row seat reserved for me? Would he introduce me? *Ladies and gentlemen, I'd like you to meet my girlfriend, Diana Goodman.* In my mind, I saw the spotlight find me in the front row as I stood up waving to the crowd. Maybe he'd even sing to me. I knew exactly which song it would be. *Wise men say only fools rush in, but I can't help falling in love with you. . .*

A bustling in the cockpit, pulled me from my imagining. The co-pilot stepped into the cabin and sat in the seat beside me. "I just want to let you know that we're not going to make it in time for you to go to Elvis's show."

My face must have shown my disappointment, because he continued, "Instead, we are flying you into the airport, where you will board Elvis's plane and fly on to his next stop."

After he went back into the cockpit, I sat there trying not to cry, telling myself that it wasn't a total disaster, I was still headed for Elvis, but the truth was that this changed everything. None of my imaginings had been correct. He wouldn't be introducing me to the audience or singing "Can't Help Falling" to me, because I wouldn't be there. Worse, I had no idea where I would be or where I was going, or even when I'd be seeing him. Once again, I was in Elvis limbo.

But I didn't have long to fret. I'd barely had time to realize we were descending when the pilot announced, "We'll be on the ground in a few minutes."

It was dusk when we landed. I came out of the plane, searching the crowd on the tarmac for his distinctive head of velvet-black hair, and checking windows of the parked planes for a glint of the heavy-metal sunglasses he'd worn on the way to the Memphian Theater. There was no sign of Elvis, but my heart leapt at sight of a couple of familiar faces from his Memphis entourage. One was a rock-star looking guy with long surfer-blond hair, and the other had darker hair with mutton-chop sideburns.

The "rock star" took my hand as I stepped onto the tarmac. "Hi, Diana, I'm Ricky Stanley."

Mutton-chop came forward, "And I'm Sonny West." Then he turned to Ricky and said, "Grab her bags."

Ricky shot back, "Darn. I forgot to wear my bellboy cap today. Get 'em yourself," and the two stepped aside, arguing.

I glanced at my heap of luggage a few feet away, and grimaced. For the trip, I'd scavenged the biggest suitcases from all my family and friends, but even that wasn't room enough. Remembering my wardrobe malfunction in Memphis, I was determined to be prepared for any eventuality that might come up on my first trip to Hollywood, so every day, I'd think of another item or ten that might come in handy, until the cardboard sides of my sister's K-mart "two-suiter" literally burst at the seams, and I fixed it by winding duct tape around it, mummy-style, tossing the roll of tape in another bag for re-wrapping on the trip home. *Smart, huh?* At the time, I was so proud of my creative solution, I called in my brothers to view my handiwork. I even preened a little when Gary patted me on the back and said, "Good girl, sis. That'll hold it." Staring at it sitting on the tarmac, it was hard to imagine what I'd been thinking back then, when right now the picture that kept popping into my head was my "heap" of luggage roped onto the top of the plane like the *Beverly Hillbillies'* teetering stack of old trunks tied to their jalopy. Maybe I should deny the bags were mine. Elvis had told me not to pack anything, and mama always said I should learn to listen. She also said it was never too late to learn, so maybe this was a good time to start. For sure, there was nothing of any real value in all that mismatched cardboard and cheap plastic, but I'd packed so much in such a hurry, I couldn't remember whether I'd packed something I couldn't live without, something like my Miss Georgia crown, for instance. Why I would have packed it to go to Hollywood I'm not sure, but you never knew, and the pageant folks wouldn't be happy to find out that I'd left it sitting on a hot tarmac in New Jersey. No, disavowing the bags was not an option, so I went to Plan B, and sidled over to them, easing my hand out and wrapping it around one of the handles. If I couldn't keep Elvis's guys from knowing this was my luggage, I could at least keep them from getting a good look.

Sonny raised his palms. "No, no, you don't! Ricky'll take care of those."

I let go of the bag, and turned away from the "heap." Oh, well, it wasn't really my fault. How was I to know those bags would be going on tour with Elvis? I'd thought their final destination was my friend Paulette's house, and duct tape wouldn't bother her a bit. *Paulette!* I hadn't called to tell her I was leaving. Then again, she hadn't exactly been keeping close tabs on me, and I didn't remember her checking with me when she rushed into the arms of B.J. Thomas. Back to matters at hand, from the corner of my eye, I watched Ricky loading my bags, and cringed when he held the duct-taped two-suiter in the air, shaking his head, chuckling to himself.

Worse than showing up in a Daisy Mae costume for a movie night in Memphis, now I'd arrived dragging all my worldly possessions behind me in duct-taped suitcases like some kind of redneck bag lady. *Do these things happen to everybody, or just to me? No, Diana, these things do not happen to everybody. Not everybody goes on tour with Elvis.* Good point, but Lord have mercy, was I going to have to be prepared to meet Elvis Presley every time I stepped out the door for the rest of my life? *You should be so lucky.* I crossed my fingers behind my back, making a wish that he'd be behind the next door I stepped through, which was the portal of the plane.

Comparing this jet to the others parked nearby, size-wise, it fell somewhere in the middle, but the interior was a far cry from average. If I'd woken up here from a drool nap, I would've thought I'd fallen asleep in a Waffle House. Since nobody had told me any better, I'd assumed I'd be getting on a commercial jet, but in place of the rows of seats I expect-ed, were upholstered benches and chairs, surrounding wooden tables in groupings, where several men sat talking and tossing comments to guys who were loading things into the cabin. Inside the cockpit, one of the pi-lots nodded a greeting to me, as did a young woman wearing a uniform, who was stepping through a curtained area in the same spot as the galley on a regular airplane. The peanuts I'd snacked on the Learjet hadn't added much fuel to my banana and diet-cola breakfast, so I smiled hopefully at the woman coming from the "kitchen," and asked Sonny, "Where should I sit?" hoping he'd reply, "Next to Elvis."

From what the co-pilot of the Learjet had told me, I gathered they were bringing me to this airport to meet Elvis, but I'd been too shy, and too shocked, to inquire whether that meant we'd be flying from here to meet him somewhere else, or that he'd be meeting us here later, or maybe even that he'd be here to greet me when I arrived. *God, please let it be the last option.* But as hard as I looked, I saw no sign of Elvis, and nothing to give me a clue where he would sit, when he showed up, *if* he showed up. I caught the eye of one of the men with the group in the back, hoping he'd signal me to come over, but he only gave me a half-smile before continu-ing his conversation with the others, so I walked a few steps further, and scooted into a booth midway down the aisle, stashing my shoulder-bag on the seat beside me, next to the wall, so that if Elvis boarded, I could move over for him to sit beside me and my bag would take up the extra space on the seat, leaving me no choice but to make "accidental" body contact.

I rested my head on the back of the bench and thought about that moment of first body contact. I'd been mistakenly imagining him greeting me when I got off the plane, but as usual, I'd had it backwards; instead of Elvis greeting me, I'd be greeting him. This scenario reminded me of the movie night in Memphis when I'd waited in the limo outside Graceland. *Please, God, don't let it turn out like that.* On the other hand, that night in Memphis was what got me here. *Forgive me, God, that night in Memphis turned out perfect. Please forget my ungrateful thought and keep right on planning things for me.* I gazed upward and signaled thumbs-up.

Glancing to my left, I saw that the stewardess was standing by my seat.

"Excuse me," she said, "Would you like something to drink?"

"Do you have root beer?"

She raised a finger, "Let me check," and in a few seconds, returned with a glass of ice and a can of root beer that happened to be Shasta, my favorite brand. I took the coincidence as a good omen, and considered it confirmed when, just as I was taking the last sip, I heard a commotion on the tarmac and looked out the window to see cars careening to a halt among the flashing lights of police-cruisers. Elvis was arriving.

I held my breath at the sound of car doors slamming and footsteps running up the metal stairs. A man stepped aboard. *Not Elvis.* Another man. *Not Elvis.* Then the velvet-black hair I'd been looking for ducked through the door and a flash of rhinestones streaked into the curtained area. Elvis was on the plane, but what was he doing in the kitchen?

I kept my eyes on the door, watching the men who followed Elvis onboard, hoping one of them would say something to clue me in, but they sailed right past me, joining the buddy group further back, leaving me to sit there all by myself, with Elvis only a few feet away. This gave "too close for comfort" a whole new meaning. After the twists and turns they'd put me through today, how dare they expect me to sit here calm as cream, with Elvis Presley doing who knew what behind the kitchen curtains. It would serve them right if I tossed Miss Manners out the porthole, then took off up the aisle, charged through that curtain and flung myself at the King. I just might have done it if a voice hadn't come over the intercom and knocked me back in my seat. I was too unraveled to understand exactly what the pilot was announcing, but "approach" and "destination" caught my ear. *What? Landing?* So, my one single glimpse of Elvis was *it,* that's all I was going to get? My heart nearly stopped with the thought that he might have escaped through a secret exit. Then the curtain parted, and he stepped through. His eyes flicked right then left, and locked on mine, never blinking as he came toward me with a slow swagger.

I couldn't even smile. The only part of my body capable of movement was my stomach threatening to spew a hot mess of Shasta root beer and Planter's peanuts all over Elvis's shiny black boots, now standing in the aisle next to my seat. With a quick prayer to the guardian angel of nervous stomachs, I managed to scoot sideways without throwing up, and Elvis sat down.

"Hey," he said.

I'm sure I wasn't the first girl to be struck dumb by his presence. He gave me his signature lopsided smile, and took my hand. His other hand held a small black velvet box, which he placed on the table in front of us. It was about the size of a ring box, so I couldn't help wondering what was in it, but he didn't mention it, didn't even glance at. His eyes were totally focused on mine. "I'm sorry for all the confusion today", he said, "I had to do a good bit of arranging, but I really wanted to see you. I just wish I'd been able to get you here in time for the show. But there'll be plenty of others.

My mouth thawed into a smile and he squeezed my hand. "You must've been wondering why I stayed behind that curtain so long, but after a performance, I'm so keyed up I have to take some time to get out of my stage clothes and relax a few minutes. That room back there has a place for me to lie down and a place for me to get cleaned up."

I lowered my eyes, "I thought it was a kitchen," my voice came out in a whisper.

He laughed. "Naw, I'll show it to you sometime. That's one reason I wanted you to come to the show, so you'd understand what goes on." He smiled and touched my hair with the tip of his finger, "I like long hair. "Then he rubbed his thumb across my pinkie nail. "I like long nails, too. But you know what I don't like?" He made a point of peering down at my pants-leg. "Jeans. You see, growing up, we were real poor and the only kind of clothes my mama and daddy could afford to buy me were dungarees and overalls, so blue jeans remind of that, and I don't like thinking about being poor, so I'd rather see you in something else when we're together. Not that you don't look cute in those, 'cause you do. You'd look cute in anything, but I'd prefer something else, if you don't mind.

"I don't mind at all," I said. No more blue jeans."

Now he turned my hand over to examine my rings and bracelet. "I see you like turquoise. I like it, too."

Until that moment, other than his boots, I'd been too brain-frazzled to notice what he was wearing, but now I saw that with his navy-blue leisure suit, he had on a number of pieces of jewelry. I recognized the TCB necklace that I'd seen in movie magazines, and the heavy gold cross he wore around his neck. Looking at his rings, I noticed that the ugly fingernail bruise – the one that had disturbed me in Memphis – had shrunk to a small dark crescent, but I still found it disturbing, and I vowed to myself that nothing like that would ever happen to him as long as he was with me.

Realizing he saw me looking at the bruise, I shifted my gaze to one of his rings. "This is pretty."

"Thanks. Lowell made that one." He turned in his seat and called to the group of men, "Hey, Lowell, come on up here and meet Diana."

A dark-haired man with glasses set a black bag on the table in front of us and slid onto the opposite bench.

Elvis said, "Diana Goodman, meet Lowell Hays." Then to me, he said, "Lowell's from Memphis. He makes all my jewelry."

That would explain the black bag, but if the intention was to show me its contents, he never got the chance, because before either of us could say more than, "Nice to meet you," Elvis asked the stewardess to bring a couple of Shasta Colas, pulled out a cigar, and the two of them talked "men talk" until we landed.

Outside the plane window was the same commotion I'd seen when Elvis arrived before we took off, but this time, in addition to limos and police, was a barrier restraining a crowd of fans and photographers. Exiting the plane, Elvis grabbed my hand and said, "Just stay with me." At the foot of the staircase, a limo waited with doors ajar. Elvis dove into the backseat, pulling me after him.

I didn't know exactly where we were, nor did I care, and if I had been expecting a red-carpet arrival to a grand hotel lobby, I was wrong. We entered a mid-size Hilton Hotel through a side door off an alley, and took a service elevator up to our floor, escorted by hotel security officers.

Walking down the hallway to our rooms, my nervousness returned. All this while, I'd been thinking of Elvis as the "white knight" who rescued me from the "black knight," Anthony Herrera, but now I realized that I didn't know Elvis any better than I'd known Anthony when we first met, and I'd thought Anthony was as nice as they came. If I could be as wrong as I'd been about that, I could be just as wrong about this, and I wasn't up to handling another situation like the one I'd just been through.

What a relief when the security officer ushered us into the living-dining-kitchen combo of a suite that had adjoining bedrooms left and right. Even so, it was awkward, waiting in the living room with Elvis, neither of us looking at each other, while the security men checked the suite, and as anxious as I'd been to find myself in this situation, when everyone said goodnight, leaving only Elvis, Sonny and me, I came close to fleeing into the hall.

Elvis must have sensed my fight-or-flight response, because he stepped over and took my hand, holding it tightly, so I couldn't have fled, even if I'd wanted to, which I no longer did. "Hey, Sonny," he said, "Wait here a minute, while I show Diana her room." He led me to the door on the left, which opened into a bedroom of yellow ruffles that made me squeal with delight. *Every little girl's dream* was my first thought, and even though I wasn't a little girl, I had a feeling it had been done especially for me, and I loved it.

Entering the room, Elvis had left the door partially open; now he narrowed the opening to give us privacy, and took my hands in his, looking deeply into my eyes. "It's important to me that you know I'm not some kind of make-out artist," he said, "and you are under no pressure whatsoever. But you're going to find out that my suite is like Grand Central Station, people coming and going all the time, so I wanted you to have something you'd be comfortable wearing while we're in the hotel." He pointed at two big white boxes on the bed. "You've had a long day, so I'll leave you to freshen up. I'll be in the living room, so whenever you're ready, just come on out and we'll order some dinner." He winked at me. "I better go get rid of Sonny before he makes himself too comfortable in front of the TV."

I spread my arms and fell backwards into the softness of that fluffy yellow bed and could have stayed there the rest of the night, crying for joy, but Elvis was waiting for me in the living room, and I had presents to open. I pulled the boxes onto my lap and leaned against the ruffled pillows, untying pink satin ribbons and rustling tissue paper, hardly believing what I saw. Each box held a wedding-night peignoir so obviously delicate and fine that for a few minutes, I sat there staring into the boxes, afraid to touch them. These were not flimsy see-through sexpot nighties, as I might have feared, these were the kind of things I envisioned a woman like Princess Grace or Jacqueline Kennedy wearing on her honeymoon. I'd always loved the word "demure" but I never dreamed I'd have the chance to embody it. Taking great care, I placed two fingers on each shoulder of a white satin robe, then oh-so-gently lifted it from the box, then laid it across my body, closing my eyes and running my hands over the silk satin, smoothing the lustrous fabric down my torso. I'd never owned real silk. It was too expensive. But feeling this slippery softness, I understood the expense. In the other box was a similar white gown and robe, but instead of satin, this robe was layers and layers of chiffon, tied with a loopy satin bow at the empire waistline. After bathing and freshening my hair and makeup, I put on the frothier of the two, and floated across the living room to the bedroom that was Elvis's inner sanctum. Through the open door, Elvis was not visible, but in the center of the room, I spied a king size bed with a fluffy comforter and lots of blue and white throw pillows. As I neared the doorway, to the left of the bed, a seating area came into view with an oversized sofa and coffee table, and further to the left was a dining nook, where Elvis sat at the table, wearing baby-blue silk pajamas. His eyes followed my every step as I crossed the room to stand before him, then he took me by the hand, his eyes rising slowly from my bare feet up the length of my body, before lingering on my face. "Do you like your present, baby?"

I touched the satin bow between my breasts and smiled. "I love it."

"And I love you in it," he said.

The only light in the room came from a lamp beside the sofa and a pair of flickering candles on the table, which was set with white linen and china, and a centerpiece of white roses. He led me to my place across from him, pulling out my chair like the perfect southern gentleman he was, then he swept his arm, indicating a room-service cart loaded with silver-domed dishes. "I didn't know what you'd want to eat," he said, "so I ordered everything on the menu."

*Oh, my god!* It was exactly the kind of gesture I should have expected from Elvis Presley, but still, I was flabbergasted. Stepping to the cart, he began lifting the domes to show me my choices: Hamburger and fries; onion-smothered hamburger steak, with mashed potatoes and gravy; fried chicken; fish and hushpuppies; and a T-bone steak with a loaded baked potato. Somehow, he'd managed to come up with all my favorite foods. My only problem was which to choose. I thought quickly and decided the burger and fries would be easiest to eat, because I didn't really plan to eat it. As hungry as I'd been before, with this feast staring me in the face, the butterflies in my stomach fluttered, and swept away my hunger. Picking at a few French fries would make it look like I was eating, even if I wasn't. Elvis chose the smothered steak. *Well, I'll be darned.* This was one king who ate just like us common folks.

Elvis took my selection from the cart and set it before me with a flourish – *Oh, my goodness, Elvis Presley just served me dinner!* – then he sat down and tucked into his steak and onions. Accustomed to watching my brothers wolfing down their meals, it struck me that although Elvis was eating heartily, he was doing it in a mannerly way, chewing thoroughly and swallowing before speaking, holding his knife and fork the way Mama taught, which I thought was pretty impressive for a boy raised in a shotgun shack in Tupelo.

I had used the French-fry trick on other occasions when I wanted to give the appearance of eating what I wasn't, and so far, no one had ever caught on, but after a few minutes, Elvis laid down his fork and said, "Don't you like your food?"

"It's delicious," I said, but, I'm happy just watching you eat yours."

That seemed to please him because he gave me his lop-sided grin and said, "What did you eat at your house growing up, what did your mama like to cook?"

"Aw, we just ate southern food, the usual stuff," I answered, "but I can tell you for sure that Friday-night supper was always fried chicken, and Sunday dinner was always a roast that Mama would put in the oven before we left for church, timing it to be done when we got home."

Then he started talking about favorites that his mama used to cook, and when his face went all soft, remembering, my heart swelled, thinking about him as a little boy, his twin brother dead and buried, leaving him an only child, living in that rundown old place with just his mama and daddy for company. What a big difference in that and my family's rowdy household with constant coming and going and one child or another either laughing or crying every second of the day. No wonder Elvis wanted to hear about my family. So, I told him about mine, and he told me about his, and we talked on, until he finished his last bite of hamburger steak. Then he tilted his glass to his mouth swallowing the last of his ice-tea, then he placed his napkin on the table, stood up and walked over to the bed. My eyes followed him, and when I saw him reach for something on top of the nightstand, I realized it was the little black box he'd been carrying on the plane, but instead of picking up the box, he palmed a tiny bottle, and brought it back to the table, unscrewing the cap to squirt liquid into his mouth. Then he chuckled. "I love steak and onions, but I can't stand to have it on my breath, so I always use this." He offered me the bottle. "Want some?"

I turned the bottle over in my hand and saw that it was Binaca breath drops. *How cute, and how considerate.* I was loving him more every minute. But I did wonder about that little black box.

Then he said, "These chairs are getting a little hard," and that's how we got to the sofa. But he didn't make himself comfortable just yet. Instead of sitting beside me, as I expected, he walked back over to the nightstand, and this time, he picked up that little black box. Now he sat beside me on the sofa with the box in his hand, and if that wasn't a ring box, I didn't know what.

"I had a little something made for you." He opened the box and presented it to me on his palm. The ring inside was the most beautiful thing I'd ever seen. Alternating squares set with sapphires and diamonds were stacked in a pyramid at least two inches high and wide. I held my breath as he took it from the box and slipped it onto my finger.

"Is this real?" I squealed.

Elvis shrank back. "Do you think I'd buy you a fake ring?"

"Well," I said, "I've never seen a piece of jewelry like this close-up. I don't even think I've seen anything like this from far away, and I've surely never been given anything like it." My shoulders slumped, "Oh, I really don't know what I'm saying, whatever's coming out of my mouth, sounds all wrong."

His face softened, and I ventured a sideways glance from beneath my lashes, "You even got the right size. How did you know?"

He scooted closer, looking into my eyes. "I know a lot about you. I know you have two sisters and two brothers and that your dad is a truck driver and that you're Miss Georgia. I can't bring just anybody into my life, you know."

That made me remember something I'd forgotten, something from that first night at the Memphian Theater. On the way to the movie, Dave had given me a spiel that sounded rehearsed, some sort of Elvis Rules: "Don't take pictures of him, don't grab him, no sudden moves," stuff like that. I didn't think much of it at the time, because who could be scared of me? And I wasn't going to do any of those things anyway. But sitting here now, wanting to hug him, I remembered and refrained.

So instead of the big hug and kiss he deserved, all Elvis got was my simple, "Thank you very much," and as I've said before, the only time I seem to do anything right is when I think I'm doing it wrong. This was one of those times. I thought a simple "Thank you" was not enough, but Elvis must have thought it was *just* enough, because he put his arm around my shoulders and started running his fingers through my hair. Then he touched my chin, turning my face to his, and said, "Can I kiss you?"

I answered with my eyes, and he placed his lips on mine in a sweet soft kiss that grew more intense, until finally, he pulled back and said, "I need to get plenty of rest for the show tomorrow night, so it's time for me to go to bed. I'd like you to join me, but as I told you earlier, it's up to you."

I'm sure he could feel my heart pounding, while he waited for my answer. The smart thing would be to leave him with a sweet "goodnight" and a kiss that would light such a fire in him he wouldn't get a wink of sleep, for wanting me. But I wasn't smart, I was in love.

"I'll stay."

Elvis stood up and went to the wall switch, turning off all the lights except for the lamp by the sofa, then he led me to the bed, throwing back the covers, and untying my robe so that it fell to the floor.

Mesmerizing me with a deep kiss, he pulled me down to sit beside him on the bed, gradually moving his lips from my mouth to my cheek and down my neck to my shoulder, until I was tingling all over.

"Are you okay?" His warm breath on my skin made me shiver.

"Very okay," I whispered.

Taking the straps in his teeth, he removed my gown from my shoulders, letting the top fall to my waist, as he kissed his way down to my navel. I stroked his hair and lowered my head, nuzzling the back of his neck, breathing the warm, spicy smell of him.

"Can we lie down?" he murmured against my bare stomach, and we slid beneath the covers.

For a few moments, we lay very still, in each other's arms, and I'd never felt safer than right there, with Elvis holding me while I trembled like a virgin bride on her honeymoon. When he peeled off my gown and removed his pajamas, it was the most natural thing in the world, coming together, skin to skin, not as Elvis the King and his Georgia Beauty Queen, but as a man and a woman, making love.

\* \* \*

Waking the next day, I came out of sleep lying on my side, facing the seating area of the bedroom, and in the dim light of morning, I did not recognize the scene until I moved my foot and touched Elvis's leg. Daring not to wake him, I eased slowly onto my back, and turned my head to gaze into his face. Although he seemed sound asleep, he must have felt my eyes on him, because suddenly, he rolled onto his stomach and threw his arm over me. I held my breath, keeping perfectly still, afraid I might rouse him, and take away my opportunity to lie there memorizing every single thing about his face, things like the way his thick dark lashes curled up at the tips, and the softness of his mouth, relaxed with sleep, childlike, almost angelic. I ran my eyes across his exposed back and shoulder, the skin so satiny it seemed to glow. The word "supernatural" occurred to me, and I smiled remembering the night before. Last night, he had certainly been all man, and glancing around the room, reminders of our romantic midnight supper remained, in a mess of dirty dishes and garments littering the floor, a sight that would normally bring that awful *Oh my God what have I done* moment when I'd snatch up my clothes and flee the scene. But instead, I felt the perfect peace of Elvis's arm encircling me, protecting me, and the wonder of realizing that Elvis Presley, the biggest star in the world, had bestowed a sacred trust, taking me into his bed, literally to his bosom, while he slept, completely and utterly vulnerable. The awe of it made me want to cry.

I batted my lashes in a flurry of blinking back tears. The last thing I wanted was for Elvis to see me first thing in the morning with my face smeared from bawling. My hands flew to my face and I began to rub furiously at my cheeks. Our lovemaking had been nothing if not tumultuous, then I had slept like the dead, which undoubtedly created more smeary, bleary havoc, but there was no mirror handy to assess the damages. I touched the top of my cheekbone, wondering if by some miracle the mascara had clung to my lashes instead of painting Rocky-Raccoon rings around my eyes. Very carefully, I twisted my head to check the pillow, and sure enough, there were the tell-tale black streaks. What a pickle. I couldn't possibly slip out of bed and dash to my room for a clean-up, without waking Elvis. As a last resort, I stuck my finger in my mouth and wiped my eyes with saliva, then blew in my palm and sniffed. My breath was not as bad as I expected, but it wasn't as fresh as I would have wished, either, so I stuck my finger back in my mouth and wiggled it around, scrubbing my teeth the best I could without a toothbrush, then cleanup complete, I went back to studying Elvis.

Although, after our love-making, he hadn't wanted me to leave, I couldn't help wondering if he would be pleased to find me in bed with him the next morning, and sure enough when his eyes fluttered open, he did look surprised to see me. But only for a second. Then he smiled and asked, "Did you sleep well?"

I nodded. "Best night's sleep I've had in a while."

"Same here," he said, gathering me into his arms, and my finger-toothbrush must have worked, because he kissed me like he wanted to eat me up, and made love to me like he could never get his fill.

Afterward, lying side-by-side, recovering, I wondered what to expect now. This wasn't the usual situation where one or both of us had to jump out of bed and get ready for work. Elvis was a creature of the night; it was hard to imagine him doing anything in the morning, anything at all.

He cut his eyes at me. "You hungry?"

I giggled, "For what?"

He ruffled my hair, "Breakfast, silly," and swung his legs over the side of the bed, pulling on his pajama bottoms. Then he headed to the bathroom, graciously allowing me time to get into my gown and robe, before he came back, saying, "I usually order pancakes and eat them sitting on the sofa, watching game shows."

"Pancakes sound great," I said, when in fact, I rarely ate breakfast. But whatever Elvis was having, was exactly what I wanted, or at least what I wanted him to think.

He took my hands, pulling me to my feet, and led me to the door of the living/dining/kitchen area, where we'd entered the suite the night before. Then he opened the door, and hand-in-hand, we stepped from his bedroom into a room filled with people.

As demurely as my beautiful peignoir covered my essential parts, it would have taken a full suit of armor to hide what Elvis and I had been doing all night, and even that wouldn't have fooled this crowd. As of yet, I hadn't even gotten a chance to brush my teeth, much less my hair, so the evidence was plain to see. I couldn't raise my eyes without catching a knowing look from somebody, but if Elvis caught any snickers or stares, either he didn't notice, or he didn't mind. He greeted everybody with a good-morning grin, traded a few quips with his guys, and shook the hands of several policemen, who were there I knew not why, then he tossed a wave to the group, and we strolled over to the seating area, to make ourselves comfy on the sofa.

"Good," he said, clicking on the TV, "The *Price is Right*'s just coming on. One of my favorites. You like it?"

"Mm-hm." I nodded enthusiastically, even though game shows were not really my thing. I was more interested in watching our greeting party to see if they were watching me, but thankfully, one-by-one, they dispersed, until by the time Elvis picked up the phone to order breakfast, we were alone.

"What do you like on your pancakes?" he asked. "I eat syrup, butter and jelly on mine."

I really didn't know what I liked on my pancakes since I couldn't remember the last time I'd eaten one. "Syrup," I said, and snuggled next to Elvis, until he got up to open the door for room service.

Apparently, this wasn't the first time the waiter had served Elvis breakfast, because, instead of steering his cart into the dining area, he headed straight for the sofa, cleared the coffee table, set it for breakfast, and left without getting Elvis to sign for our meal. So, either being Elvis Presley meant you didn't have to pay for your food, or somebody else did the paying for you. *Gee, you'd think the guy would've at least asked for an autograph, or something.*

Watching Elvis remove the dome from the large platter, I said, "Would you like me to butter your pancakes?"

His hand stopped mid-air, the dome hovering over the platter. "Oh, I think I sure would." He gave me a slow wink and a wicked grin, as if I'd said something naughty.

I couldn't imagine what could be sexy about buttering pancakes, but the wicked grin remained as he watched my every move while I painstakingly spread butter and jam on each one and stacked them atop each other. Then I picked up the syrup pitcher, "Say when."

"Pour till it makes a puddle around the rim of the plate," he instructed.

"Good?" I asked, watching him take the first bite.

"Mm-mm," he answered, chewing while he forked another and another, talking to the TV between mouthfuls. "Aw, naw, you shoulda stopped there, dummy!" he'd coach the contestant, or turn to me, "Can you believe she bid that? How could an Amana Radar Range cost three-thousand dollars?" then back to the TV, "What bus did you come in on, lady?"

I only smiled and nodded *yes*, or shook my head *no*, trying to gauge which answer he wanted, because I wasn't paying any attention to the show; I was too busy marveling at this superstar sitting here all twisted up in the pricing of appliances he'd never use in his life, and automobiles he wouldn't be caught dead driving. This was a whole 'nother Elvis, and of the several sides I'd seen in the past twenty-four hours, I thought I might like this one best of all.

Right about the time the networks went from morning game shows to afternoon "soaps," Elvis's guys started drifting in, to discuss the day's schedule, which interested me not in the least, since I didn't care where we were going or what was happening when, as long as I was with Elvis, so my attention wandered to *One Life to Live*, until suddenly I felt Elvis's finger touch my chest.

"Be ready on time," he said. "*Do. Not. Be. Late.*" A tap on my chest punctuated each word.

In those days, one of my brothers' favorite jokes was, *Diana's extremely reliable; you can always rely on her to be late.* Ba-da-bum. But I had a feeling it would be no laughing matter to Elvis.

"Then, I'd better go to my room and start getting dressed." I got up from the sofa, dragging my bare feet on the carpet as I went. Walking away from Elvis would never be easy, but after being glued to his side for so many hours, I almost literally had to tear myself away. I did want to have time to make myself perfect for our first real date, though. As many hours as I'd spent dreaming of the night to come, I never would have imagined that my first evening out with the King of Rock-and-Roll would be one of his own concerts, and I wanted to look every inch Elvis's dream date.

With over two hours until time to leave, I had the leisure to polish and puff myself into perfection, but leaning over the sink to brush my teeth, I glanced up and noticed the wide-track-tire stripe running down the top of my head. Maybe I should have brought my pesky little sister along to remind me when I needed a touch-up. Two hours was a lot of time, but was it time enough? The stripe splitting my head seemed to widen as I stared at it. I parted my hair this way and that, wondering if perfection was worth risking being late. Elvis had sounded deadly serious about that, but between perfectly beautiful and perfectly punctual, I made the choice that any girl in my position would make. I reached into my cosmetic case for the bottle of Clairol Baby Blonde.

Anybody who's ever gone blonde knows that the color in the bottle is a far cry from the finished product, so twenty minutes later, I was standing in front of the mirror with my hair fully coated in purple dye, when I heard a knock at my door. *Hotel Maid?* I surely hoped so. The only other person it might be was – Oh, dear God no, it can't be – But it was.

"Hey, Diana, it's me."

*Lord have mercy!*

I'd made it through the morning-after gauntlet with flying colors, but in certain circumstances, bed-head and smudged eyes could be considered sexy. "Flying Purple People Eater?" Any way you looked at it, that was nothing but scary.

Elvis knocked again. "Diana?"

I grabbed one of the extra-thick-and-fluffy white towels to wind around my head in a turban. I wound once, then twice, then again and once more. Nobody could accuse the Hilton of short-sheeting the towels; the twist atop my head rose two-feet in the air. *Great*. Now, instead of the Purple People Eater I looked like a Conehead. *Whatever*. I pulled on a terry-cloth robe and opened the door.

At sight of my do-rag, Elvis's mouth crooked up at one corner, but all he said was, "I need some help, I can't get the shower to work."

*What?* He's got fifty or so big strong guys along for the ride on this tour, and he's dragging me out of the bathtub to fix his shower? Given my state of undress it would've been reasonable to suggest he call Housekeeping, but I tightened the belt of my bathrobe and followed him to his room, thanking God that none of the guys were lounging in front of the TV as we crossed the common area.

I'm not sure what particular quality Elvis saw in me that led him to assume I was the kind of girl who was handy with plumbing. Maybe since my brother was a handyman, he thought it was genetic. At any rate, he soon found out otherwise.

I stood beside him staring at the shower handle, as mystified as he was.

"What's the matter with it?" I asked.

"I don't guess anything's the matter with it," he said, "but look at that shower knob, if that's what you call it. It's some kind of newfangled thing I've never seen before. I've twisted it every way I know to twist, and it hasn't given me so much as a trickle. I thought maybe you could figure it out."

That made me feel better. It wasn't that he mistook me for a plumber, he mistook me for somebody that was smart. Wouldn't it be amazing if I proved him right? So, I twisted and turned the knob this way and that, then the other, and lo and behold, water!

"Gosh, thank you," he said.

I beamed proudly, "You're quite welcome," and scurried back to my room to get the hair-color rinsed off before Flying Purple People Eater ate holes in my scalp.

Even though my hair was a couple of shades lighter than it would have been without Miss Clairol's help, the Miss Georgia officials had dubbed me Little Miss Au Naturel, for my dislike of makeup. It may sound vain, but I truly thought I looked better without it, and it sure was nice that I didn't have to spend hours putting on a bunch of goop that didn't improve on what nature had provided, anyway. My hair though? That was another matter. Nature had provided me so well in that department that it took forever just to get it washed and dried. Then I had a laundry bag full of curlers to put in, and comb-out was a chore of its own, so there went the better part of an hour. Thank God, I had my outfit for the evening selected and hung out, ready to slip into. Back then, in the early disco era of 1975, an evening on the town called for satin and sequins, so anticipating glamorous Hollywood nights that didn't happen, I had packed a couple of sexy shimmery outfits in my suitcase for L.A., never suspecting I was actually packing them for the biggest and most glamorous nights of my life, this particular night most of all, so after consideration that may have crossed the line into obsessive over-thinking, I chose a simple white satin halter-neck jumpsuit, with a neckline that plunged to my naval, and made my waistline look about eighteen inches. Giving myself the once-over in the full-length mirror, I said "lean machine."

When I heard Elvis's knock, I took a moment to strike a hand-on-hip pose and to stretch my smile into beauty-queen brilliance before flinging open the door.

Looking me up and down, he said, "You look great in that jumpsuit," and the way he licked his lips and swallowed hard, if he had been any other man, he would have tossed me onto the bed and forgotten all about the show. But with Elvis, the show always came first.

\* \* \*

I had never been in a star's dressing room, so I really didn't know what to expect. I wasn't surprised at all the flowers, because the backstage at a beauty pageant was always covered with "good luck" bouquets and Elvis surely had more well-wishers than even the most congenial Miss Congeniality, but what did surprise me, was all the food; fruit baskets, cakes, cookies, cheese and crackers, chips and dips and every kind of sandwich meat, and even more surprising was that the first thing Elvis did when we entered the room was circle the counters, looking at every card on every floral arrangement and every gift-basket of food. It struck me how very gratified the senders would be to know that their gifts meant so much to him, and I wished I could tell them somehow. But as much as he appreciated them, if I expected Elvis or anybody else to take time to smell the roses or to sit down and eat any of the food, I was wrong. No sooner had we gotten there than Red and Joe ushered me out of the room, into the auditorium, where they showed me to my seat on a little balcony attached to the stage, which would put me to Elvis's left when he came out to perform.

The band was already onstage, getting things situated exactly the way they wanted, and most of the audience was in their seats. I was very close to the first few rows, and you can bet they did not take their eyes off me. These were thousands of Elvis fans who had probably recognized Red and Joe as the ones who brought me out, so they would know I was with Elvis's entourage, but they surely must be wondering exactly who I was. The buzz in the room had increased as soon as I sat down, so I knew they were talking about me, which made me sit that much taller. I wanted to stand up and shout, "I came with Elvis and I'm leaving with him, too!" and pretty soon I got the chance, when a woman in the front row shouted at me, "Are you Elvis's girlfriend?"

I sat even taller in my seat, so everybody could see me, cupped my hands around my mouth and called back to her, "Yes, I'm Elvis's girl-friend!"

Then, as if on cue, the lights went down, and the band started playing – not that they would try to shut me up, at least I hoped not – but it did keep me from carrying on any kind of conversation with the front row, which didn't matter anyway, because before I could even get myself settled down to pay attention to their performance, they were playing the opening to *2001: A Space Odyssey*, and spotlights started swooping and circling all around the room, and everybody in the place was going wild, screaming for Elvis, then suddenly there he was on the stage like a god had descended, and the excitement went from electric to super-sonic. The screams were deafening and the flash of cameras so continuous that the whole coliseum looked like some crazy '60s LSD flashback. I didn't know that kind of excitement was humanly possible. Shockwaves buzzed up and down my body until I thought I would either burst through my own skin or fly right up into the rafters. To this day, if somebody told me they actually saw me levitate that night, I wouldn't doubt it one bit.

I was too out of my mind even to notice what song Elvis opened with, but I wouldn't have been able to hear it anyway, with all the screaming. Finally, he started talking to the audience until they quieted, and I drifted down from the rafters, into my seat, taking long shuddering breaths, trying to calm myself, because the tiny bit of my mind that remained rational told me this was the most important night of my life, and that I should try my best to remember everything about it. But try as I might, I was just too excited, and the whole thing passed in a blur, with only a few stand-out moments pressed into my memory, like when he sang, "I've Got a Woman," and instead of singing "I've got a woman, way cross town" changed it to "I've got a woman Waycross Georgia," and caught my eye. Then, when he picked up a teddy bear that a fan had thrown onto the stage, and tossed it to me, I looked out at the audience and thought, *Okay, ladies, you see who's got his teddy bear, dontcha?*

Elvis must have performed for an hour-and-a-half or longer, but it didn't seem five minutes before he was coming out for his encore and Red and Joe were helping me up from my seat, ready to leave, and I can tell you that when they say *Elvis has left the building*, they're not kidding. From the second I stood up from my seat, it was a mad dash to the exit into a tunnel where the limo waited, with Elvis somehow winding up beside me in the middle of his bodyguards, everybody quick-stepping in unison, like a monster with a hundred legs, plowing through the massive crowd.

Safe inside the human walls of policemen and guards surrounding us, I couldn't see the faces of the people in the crowd, but I could see their arms and hands straining to reach over the guards' heads to get to Elvis, and I could hear their screaming and sobbing, calling his name.

Then, before I knew what was happening, our "circle" halted, and somebody shoved me into an open car door, Elvis diving in behind me. Now I could see the faces of the fans that had surrounded us, because they were shoved against the car windows, with their noses smashed into the glass and their fists beating on it.

"Get down!" Elvis slung his elbow around my neck and pulled my head onto his lap, leaning over, covering me with his arms.

Now I couldn't see anything at all, but I could hear men's voices shouting "Out of the way! Get back!"

The limo made slow progress, lurching forward, then slamming on brakes, until at last, we gained speed, and Elvis relaxed his grip on my head. "We're safe now."

I sat up, brushing my hair from my face, and he gave me a cute little grin. "People think I wear these sunglasses to look cool; they don't understand I really wear them for protection in case my fans get overzealous and break out the car windows."

A chill went down my spine and even though Elvis told me we were safe, my goosebumps didn't subside until we were on the plane, and it was just the two of us behind the curtained area, where he had disappeared that first night on the flight out of New Jersey. Now I understood why he had come straight into this private niche instead of immediately greeting me. This provided the sanctuary he needed after that harrowing escape, which I now realized was a regular occurrence for him. Sitting there beside him, in his cozy little den, I thought back to the evening's performance, remembering the place in the show when the security men allowed a pre-selected group to come down from the audience to the stage, so that Elvis could touch his fans. At the time, it had warmed my heart to see that he didn't just breeze along, brushing his fingers on their outstretched hands; he took time with each one, making sure to give them a scarf, or a flower, or for a few lucky ones, a kiss. Looking at him now, resting his head on the back of the sofa, with a towel around his neck, trying to relax, it made me sad to think of how that stage-moment of shared love with his fans had morphed into the threat of danger.

I sat quietly looking at him for several minutes, allowing him the peace he deserved, until gradually, his breathing slowed, and he raised his head, and looked me straight in the eyes. "So, what did you think?"

I returned his gaze, without speaking. Could he be serious? My only thought was that it was unthinkable for Elvis Presley to ask my opinion of his performance. But clearly, he was waiting for my answer. I did the only thing I knew to do. Very gently, I raised my lips to his and kissed him.

To my surprise, he barely returned my kiss. The question in his eyes remained.

*He really does want my opinion*, I thought, but the more I searched for words, the more tongue-tied I got. Then just as I was about to panic, clear as a bell, I heard Mama's voice, *Honesty is always the best policy*. With that, I cleared my throat, squared my shoulders and returned his straight-on gaze. "I have a confession to make," I said, "Tonight was the first time I've ever seen you perform. Can you imagine how overwhelmed I was?"

I studied his face, trying to figure out his expression. He was sur-prised for sure, but there was something else, too. Hurt? Annoyed? An-gry? Finally, it dawned on me that what he could not imagine was that I had never been to one of his concerts, so I tried again, saying everything I thought he'd like to hear, rambling on about him being the greatest per-former ever, which songs I liked best, how special I felt when he sang the part about woman Waycross Georgia and tossed me the teddy bear, but it wasn't until I mentioned how touched I was by the part in the show where the fans came down to the stage that he seemed to pay attention to what I was saying.

At that point, he stopped me by putting his finger to his mouth and pulling down his bottom lip. Inside, was a small cut. "See that?" He pulled his lip lower. "Tonight, when I tried to pull away from one of those fans below the stage, the woman wouldn't let go, and her tooth scraped my lip." Then he rolled back his cuffs to show me the tops of his hands, which looked like he'd had a fight with a tomcat. "These are from those same fans trying to hang on to me."

"I'm sorry you got hurt." I slipped the towel from his neck and began blotting the beads of sweat on his forehead. When I got to his hairline, I noticed a thin trickle of something dark. *Hair dye.* The scales fell from my eyes. Godlike onstage, yes, but when he came offstage, this superstar was a middle-aged man, going gray, a little overweight, whose ego needed massaging, and I was his chosen masseuse. Suddenly, I didn't feel so over-whelmed. Soon we would arrive at the hotel, and I would make sure he got the best massage of his life.

*  *  *

On the evening of Elvis's second concert, when I opened the door to his knock, instead of greeting me with his usual "Hey, baby," he said, "Hold out your hand."

Thinking he wanted to make sure I was wearing the ring he had given me, I held out my right hand.

"He shook his head, "left hand," and pulled a ring box from his pocket.

# Chapter 5

*A RING FOR MY LEFT HAND? Good Lord in Heaven.*

Even after he slipped it on my engagement-ring finger, I could only guess its meaning. This wasn't a traditional diamond solitaire, but it was a stunning starburst of opals and diamonds, and I knew that opals were an alternative stone for engagement rings, so when he didn't drop to one knee, I wondered if he might be planning an engagement announcement from the stage during his show. Oh, my goodness, if he did that, I hoped he'd send a couple of the guys to my seat to catch me when I fainted.

If such thing should happen, I was glad he had chosen this night, because I had packed only two evening outfits, the first of which I had worn to last night's show, leaving just one fancy dress for tonight, and if I was going to be in the spotlight, I thought the purple satin thigh-slit evening gown was perfect, and Elvis need never know it was a six-dollar markdown from the sale rack at Zayre's.

But if Elvis had been planning to announce our engagement during his show that night, what happened as soon as we got to the auditorium surely erased it from his mind.

Everything had progressed exactly as the night before, leaving the hotel through the service entrance and climbing into a limo to the auditorium, where we waited in the hallway for Elvis to change into his costume, before joining him in his dressing room. Which is where it all went crazy.

When we walked in, Elvis was rubbing his chest. "I'm itching." He undid two of his shirt buttons, and scratched his breastbone. "I mean it, y'all, I'm on fire."

One of the guys laughed, "Just a hunka burnin' love."

"It's not funny." Elvis reached beneath his shirt, clawing his back.

Joe said, "Diana, you stay, but rest of y'all excuse us for a minute." When everybody had left he said, "Elvis, take your clothes off, and let's see what's going on."

"Oh, my goodness!" I exclaimed, as he stripped, revealing the red welts covering his body, head to toe.

Out in the auditorium, the audience had begun their chant. "Elvis! Elvis! Elvis!"

"We gotta do something, Joe! I can't go onstage like this." Elvis clawed his skin, which was now streaked with scratches from his nails.

Joe threw up his hands. "What do you want me to do?"

I picked up his costume jacket and sniffed. "This reeks of cleaning fluid. Maybe if we shake it and let it air for a few minutes, and could you get me some baby powder?"

Joe snapped his fingers at me and stuck his head out the door, into the hallway. "Get some baby powder! Quick!" and like magic, a bottle of baby powder appeared.

"Here." Joe handed the powder to me and I started sprinkling it all over Elvis, gently patting it into his skin, asking, "Is that better?" until finally he let out a whoosh of breath. "I think I can go on now," and the audience never had the slightest clue that a crisis had been averted.

\* \* \*

For the first couple of days on tour, Elvis's entourage had respected our time alone. Once Elvis closed the door to his bedroom each night, no one disturbed us. The first indication that things were about to change, was a knock at Elvis's door on the morning after his second show.

Elvis was still asleep, but I knew it had to be somebody who had a key to the suite, so I called, "Come in," and Joe came through the door carrying a glass of water, tossing "Good morning," at me, heading for the other side of the bed. "Come on, wake up," he said, shaking Elvis's shoulder, "you got a show to do."

Elvis moaned, "Mm-hm," and raised himself on his elbows.

"Here you go." Joe handed him two pills and the glass of water.

Elvis popped the pills in his mouth and washed them down without question.

*Who's in charge here?* I wondered. "What were those pills?"

Before Elvis had a chance to answer, Joe said, "Something to help him wake up. We've got an early show today."

I had heard of sleeping pills, but wake-up pills were news to me. So, when Elvis woke up, which he did very soon, I was relieved to see no change in his behavior, and that our day proceeded as usual.

Getting dressed for the show, I thanked my lucky stars that today's performance would be a matinee, since I had quickly run through my two-outfit supply of evening wear, and just happened to have brought along a mini-dress that I hoped would suit the occasion. Like my bargain-rack purple satin that I'd worn last night, this one was a find from the Family Dollar Store, but it seemed to me that the thigh-high yellow knit might hit the right degree of sexy for the girl on Elvis's arm at an afternoon performance.

Even so, when he came to my door, ready to go, I felt the need to explain. "I hope this dress looks all right. I didn't bring very many dressy clothes, and with all the photographers, I didn't want to wear the same thing twice, but I can change if –"

Elvis slapped his forehead. "Dang it! I am so sorry. I promised to buy whatever you needed when you got here, didn't I? And then I went and forgot all about it, but you can be sure that tomorrow I'll get one of the guys to take you to the mall."

Maybe I should have been excited at the thought of a shopping trip, but at that point even a supermarket-sweep at Tiffany's wouldn't have excited me if it meant I had to be away from Elvis. "Will you be going shopping with us?"

Elvis said, "Baby, you know I can't go to the mall."

Yes, of course I knew Elvis couldn't go to the mall like any other person, but I hadn't thought about it till right then, and a sadness came over me as we headed down the hall. Then when we joined his entourage at the elevator, they looked me up and down, and I heard one of them say something about *short skirt* and *legs*.

Elvis must have heard, too, because he snickered and said, "Yeah, she's got some legs, doesn't she?"

Now on top of being sad, I felt naked, and in the back of my mind, something about the pills he'd taken that morning nagged at me, so that even though his show was as electrifying as ever, our lovemaking as passionate as always, and the diamond bangle he gave me the most extravagant gift of all, during the next couple of days, the golden haze I'd been floating in seemed a little less bright. We even had our first lovers' quarrel. It happened on the afternoon I was supposed to go shopping. Elvis walked into my room and tossed a fistful of hundred-dollar-bills on the dresser. "Here's the money I promised you."

I glanced at the money and back at him, "What?"

"To buy clothes."

"But, I can't take money from you."

"Then how am I supposed to buy you some clothes? I told you I can't go to the mall."

I stared at the floor. "It doesn't feel right."

"Aw, for cryin' out loud," he said. "I'm the one who asked you to fly out at the last minute, so I should be responsible for making sure you have everything you need."

His voice sounded tense in a way that I hadn't heard before. I bit my lip for a few seconds, trying not to cry, before I was able to say, "I don't mean to sound ungrateful. I cherish the gifts you've given me, even the teddy bear, but money is not the same thing."

"Well, there it is," He swatted the wad of cash, sliding it closer to me, "If you don't pick it up, I guess you'll be leaving a mighty fine tip for the maid." He opened the door and walked out, mumbling, "See you later.

\* \* \*

Then came the night that Joe Esposito walked into Elvis's bedroom carrying a hypodermic syringe.

After experiencing the energy he generated onstage, it wasn't hard to understand that post-performance, it was possible for Elvis to be exhausted and wired at the same time, especially if you added pain into the equation. Somehow during the show, he had chipped a jaw tooth, and as we drove away from the coliseum, he complained that it was scraping the inside of his cheek.

"Let me see if I can feel it," I said.

Elvis opened wide and I stuck my finger in his mouth and rubbed the tooth he indicated. "Ouch, that's sharp."

"Yeah. Hurts more than you'd think."

"Are you going to need something to help you sleep?" Joe asked.

Elvis nodded, "Probably."

I wanted to say, *Not as long as I'm around; I've got my own ways of helping him relax.* Although Elvis and I had made up quickly after our spat, I wanted to give him the kind of loving that would ensure he forgot it ever happened, and sleeping pills did not fit my agenda. But if I thought sleeping pills were the worst of it, my blissful ignorance was about to get sucker-punched by reality.

My face must have shown my horror when Joe came into Elvis's bed-room later that night, carrying something I didn't know existed outside a doctor's office.

"Just something to help him sleep" he explained, heading for Elvis's side of the bed.

"Why does he have to have a shot?"

"Works faster."

"Well, he seems pretty tired, and he's relaxing in bed, so I think he could probably go to sleep on his own," I smiled at Elvis, "or with a little help from me."

Joe rubbed alcohol on Elvis's arm. "I know what I'm doing."

I couldn't watch him put the needle in. I looked away, and kept my face turned until Joe was leaving, and Elvis pulled me into his arms. "It's all right, baby," he said. "Sometimes I have to have something to get the rest I need."

"How fast does it work?" I was thinking of all the good-loving I had in store for him.

"Pretty fast," he said. His voice was already sounding lazy, and it couldn't have been more than a minute or so before I felt his arms around me go slack, and his breathing slowed into deep sleep.

Lying there, beneath the dead-weight of his arms, I could have gladly strangled Joe Esposito.

Next morning, Joe didn't bother to knock, he just strolled through the door and shook Elvis awake. "Come on now, here you go."

Elvis took his "wake-up" medicine like a good boy, while I lay there silently staring at the ceiling. When Joe left, he turned on his side looking at me. "How'd you sleep?"

"Probably not as soundly as you did," I answered.

"I'm sorry," he said, "the shot took effect more quickly than usual, but I really do have to have help sleeping and waking up when I'm touring. Life on the road is not as much fun as people think, but I promise you it won't always be like this. When we get through with the tour, I'm going to take you to L.A. with me and we'll buy you those clothes I promised. See, in Beverly Hills, I can walk around and shop just like anybody. Out there, everybody's a celebrity, I'm no big deal."

My pique melted, and I rolled onto my side, so that we were face to face. "You're a big deal anywhere, especially right here with me." Then we were kissing, and the world was wonderful again, and I wanted to believe the dream he'd woven about our life together after the tour.

So maybe he was trying to make up for the disappointments of life on the road, when on the way to the show that night, out of the clear blue, he asked, "Do you have a car?"

"Yeah, I've got a 1973 Gran Prix."

"You like it?"

"Yes, I do. It's a really nice car, but lately it's been making some funny noise, so I need to take it to a mechanic when I get back."

"Wouldn't you rather have a new Cadillac?"

"A new Cadillac? Where would I get one of those?"

"I want to buy one for you."

"Well, that's awfully sweet, and of course I'd love to have a new Cadillac, but what will I do with the car I've already got?"

"Give it to your sister, the one that's having that baby you're always talking about."

I smiled, "Well, I guess I could do that," but I wondered why Elvis would buy me a new car instead of giving me one of the many he already had, like maybe the Stutz Blackhawk I'd spied in the garage at Graceland.

During his show that night, I couldn't concentrate on Elvis as I should have because my mind kept wandering to images of myself driving a shiny new El Dorado or that sexy Blackhawk, so maybe I was lost in my head when the show ended, and I realized it was time to leave and that nobody had come to escort me backstage to get into the limo. Then it struck me that on this night, instead of one of Elvis's guys bringing me to my platform seat, one of the venue's security guards had accompanied me. Could he possibly have put me on the wrong side of the stage? Maybe they were searching for me over *there. Surely, they wouldn't leave me behind. Or would they?* To make it worse, before the show, Elvis had entrusted me with the safekeeping of his trademark sunglasses, which I was supposed to hand to him before we got into the limo. And hadn't he told me that he wore those glasses for protection? What if Elvis were to get injured because I was daydreaming and got lost? Feeling sure they were searching for me on the opposite side of the auditorium, I found my way down to the roped-off section in front of the stage, planning to make a short-cut to the other stage entrance, but too soon, someone in the audience spotted me and yelled, "There's Elvis's girlfriend," and suddenly thousands of hands were stretching across the barrier, thrusting programs at me, asking for my autograph. I ignored all of them except one woman who kept shoving a big rolled-up poster at me. Every time she stuck it in front of me, it came down like barricade, halting my progress, until finally I took it from her.

And wouldn't you know that in the few seconds I paused to scribble my name, Sonny West came up behind me, yelling in my ear. "Where have you been?"

He took me by the arm, pulling me along. I went willingly, if not gratefully, and at last, there was Elvis, but he didn't look happy to see me. "Where were you all this time?" You've thrown us off schedule."

I could hardly bear the anger in his voice, but I didn't have time to answer before Sonny cut in, "I found her down in front of the stage, signing autographs."

*That's not true*, I wanted to say, but I was stunned into silence when Red came into view and I saw that the girl with him was the same girl whose poster I had signed, the one who had seemed intent on keeping me from getting to the stage door. Watching the two of them whispering together, I wondered if it was possible that none of the guys came to get me after the show because they wanted to make me late. Or maybe they had planned to leave me behind, altogether. Now I was too confused to defend myself, and this was no time to make excuses, anyway, because we were having to fight our way through the mob of fans who were a zillion times worse than on other nights. *Of course, they are worse tonight. There are a zillion times more of them because Elvis didn't have time to make his getaway before they became a mob, and it's all your fault.*

When we got to the limo, was it my imagination or did he really shove me into the car with a little more force than usual? Sitting beside him as we inched along with fans swarming the car like termites on rotten wood, Elvis continued badgering me about where I'd been, until I hunched over with my hands covering my ears.

He put his arm around me. "Aw, don't do that. It's all right. I just wanted to know where you were."

Did he honestly expect me to explain with Joe and Sonny sitting there? I was beginning to think his bodyguards might really be the Memphis Mafia, and I was pretty sure they wanted to get rid of me.

Finally, we arrived at the hotel. I couldn't wait for us to be alone, so I could explain that it hadn't been the way Sonny made it sound. But when we got to the door of the suite, Elvis started searching through his pockets, and said, "Have you got the key, Red?"

Red searched his own pockets, "No." Then everybody was searching for the key. They even asked me to check my bag.

Just when I thought this night couldn't get any worse.

"Aw, heck," Elvis said, "Y'all give me some room."

The rest of us moved a few feet away, and for several seconds, Elvis stared at the door, moving his hands around in the air. Then like lightning, he jumped and karate-kicked it. The door didn't budge an inch. Elvis grunted, and got into another karate stance for one more try. Bam! He kicked the door and there was a loud ripping sound. But it wasn't the door coming apart, it was Elvis's pants splitting front to back.

I tried to hold my laughter, but nobody else did, not even Elvis, so I let go and we all laughed until we ran out of breath. When we recovered, Red sauntered over to Elvis and clapped him on the shoulder. "Man, get out of the way and let an expert handle it." Which Elvis did. It took Red several kicks, but finally the door gave, and with it, the mood lightened, so that while the hotel maintenance crew fixed the door, we all ordered room service and ate dinner together, joshing like buddies, even though I still wasn't so sure. Especially when I heard Red ask Elvis, "What did you think about that girl I introduced to you?"

It helped a little that Elvis waved it away. "Nah, she had short hair, looked too much like Sheila.

I had no idea who Sheila was, although later I would hear the name Sheila Ryan, and it was nothing to me, because Elvis didn't sound interested in either Sheila or the girl who had tried to make me late. Something told me that girl – the fan whose poster I'd signed – was one and the same as the girl Red had introduced to Elvis earlier, and was now asking him about. Still, even if Red was in on the plot against me, I couldn't believe he would be bold enough to talk in front of me about somebody he was trying to fix up with Elvis, so I chose to assume he had been asking Elvis's opinion on a girl he was interested in for himself. None of it mattered anyway, because literally at the end of the day, I was the one who would be alone with Elvis, and have his undivided attention.

Thankfully, the maintenance crew fixed the door in record time and everyone departed for their own room. Now was my chance. Not wanting to let the moment evaporate in the heat of passion, I asked if we could sit and talk for a few minutes before going to bed. Elvis suggested we take the pair of bedroom chairs, and sitting down, I couldn't help noticing the black velvet box on the small table between us. This one was larger than the other jewelry boxes he had presented, so I wasn't sure, but I did hope it was another "little something" for me, and that after he heard my explanation he would still want to give it to me.

I began by apologizing for being late, speaking softly and slowly, choosing my words carefully, before going into the story of what caused me to be delayed. Then I paused, giving him a chance to respond.

"Aw, baby, I feel bad that you were upset. If I sounded mad, it was just that I worry that somebody I care about might get kidnapped."

I had hoped he'd be sympathetic, but this was more than I could have imagined. He hadn't said the L word, but he had just told me he cared for me, and that was pretty close. Close enough to give me the courage to ask, "Who was the girl Red was talking to you about, the one he said he introduced to you?"

"Oh, shoot, they're always trying to fix me up with somebody or other, thinking they'll get brownie points, but you don't need to worry about that, they can't fix me up with anybody, 'cause I'm already with somebody, I'm with you." He reached and gave my hand a squeeze. Then he passed me the black velvet box.

I opened it and gasped, "It's big," then took longer than I should have adding, "and beautiful." The thing in the box appeared to be made for a man, and I had never seen a gemstone the color of the silver-dollar-size disc that looked like a bright blue flat rock attached to a gold chain so heavy it reminded me of something you'd see in a mechanic's garage. I did, however, recognize the diamonds surrounding the rock.

I gave him a playful smile and said, "I love it, but what is it?"

He touched the blue rock. "That's lapis lazuli."

"Lapis what? I've never heard of that."

"Oh. Well, it's sort of exotic. I helped design this piece."

"You did? Wow."

"Yeah, I thought you could wear it tomorrow night. Now you've got a ring for each hand, a bracelet and a necklace."

I thought for a minute, mentally scanning my wardrobe, and realized that I had run through all the clothes I'd packed for Hollywood. The only thing I hadn't already worn on the Elvis tour was my Daisy Mae, and somehow, I didn't think a big blue rock hanging on a motorcycle chain was the right accessory for a red polka-dot party dress. "Um," I paused, wondering how to say it. "I don't think this goes with the outfit I'm planning to wear tomorrow night."

"What are you talking about?" he said. "This is a work of art. Art doesn't have to match anything."

He might as well have called me a heathen. I tightened my grip on the box, afraid he might snatch it away from me. Even if I didn't know much about art, and had never heard of Lapis Wazooly, or whatever he'd called it, I knew that a hunky bright-blue rock didn't go with a red polka-dot party dress.

I also had enough sense to know that it was exactly what I should be wearing the next night when Elvis came to my room to escort me to the limo for the concert. Staring at my image in the mirror I had managed to convince myself that people would be so blinded by all the jewelry I was wearing they wouldn't even notice that none of it matched. So, when Elvis knocked, I opened the door, with my bosom thrust out in a way that could leave no doubt how proud I was to have that big blue rock hanging between my breasts.

"Oh," he said, "you decided to wear the necklace. I'm glad."

I just smiled and took his arm. He was right that the necklace didn't need to match the dress, but it had nothing to do with art and everything to do with making him happy. I had decided that his happiness was my mission in life. It had become clear to me that if somebody didn't save him from himself he wouldn't live long enough to find the happiness he so desperately wanted. I knew I was the one to save him, and I'd proven it the night before when he gave me the necklace.

My mama didn't raise no fools; I knew I had put my foot in my mouth, and I knew I'd better remedy my blunder, and fast. So, I closed the necklace box and hugged it to my breast, vowing, "It's the most amazing thing I've ever seen." Which wasn't a lie. "I'll cherish it forever." Then I set the box on the table, went over and snuggled onto Elvis's lap, gushing appreciation. What a lesson in gratitude when he scooped me up in his arms, carried me to the bed and laid me down gently, then called Joe and told him to wait, saying he'd call him back in an hour or so.

I knew what that meant, so when he climbed beneath the sheets, I was determined that when I got through with him that night he would be too exhausted to pick up the phone and call anybody, especially not Joe Esposito.

The next morning, I felt a thrill of triumph when Joe strolled into the room complaining, "You never called me last night."

\* \* \*

No matter how much I hated the vicious cycle of sleep/wake drugs, I couldn't bear to see Elvis in pain, and the chipped tooth situation had gone from bad to worse. Now it wasn't just the rough edge scraping the inside of his mouth; in trying to eat "around" the bad tooth, he'd bitten his jaw bloody, which would be inconvenient for anybody, but for a singer catastrophe.

So, I didn't protest when, after the show one night, Elvis asked Joe to come in as soon as we got back to the hotel. As usual, I couldn't watch while Joe gave him the shot, but instead of getting sulky when he immediately passed out in my arms, I held him with extra tenderness, knowing that he was sleeping through the pain. Or at least I thought so.

I had come to the conclusion that whatever Joe was injecting into Elvis's arm, was less like a sleep medication, and more like anesthesia, so it would take pain strong enough to wake the dead to rouse Elvis from that depth of unconscious. But that's exactly what happened.

"Diana, Diana." Elvis was shaking my shoulder and moaning.

I'm not one to come awake instantly, and even with my eyes closed, I could tell it was still dark.

Elvis switched on the lamp. That did it. I sat up and saw that he was sitting up, too. His head was hanging limp on his chest and he was holding his jaw.

"I heenh hunh henhinh."

I couldn't understand his words, but I knew what he was saying. Leaping out of bed, I pointed at him. "You lie down, and stop trying to talk. Not one more word. I'll call Joe to get a dentist, and meantime I'll make an ice compress."

The knock-out drug may have lost the battle with the pain, but it hadn't given up trying to put Elvis under. It took three big men to put pajamas on his dead-weight and get him downstairs into the hotel security guard's car. Then, at the dentist's, Joe and the guard had to haul him into the office bodily. The most heartbreaking thing I've ever seen was the superman I watched onstage being held upright by men's arms looped beneath his shoulders, with his head lolling and his house-shoes scraping the concrete, as they dragged him inside. The nausea I felt only strengthened my resolve to save him.

Once they got him in the chair, the dental assistant ran everybody out into the waiting room, only to return a little later, saying that Elvis wanted to see me. When Joe got up to go with me, the nurse shook her head, "Just Diana."

Tossing a triumphant look at Joe, I hurried to Elvis's side. He flapped his hands at the dentist and nurse, and when they left us, Elvis clutched my arm and pulled me down, so that my head was touching his. "Hnay, hneer." Now, on top of the drugs, his mouth was shot full of Novocain and stuffed with cotton. I removed the wadding and put my ear to his mouth. His words were still slurred but I understood, "Stay here. That nurse tried to kiss me."

*What?* How dare she take advantage of him when he was in this state. "Where is she?" I turned to go find her, but Elvis pulled me back, and looking down at him, his eyes pleading like a little boy afraid to face the dentist alone, I decided it was more important to stay by his side, than to give that dental assistant a piece of my mind.

Even though I knew how much Elvis's fans loved him, the longer I was with him the more I understood how quickly that love could turn on itself, and on him. Our dawn exit from the dentist office was a sickening example. Although Joe had given strict instructions that Elvis's visit to the dentist's office should be kept top-secret, when we walked out, it was clear that someone – *Nurse Wretched* I thought – had blabbed. The foyer was full of gawkers. "Elvis is drunk, he can't even walk," they sneered, while Elvis tried his best to smile at them, when he could barely hold up his head and put one foot in front of the other.

\* \* \*

Thank God, after sleeping off the load of medication, Elvis got up ready for business, heading out to meet with Joe, and although their regular afternoon session was usually my least favorite part of the day, this time I was happy to see Elvis back to normal, besides which, I welcomed a few hours to myself for a badly needed relaxing soak in the tub. So, I was a little annoyed, and a lot surprised, when before I had a chance to run my bath, Sonny showed up at my door, saying that Elvis wanted to see me in his office.

My only experience with a summons to an office was in high school when unruly students were sent to the principal for a paddling. I couldn't think of anything I had done to deserve that, so I slipped into one of my little knit dresses and hurried to the business area of the suite.

Elvis sat facing the door with his back to a desk, his elbows propped on top. Joe was sitting to Elvis's right, and even though there was another chair in the room, neither of them offered it, so I stood facing Elvis, feeling more and more like that student in the principal's office, especially since Elvis had a stern look on his face.

"I'm going to have to send you home." He spoke so fast, I wasn't sure what I'd heard, until he went on explaining that his dad and Colonel Parker were flying in for a few days, which meant he'd be spending all his time with them, and it wouldn't work to have me around.

I opened my mouth, intending to reply calmly, but before I could speak, a huge lump clogged my throat, and I fled to my room, flinging myself onto the bed, in a fit of crying that, even with the door closed, Elvis must have heard, because pretty soon he was sitting beside me, stroking my hair.

"I don't want you to cry like this," he said. "I'm not sending you away forever, I just have some things to do." He waited to see if the reassurance had worked, and when I continued to snivel, he said, "Tell you what, how 'bout if we postpone you leaving? Let's do that. You can stay tonight and go home tomorrow, okay?"

I rolled onto my back, looking up at him, wiping the tears from my cheeks. "Okay."

He put his hands beneath my shoulders and positioned me against the pillows. Then he took me in his arms and told me again about the plans he had for us, how he was going to bring me out to visit him in Hollywood, and all the fun we would have, and as I listened, the crisis passed, so that later, as usual, he collected me at my door and, also as usual, handed me a black velvet box. This one contained a diamond teardrop pendant, which perfectly complemented the simple white silk blouse and black pants I was wearing, forever laying to rest the big blue rock mismatch. Peace at last. Walking to the limo with Elvis and the gang, laughing and joking like always, I could never have imagined that before the night was through, I would heartily regret not getting away while I had the chance.

When we got to the auditorium, things progressed as expected, with Red seeing me to my special seat, then Elvis came onstage, as powerful as ever, and all seemed well until he got to the point in the show where he introduced his singers. First up was Kathy Westmoreland, and as he did every night, he praised her beautiful high soprano, but on this night, added a little rhyme that went something like, *Kathy doesn't have a man, so she gets it anywhere she can,* which struck me so odd that I thought I had misunderstood until I saw the look on Kathy's face. Then when he introduced his three other female vocalists, he teased them about smelling like they'd been eating catfish, which must have been an inside joke, because I didn't get it, and neither did they. Or maybe they did get it and didn't find it funny because their mouths flew open and they sat down hard in their chairs, leaning forward, putting their heads together in a way that made me feel like something bad was about to happen.

A few seconds later, Kathy Westmoreland walked off the stage. Then two of the Sweet Inspirations got up from their chairs and followed.

All of this had taken place behind Elvis's back while he was introducing the male vocalists, so he was clueless until he started the next song and the female vocal parts were missing. He whirled around, and seeing that the three singers were gone, turned to the band, lifting one palm in a question. *What's happening?* The band started nodding and mouthing *it's okay.* But it wasn't.

They got through the rest of the show, and after a few songs, Elvis hit his stride, pouring it on thicker than ever for the audience, but once we got inside the limo he made no attempt to hide that he was livid. It quickly became apparent to me that this incident was unprecedented, and that, like me, the others in the limo had no idea where Elvis's rage would take him, or them. We rode in uneasy silence to the hotel, then glumly trailed Elvis's wake into the great-room of the suite, where Joe, Red, Sonny and I stood, watching Elvis stare at the floor, while we waited for him to speak. Then, all of a sudden, in a rapid-fire so fast it made me flinch, he spat out, "Nobody's going to bed until we get this fixed. I mean to-*night*. I want to see everybody one-at-a-time." He turned to me. "Everybody but you, Diana. You'll need to go to your room and wait while I get this mess straightened out. I'll come and get you as soon as I'm done."

I'd held it as long as I could; I went to my room with tears streaming, and there I lay, crying all alone, fearing what might happen.

Then at last, there was a soft knock at my door. I ran and flung it open, expecting to fall into Elvis's arms.

Instead it was Dr. Nick. "Elvis asked me to come check on you," he said.

"Oh." I swiped at the wetness beneath my eyes. "Come in."

I sat down with him at the small table across from the bed, and soon his bedside manner had all my worries and fears spilling out my mouth, right into his lap, as he listened in his doctorly way, reassuring me all the while.

When I had spewed my last, he said, "Would you like a nerve pill?"

I considered for a minute, then said, "I've never heard of a nerve pill. What is it?"

"It'll help you calm down. I think you need it." He walked into the bathroom and came back with a glass of water, which he handed to me along with a pill that was broken in two. "Why don't you just take half?"

I swallowed one of the halves like a good patient, exactly the way Elvis took his medicine from Joe. I should've known better. Whatever I may have expected the pill to do to me wasn't what happened at all. At the time, I didn't even realize the pill had taken effect, I only knew that after Dr. Nick left, I stopped feeling scared and sad and started feeling outraged. How dare Elvis leave me alone this long in here with nothing to do?

Why, even the TV channels had signed off. I was not one of his lackeys to order to my room, I was his girlfriend. If he was the King, then I was his Queen, and the Queen should be by the King's side, shouldn't she?

By the time Elvis finally came for me, I was in a lather.

"We did it," he said, "Everything's going to be all right."

I sat on the bed with my arms crossed, refusing to look at him.

He held his hand out to me. "You ready to come to bed?"

I glared at the floor.

"I'm talking to you," he said. Then he turned to Sonny, who was standing behind him, "What's wrong with her?"

Bringing Sonny into it was all the prodding I needed. "*You* are what's wrong with me," I punched my finger at Elvis, "*You* left me in here for four hours with nothing to do and nobody to talk to, and that is not *right.*"

One corner of his mouth twitched. "Are you serious? I've been in there for that same four hours, wringing my guts out, trying to salvage my show, and when I finally get it fixed, now I'm supposed to fix you, too?" He spun on his heel, motioning Sonny to follow.

*Oh, my god!* I ran after him, pleading how sorry I was, trying to explain that I didn't know what I was saying, that it was the pill talking.

He stopped short and slung his arm toward the sliding glass doors. "I ought to throw you over that balcony," Then he stalked off to his bedroom, yelling at Sonny, "Book her on the first flight out."

I knew it was an empty threat because the next flight didn't leave till in the morning, and I was already booked on that one, anyway, which gave me the rest of the night to work on him, and although he may have been mad enough to toss me off the balcony, I had a feeling he wasn't mad enough to toss me out of bed. Suffice to say that when morning arrived we parted sweetly, with his promise to call and check to make sure I got home okay, which he did. My parents' kitchen phone rang shortly after I arrived from the airport; Elvis was on the phone, God was in His Heaven, and all was right with the world.

When several months went by without another word from him, I told myself that he couldn't call because he was sick, and he did, in fact, cancel the rest of his tour and check into a hospital, so I waited, although not very patiently. I had the phone number at Graceland, and I was not too proud to try to reach him, especially since he was sick, but the only people I ever got were the maids or Charlie Hodge. Charlie encouraged me to send cards, so, I began doing as he suggested, and when I followed up, he always said that Elvis liked the things I sent, but when the months lengthened into a whole year with no word from Elvis himself, I heard that he was performing at the Omni in Atlanta, and knew the time had come. If things were over between us, he owed it to me to tell me straight to my face. I pranced into the hotel lobby, wearing a white tank top with my short-short cutoffs, and approached the desk clerk with every bit of confidence I could muster. To my amazement, she divulged that Elvis was rehearsing in a ballroom right down the corridor, and who should I find there, but Dave Hebler and Red West.

Dave greeted me with, "What are you doing here?"

I lifted my chin. "I want to see Elvis."

"But Elvis doesn't want to see you," he smirked.

"Since when do you speak for Elvis?"

"Since we showed him that news photo of you with Burt Reynolds."

"That was a publicity photo," I said, "I had a bit part in *Gator*, his new movie."

Red said, "That's not how it looked, and Elvis does not want to be seen with anyone who is so publicly dating someone else."

"I wasn't dating Burt Reynolds," I argued. "I can't help how the newspapers made it look. Elvis knows that better than anyone, and if you'll take me to him, I'll clear this up."

Staring at my cutoffs, Dave sneered, "I see you really fixed yourself up to pay a call on the King."

The two of them looked at each other and started laughing like I was an inside joke. When I turned to walk away, Dave called out, "You've let yourself get fat."

Clearly, they hated me even more than I realized, and I still had no idea why.

The next day, a friend called and said he had tickets to Elvis's concert, thinking I would jump at the chance to go.

"No-o-o!" I wasn't sure I could stand it after my encounter with Red and Dave, but my desire to lay eyes on Elvis won out and I spent the better part of the afternoon searching through my closet for something to wear that would disguise my fat body, as I now perceived it. Eventually I settled on a floor-length flowered sundress and set off to see Elvis for the first time in a year.

When he burst onto the stage I threw up in my mouth.

"Please take me home," I said to my friend, and kindly, he did as I asked.

Not long after that night, I saw a magazine featuring Elvis and his new girlfriend Ginger Alden, and a phone call from my sister Rhonda on August 16, 1977 put the matter to rest for eternity.

"Are you watching the news?" she asked.

3. Elvis was dead.

\* \* \*

From the moment I met Elvis, all my ambition for the future had centered around him.

Even after the cruel encounter with Dave and Red, a part of me was still waiting for his call. Now, I could finally stop waiting, if only I knew how.

As usual, my family came to the rescue. Rhonda urged me to come visit her in Houston, and even though I didn't think getting out of town was the answer to my problem, when the plane lifted off, my spirits rose with it, so that by the time we landed, I was in a mood to throw my arms around Rhonda and her husband Ron as soon as I spotted them waiting at the gate. Then, at the baggage carousel, when Ron struck up a conversation with a friendly group of guys, for the first time since that night at the Memphian theater in 1975, I spotted a guy that knocked my socks off. I looked at him, he looked at me, and strolled over to where I was standing.

"Hello, I'm Rick Nelson."

He was performing in Houston that night, so instead of sitting at home, wallowing in grief, I would be sitting front row gazing starry-eyed at the reigning sexiest man on the planet – since Elvis had passed on. Could anyone possibly be this lucky twice in one lifetime? Apparently so, because not only did Rick offer front row seats for the three of us, he invited Rhonda, Ron and me to his suite for pre-show drinks, after which, we would ride to the gig with him and his manager. He even asked me to help choose the black pants and shirt he would perform in that evening. As they say, déjà vu all over again.

After the show, we went with Rick's entourage to Houston's hottest disco to let him loosen up post performance, then back to his suite, where he poured drinks while I poured out my heartache over Elvis. It stood to reason that the two teen idols might have known each other, but I hadn't realized they were friends. He was also mourning Elvis, and not only in the way the whole world mourned the death of the King of Rock and Roll. Rick felt the loss personally, and what a comfort he was.

Then the conversation drifted to the breakup of his marriage. He and his wife Kristen had been together since they were teenagers, and they had four children. His sadness touched me and created a bond between us that wouldn't normally grow so quickly. Then the sun rose, and Rhonda, Ron and I headed back to their house, and Rick headed back to L.A., but we exchanged phone numbers, and somehow, I knew we would be seeing each other again.

# Part II
# Victoria

Victoria Hallman (1980). Photo courtesy of Harold McBrayer

Vicki Hallman Birmingham Skyline (1973). Photo courtesy of John Robinson

# Chapter 6

VICTORIA
*1979*

IT SHOULD HAVE OCCURRED TO ME that Buck Owens might be hanging out backstage between his matinee and evening performances, and since I was an aspiring young singer, it also should have occurred to me to arrange a run-in, but neither had entered my mind when I rounded a corner and ran smack into him.

Bam! I rocked backward on my heels, then righted myself, staring into a plaid shirtfront. Slowly I raised my eyes to his face, looking up and up, until the back of my head was almost resting on my shoulders. At six-feet-six, counting boots and cowboy hat, Buck presented an imposing edifice. Our collision hadn't moved him an inch, but he did look surprised. Before I had a chance to apologize, my manager, Bill Loeb, appeared out of nowhere.

"Great show today," he shook Buck's hand, "But you could use a girl in your act." Bill opened his palm my direction. "This is Vicki Hallman, and she's a good little country singer."

My head whipped around to Bill. *What?* My current gig as opening act for Bob Hope didn't include a single country song.

Buck said, "What do you think, Jack?" speaking to the portly gray-haired man standing next to him. "Go tell Don to bring his guitar to my dressing room and let's see how she sounds."

Jack went off to get Don and his guitar, and Buck, Bill and I trooped down the hall to a dressing room, where Buck grabbed a red-white-and-blue guitar from the corner, and sat down on the sofa just as Jack entered the room, followed by a tall, dark, bearded fellow carrying a guitar, which was not red, white and blue.

83

I had perched myself atop the dressing table, for a bird's-eye view of the action.

Buck gestured in my direction, "This is Vicki Hallman, Don, she's going to sing for us."

Don smiled, "Nice to meet you."

I returned his smile vaguely, still trying to figure out what was going on.

Then Buck said, "What would you like to sing?"

The four men stared at me expectantly, which did nothing to help me think more clearly. I wasn't so addled that I didn't recognize a lucky break when I ran into one, but while half of my brain puzzled over what was happening, the other half searched for a country song to which I could remember all the words. I swept my eyes around the faces, wondering exactly how long they had been watching me try to come up with something. *Thirty seconds? Five minutes?* Buck's hands rested loosely on his patriotic guitar as if he had nothing better to do than sit there waiting for me to decide what to sing, but Bill's smile was stretching into a grimace.

Just when I was about to betray Bill's lie, and confess that I was not really a country singer, I heard myself say, "'Help Me Make It Through the Night, key of A.'"

When I finished the song, Buck said, "Come out onstage and sing it with us."

Some other music-biz ingenue might have thrown her arms around his neck weeping tears of gratitude. I just said, "Okay."

While my manager checked with Buck and Jack on the ins-and-outs of my impromptu performance, I assessed my attire, and decided that the lavender silk blouse with skin-tight jeans tucked into brand-new stack-heeled gray suede boots was not at all a bad wardrobe choice for my debut as a country music star. Hair and makeup were another thing altogether.

I hadn't even known Buck Owens was appearing at the Orange Show that day. I had convinced my manager to let me tag along from Hollywood to San Bernardino, not so I could go to a concert, but because, as booking agent for the Grand Stand show, Bill had free ride tickets for the midway. I had still been dizzy from using up a whole roll them, when I ran into Buck Owens, and between roller-coaster and run-in, most of my hair had escaped its ponytail, and the lip gloss I'd dabbed on that morning had stuck to the caramel apple I ate for lunch. Checking my disheveled appearance in the mirror, I headed to the dressing room of a troupe of

*Solid Gold* dancers, who were appearing a few acts down the bill from Buck Owens, and when they heard the story of my lucky collision with Buck, they went to work on me, combing, powdering and polishing, until I looked like one of those beauties Buck swapped corny jokes with on *Hee Haw*.

Giving me a final once-over in the mirror, their dance captain, said, "You'll do, break a leg."

The Buckaroos were already playing, and Bill was waiting for me in the wings, stage-right. I listened to the music for a minute, then turned to him. "These guys are really good."

He laughed and nodded, "Yes. Really good." Then he kissed my forehead. "But so are you."

When Buck came onstage, the crowd went wild.

Growing up in Centreville, Alabama, with only three TV channels to choose from, I had seen *Hee Haw* a time or two, and I'd always found Buck Owens oddly attractive. Had he been a woman, the French expression would have been *jolie laide*. Now I saw that his on-camera persona revealed only a fraction of his stage presence. I was so mesmerized that I didn't realize what he was saying when he yelled into the mic, ". . . big round of applause . . ." Then I heard, "Vicki Hallman!" and I vaulted onto the stage, waving to the crowd with one hand, grabbing the mic with the other.

When I finished the song, a roar rose in my ears and the whiteness of hands fluttered in the audience. "Thank you!" I shouted.

The Buckaroos played a chaser and I turned to exit stage-right.

"Y'all want her to sing another one?" Buck's voice came from the monitors, "All right! Vicki Hallman!"

I stopped in my tracks, spinning to face Buck.

He twisted his head sideways, speaking into the microphone, looking at me, "They want another one." Then he mouthed, "What song?"

Again, I had no idea what to tell him, but somehow the words "'When Will I Be Loved,'" came out of my mouth.

"What key?" Buck asked.

I threw my hands up, shaking my head, *I don't know.* "Just play it."

He raised his guitar pick in an upstroke, calling out "'When Will I Be Loved' in D," and when his pick came down, the whole band hit the opening chord with him, then followed my every nuance down to the final "lo-oo-oved" when three Buckaroo voices blended with mine in perfect harmony.

Buck took the microphone from my hand and spoke into it: "Vicki Hallman, everybody!"

I sprinted off with my arms lifted in a double-handed wave to the audience, and watched the rest of the show from backstage.

When Buck unstrapped his guitar, and exited into the wings, I stepped forward and offered my hand, "Thank you."

"My pleasure," he nodded. "We'll be in touch."

It didn't sound like a job offer and I knew better than to get my hopes up.

\* \* \*

Buck called the next day.

My roommate, Michael Ballard, answered the phone on the dinette bar in our apartment. "Who's calling?" he asked, then said, "One moment, please, and brought the phone to the sofa, where my toy poodle, Neesh, was napping on my lap, while I breakfasted on Diet Shasta Tiki Punch and a Marlboro Light.

Michael covered the mouthpiece, "Buck Owens," and placed the phone on the coffee table, handing me the receiver.

"Hello."

"Vicki, this is Buck Owens. I like the way you sing."

"Thank you."

Michael crooked his brown mustache into a smug expression, and nodded, *I told you so.*

"I'd like to bring you into the studio," Buck said, "see about putting you in my show. Do you have transportation, can you come up to Bakersfield?"

"Sure!"

I had no idea where Bakersfield was, and no way to get there once I found out.

"Could you be here tomorrow about three o'clock?"

"Sure!"

\* \* \*

When I got off the bus at the Greyhound station in Bakersfield, the waiting room was empty except for a man and a woman behind the counter.

"Excuse me," I said, to the woman, "I need to get to the Buck Owens Studio. Is there a local bus line? Or maybe a taxi?" I hoped for the bus line, because I wasn't sure I had enough money for a cab.

The woman must have read my expression because she said, "Buck's studio is not very far from here."

The familiar way she spoke his name made me ask, "Do you know Buck Owens?"

She chuckled, "Everybody in Bakersfield knows Buck Owens. He's our claim to fame."

"Well, that's good to hear," I said, "I may start singing with him. At least, that's why he asked me to come. Sort of an audition, I guess."

Her eyebrows shot up. "Buck invited you?"

"Mm-hm, he called yesterday, and here I am."

She pointed to the row of chairs in the middle of the room. "Have a seat over there and I'll get you a ride."

A few minutes later, a station wagon pulled up in front, and Don, the Buckaroos' guitarist, walked through the door, wearing a big grin. "Hey, Vicki. Remember me? I'm Don Lee. Buck asked me to come pick you up."

Riding down Bakersfield's main drag, I wouldn't have been surprised to see a tumbleweed blow across the street, so it was hard to miss the old art deco movie theater with a marquee that read *Buck Owens Studios*.

Don drove around the building and we entered through a back door, which turned out to be the private entrance to Buck's personal office. My first impression was that the room was more suitable for a lawyer than a country singer – a chess board on a side table, a pipe rack on his desk – but what did I know, since this was the first time I'd ever seen a country music star's office. Stepping inside, we were behind Buck. He spun in his swivel desk-chair, standing to shake my hand. Welcome to Bakersfield, Miss Hallman."

"Thanks. You can call me Vicki."

"Oh. Okay." He gave me a mock-serious nod, "Then I guess you can call me Buck."

"You need me for anything else?" Don asked.

"No, you can go on in the studio with the Buckaroos."

Don gave us a little wave as he walked out, and Buck indicated a leather chair beside his desk. "Please sit down. Have you thought of any songs you might like to sing?

I had learned a good lesson at the Orange Show, and had spent the day between that and this, combing through my friends' record collections, to make sure Buck wouldn't catch me short on country songs again. I reached into my shoulder bag and handed him the list I'd made.

"Let me see what you got here." He began reading the song titles aloud. "'I Fall to Pieces,' my ol' pardner Harlan Howard wrote that one, you know."

I didn't know. I'd never even heard of Harlan Howard, but I thought it smarter not to say.

Buck continued with my list. "'Rocky Top,' 'Mule Skinner Blues,' ah, that's a good one. I wouldn't've thought you knew that song."

And he would have been right until the night before when "Mule Skinner Blues" grabbed my ear while I was listening to a Dolly Parton album.

"'For the Good Times,' 'Let Me Be There,' and I'm glad to see you included the two you did at the Orange Show. This is a good list, let's go on in and run 'em."

He got up and ushered me through a door that led to a sleek recording booth done in metal and black leather, low-lit like the night-flight cockpit of an SST. Pausing for a second, he let me look around, before stepping through another door into the brightness of a lofty studio, so spacious I thought it once must have been the audience "house" of the original theater.

Here the Buckaroos awaited us, and since the band and I hadn't had the chance to get acquainted at the concert, Buck went around the group making introductions: Doyle Singer, the bass player with prematurely silver hair; Jim Shaw, the Beatle-esque keyboardist; Terry Christofferson, a quiet young guy with wire-rim glasses, on pedal steel; and Rick Taylor, the cute drummer with thick dark hair and mustache.

"That's your microphone right there," he pointed to a boom mic. "What's your key for "I Fall to Pieces?"

I shrugged.

"Do you know your keys to any of these songs?" Buck asked.

I clapped my hands to my cheeks, shaking my head.

"That's all right, we'll get 'em."

*Well, I knew that.* But I also knew that the trial and error it took to "get 'em" would cost Buck time, and therefore might cost me the gig.

"'I Fall to Pieces' in F," he told the Buckaroos.

Since he'd nailed the key for "When Will I Be Loved," during my Orange Show encore, I wasn't overly surprised when he did the same with 'I Fall to Pieces,' but my astonishment grew with each song key that Buck "guessed" right, which ended up being all of them. Either this man had a preternaturally keen ear for music or he was clairaudient. Maybe both.

We did each song one-time through, and less than thirty minutes after we'd entered the studio, Buck said, "Okay, then, see you boys later."

The Buckaroos started putting away their instruments, and Buck said to me, "Come on back in my office. I need to talk to you before you leave."

*So, this is it,* I thought, *he'll either hire me, or not.*

Victoria performing with Bob Hope (1976)

# Chapter 7

"WHY DIDN'T YOU TELL ME you were taking the bus today? You don't have a car?"

"No."

"How did you get to the bus station?"

"My roommate took me."

"So, your roommate has a car?"

"He borrowed one."

Buck's eyebrows lifted at the word "he."

"Is that your boyfriend?"

"No, he's gay."

"Is he going to pick you up when you get home?"

"Yes."

Buck rested his head on the back of his chair, staring at the ceiling, and I wondered if he was trying to think of the kindest way to tell me I hadn't passed the audition, but instead it was another off-the-wall question. "Where do you live? I mean what part of town?"

"Hollywood Hills."

"Oh, that's nice, but I don't think there's a Greyhound Station in the Hollywood Hills, is there?"

"No, it's down in Hollywood, a few blocks off the boulevard."

"Yeah, I think I've been there. I imagine it'll be dark when you get home. How far do you live from the bus station? Too far to walk in those heels you've got on?"

I looked down at my white patent Charles Jourdan sandals with the pewter spike heels. They were my pride and joy. "I don't know. I'm good at walking."

Buck smiled. "So, I've noticed. But you say your roommate's picking you up. How will he know when you get there?"

"I'll call him."

"And then you'll hang around that bus station, a few blocks off Hollywood Boulevard, dressed like that?" He pointed at my dress, which was a spaghetti-strap baby-blue knit that I considered appropriate for almost any occasion, except maybe church, since it fit me rather snugly.

"You don't like my dress?"

He shook his head, chuckling, "Oh, yes. I like your dress, but we may have to make some other transportation arrangements for you, since you'll need to be coming up here with some regularity."

It took a few seconds for me to realize he'd just told me I got the gig.

Before my brain could get a firm grip on that piece of info, Buck was telling me about my first performance as his opening act, which would be a concert coming up the next weekend at an outdoor venue with a name that reminded me of salad dressing. Happy Valley Ranch? Apple Valley Ranch? My head was too busy processing the reality of doing a show with Buck Owens next week, to catch the exact time and place, but "a hundred dollars" caught my ear.

"You'll probably come out better that way," he said, talking about paying me per show rather than on retainer, which mattered not to at all to me. I hadn't had a steady gig since I moved from Birmingham to Los Angeles, unless you counted the tour I'd done as backing vocalist with Connie Stevens last summer, or my off-and-on performances opening for Bob Hope. I didn't worry much about the next gig or where money would come from. It always seemed that if I opened my mouth and sang, a paycheck soon materialized.

The next morning, I woke up with a sore throat. Not that it put me in a panic about the upcoming performance with Buck. I'd sung with a sore throat hundreds of times, and the audience never seemed to notice. But *I* noticed, and a singer with an ear as good as Buck Owens' might notice, too. I sent Michael on a quick run to Ralph's Supermarket for lemons and Earl Grey, neither of which worked.

When performance day rolled around, my throat was still scratchy, my voice still gravelly, and I still didn't know where I was, even when Buck and his manager, Jack McFadden, picked me up at the small airport on Saturday morning, headed for the ranch, where Buck, the Buckaroos, and I would be playing at an outdoor festival.

Sore throat or not, when the emcee called my name, I bounced onto the stage and ran through my four songs with ease, if not comfort. As I walked offstage, with applause ringing, at the bottom of the stairs, Jack greeted me with open arms, "They loved you!"

"You think so?" I rubbed my throat. "I've been sick all week."

"You hear the applause, don't you?"

*  *  *

Emmy Lou Harris was playing at the Palomino and I was going as Buck's guest. Although the Palomino was a legendary nightclub, I had never been there, and although Emmy Lou was from Alabama, I had never heard her perform, so this was cause for excitement, especially when Jack greeted me at the door and steered me to Buck's table down front, where a bright-eyed woman stood up and introduced herself as Bonnie Owens.

This, I knew, was Buck's ex-wife. I also knew that she was the ex-Mrs. Merle Haggard, and that they and their sons were all one big happy family, to the extent that Bonnie still did some singing with both former husbands, making her good graces much to be desired. I took the empty chair between Jack and Buck, eager to hear one of my favorite singers.

I'd been listening to Emmy Lou Harris since she hit the airwaves in 1975 with "Boulder to Birmingham," which may not have gotten a lot of play in other cities, but for obvious reasons, was hard to miss in Birmingham. I'd never really thought of it as a country song, nor Emmy Lou as a country singer, so clearly, I had a lot to learn. My education took a big step forward that night, when Emmy Lou, one of my idols, introduced the man sitting next to me as one of hers.

My wonder grew when, after the show, Jack went ahead of us, parting the crowd as we made our way into the parking lot, where Emmy Lou's bus waited. Jack rapped on the door, which immediately opened, with Emmy Lou welcoming us, and introducing her aunt, who was traveling with her.

In turn, Buck introduced me, and when the aunt heard my last name, she exclaimed, "Hallman? We're related to the Hallmans, where are you from?"

Can you imagine, discovering I was a country singer and also Emmy Lou Harris's cousin in less than two weeks' time? That was only the beginning.

Before the night was over, Buck informed me that he was in town to work on a new album, and he wanted me to come to the studio the next day. He also let into the conversation that some of the "pickers" on the session were Emmy Lou's Hot Band, the same amazing musicians I'd heard tonight. Oh, and Emmy Lou might drop by to do a little singing.

Her "drop by" became a duet with Buck that was his next top-ten single, "Play Together Again, Again." It was also the song that moved me into the spot as female vocalist with the Buckaroos. Although Doyle and Don's voices blended beautifully with Buck's, when it came to his newest hit song, somebody had to step in for Emmy Lou, and there I stood. So, with that change in the lineup, Buck's show ran like this: The Buckaroos opened with four songs, then I did four, then when Buck came on, I stepped back, becoming one of the band. It worked so well that by summertime, I no longer felt that I'd gone country, I felt I *was* country. Then just when I thought I'd settled into a whole new career path, up popped the devil with an offer I couldn't refuse.

Gwen Evans was a mover and shaker among L.A.'s tight-knit A-list of backing vocalists. As such, she had been high soprano to my second-soprano with Connie Stevens' show, and was calling to say that she and Merry Clayton, who had rounded out our threesome, were planning to form a trio, and wanted me to be the third.

Merry Clayton was the devil that popped up. Not that Merry was a devil, but she had played the Acid Queen in the Who's movie version of *Tommy*. She was also known as the female Rolling Stone, for her legendary duet with Mick Jagger on "Gimme Shelter." Merry Clayton didn't just stand *Twenty Feet from Stardom* – as years later she would be featured in the movie of that name – during the 1970s, she stood twenty feet from super-nova stardom, and if I accepted this offer I would be gaining entrance to that exalted circle.

When I told Gwen that I'd have to think about it, she sounded more than miffed. "All right," she snapped. "But we need to know soon." The line went dead.

*   *   *

The next morning, Buck called to say he'd decided to take me to Nashville in June, when he went to tape *Hee Haw*.

I dialed Gwen and told her I'd have to decline, even though Buck had made it clear that, although he wanted me to come to Nashville, he wasn't sure he wanted me to come to *Hee Haw*. It was his opinion that the first time I went to the set, it should be as one of the Buckaroos, and the timing for that would not be right until *Hee Haw's* taping in October, when he'd be doing songs from his new album that featured me on backing vocals. The songs he'd be doing at the June taping featured Bonnie, on vocals that were cut before I came along.

I didn't mind waiting until October. I was feeling more and more confident of my position.

"On the road" is a literal term, because only a tiny portion of touring time is spent performing. The rest is in transit: Limo-plane-limo-venue-limo-hotel, over and over, day in, day out, which leaves a lot of time to talk, and Buck was an enthusiastic conversationalist.

In explaining the rules of the road, he had offered me two choices: I could travel with the Buckaroos, flying coach and riding in rental cars, or I could travel with Buck and Jack, flying first class and riding in limousines. The catch was that if I chose to travel with Buck and Jack I was not allowed to check any baggage, and I must be prepared to carry my own bags, because although the two men would help me when they were around, I couldn't count on flying with them one-hundred percent of the time. It was something to be considered, but I didn't have to think long.

So that put me at Buck's side for hours upon hours, and we never ran out of things to talk about. I would never have guessed we'd have so much in common, but apparently Buck had me pegged even before our backstage collision at the Orange Show.

One afternoon, while we finished our selections from the sundae cart in first-class, with Jack across the aisle, taking an after-lunch nap, "Buck turned to me and said, "Have you ever seen a little newborn thoroughbred filly?"

It wasn't unusual for Buck's questions to come out of nowhere, but I'd learned they were always leading somewhere.

"Those little fillies come out of their mother knowing they're special," he said, "You can see it in the way they walk. They just prance."

I nodded, waiting for the point, and he continued, "That's what you reminded me of the first time I saw you."

Thinking back to our run-in, I didn't see where prancing came into it.

Buck nodded, "Mm-hm. Before the matinee, Jack and I were backstage, checking out one of the other acts, when a flash of sunlight caught my eye, and there you were, standing in the open stage door, with your sunglasses on and jeans tucked into those gray suede boots. You stopped a minute, looking around, and I watched you come down the hallway, stopping to talk to this person and that, and after a few minutes, I bent my head to Jack and said, "Wonder who that is walking around here like she owns the place."

"Ha. I almost knocked you down."

"Yeah. I wasn't surprised, though."

"Yes, you were."

He shook his head. "Startled. Not surprised. I knew when you walked in the door that we'd meet, and that it would be significant."

"I wish you had told me."

"I didn't know what kind of significance." He lowered his head, looking me in the eyes. "I still don't."

He held my gaze for a few seconds, as if expecting me to prod about what he meant, but I'd gotten used to Buck talking in riddles. Whenever I'd leave one of his comments hanging, he'd shake his head and call out to Jack, "I'm going to get her attention one of these days."

Jack would chuckle and say, "I don't know about this one, my man. She's got 'em running around crazy down there in Los Angeles."

That back-and-forth had become a running gag, but I wasn't sure Buck found it all that funny. He'd begun keeping tabs on me, to the point that, if he couldn't locate me in L.A. he'd call my mother in Alabama. Whether he thought she might actually be privy to my whereabouts, or he simply wanted to get to know her, I hadn't a clue, but he did seem anxious to meet my family, so the first time we played a gig within driving distance of my hometown, he extended a special invitation to them for our performance at Lake Lanier, Georgia. So, when I came out onstage, there sat Mother and Daddy and my little sister Valerie, along with my grandparents, smiling and waving from the front row. Afterward they came backstage, and soon were talking like old friends with Buck and Jack and the Buckaroos, so that by June, when time came for Buck to tape *Hee Haw*, he generously offered to fly me into Birmingham for a short visit with them before meeting him in Nashville, and it was no surprise when, one night during my stay, my sister Robin answered her kitchen phone, then craned her head around the door into the living room, and said, "Buck Owens for you."

"I'm just checking to make sure you got there all right," he said. "You've had the whole staff at Spence Manor worried, I told them to be expecting your call. They don't put just anybody through to my room, you know."

"Here I am, safe and sound," I said.

He sighed. "Well I'm glad you're finally letting me know. I've got something to tell you."

I pulled out a chair at the dinette table and sat down. "You sound awfully serious."

"No, nothing serious, I just wanted to tell you that when I got to the hotel, they brought me a message from Jana Jae." He paused, and when I didn't respond, he said, "My old fiddle player I got married to one time, remember her?" He waited a beat, "Anyway, the message was, *let's have dinner tonight; no strings, call me,* and a phone number. So, I lay down on the sofa and there was nothing on TV and I tried to call you, but nobody answered at your sister's house, so I started thinking maybe I should have dinner with Jana. It might be good to make sure there was nothing left of that old feeling. So, I met her for dinner, and what a relief. Anything I ever felt for her is gone completely. I mean nothing left. Nothing." Again, he paused for my lack of response before saying, "I just thought you might like to know."

Hanging up the phone, I walked back into the living room. "Why would I 'like to know' that he had dinner with one of his several ex-wives?"

Robin laughed. "I would think that's something you *wouldn't* like to know."

*  *  *

In the limo on the way from the Nashville airport to the hotel, I gazed at the passing landscape, thinking of my first trip to Nashville many years before, and wondering if I'd see anything that I remembered from back then. I had only been six-years-old when a Birmingham record producer named Kenneth Shackleford brought me to the Disc Jockey Convention, as his newest artist. The Christmas song I had recorded wasn't country, but I was signed with Briar Records, whose roster included country artists like Hoyt Axton and Mother Maybelle Carter. Thinking about it now, it struck me as odd that with Birmingham only a three-hour drive from Nashville, I'd had to travel all the way across the country to California, to get back to Tennessee. I kept my eye peeled for anything that looked familiar, but nothing did, and soon the driver was pulling beneath the portico of a contemporary structure that looked more like a luxury apartment building than a hotel.

The Spence Manor was designed to cater to the music industry, which meant it was in a prime spot on Music Row and boasted personal butler, valet, chauffeur and chef service, but did not house a restaurant or bar. This afforded the ultimate luxury of privacy to the superstars and music moguls who stayed there.

"If you need anything, just pick up the phone," Buck told me, as he showed me around my suite. All creamy-white Louis XVI, brocade, gilt and crystal, it was a tasteful version of Las Vegas style that would tempt someone to stretch out on the sofa and eat bonbons all day.

Buck took a menu from the desk. "Room service suggestions are in here, but they'll make anything you want. I thought we'd just have dinner here tonight, and watch some TV." He sprawled on the sofa and picked up the remote. "*Hee Haw's* coming on in a few minutes." He clicked on the TV then muted the sound. "What do want to eat? I'm having chicken-fried steak."

"You always have chicken-fried steak," I laughed, settling into the cushy club chair beside the sofa.

"Not always, but most of the time," he said.

"I make delicious chicken-fried steak and gravy` Can you cook?" I asked.

"Oh, I guess I could cook if I had to," he said, "but I don't."

"Don't have to, or don't cook?"

"Both; neither."

"Do you eat out all the time?"

"No."

I thought about that for a minute. Buck had taken me to his ranch in Bakersfield, and I had seen no sign of servants. I also saw no signs of a female occupant. "Do you have somebody who cooks for you?"

"Yeah."

"A chef?"

"Not a chef, but she's a pretty good cook."

"What's her name?"

"Jennifer."

# Chapter 8

JENNIFER WAS A NAME I had not heard him mention. "Does Jennifer live with you."

"Umm," he worked his mouth around. "She lives in a house that I own. I own several houses."

"Is she your girlfriend?"

"She is a girl and she is my friend."

"How long has she been your friend?"

"A long time."

"Longer than Jana?"

"Jana's not my friend," he said, "but I have known Jennifer longer."

Although Buck always enjoyed question-and-answer games, I was ready to get to the point. "Are you in love with Jennifer?"

He rested his head on the back of the sofa, staring at the ceiling. "I don't think I've ever been in love."

"Not even with Bonnie?"

"Bonnie and I were just a couple of kids in lust."

Buck Owens, Victoria Hallman, Doyle Singer, Buddy Alan, Charlie McCoy, Terry Christofferson, Jerry Wiggins, Martin Clayton, "Buck's Place" segment on the Hee Haw Set (1980). Photo courtesy of Becky Scott

"Okay, then, are you in lust?"

"With Jennifer? No."

"You must at least like her more than Jana."

"I don't know what makes you think that, but I will say that I'm real comfortable with Jennifer and I was never comfortable with Jana."

I got quiet, thinking about the value of being comfortable with someone, especially someone as famous as Buck Owens. "Are you comfortable with me?" I asked.

"Getting there," he said. "Any more questions?" Because *Hee Haw's* coming on and you never said what you want for dinner."

"Chicken-fried steak sounds good to me. With mashed potatoes and gravy. Milk to drink."

"You want some ice cream?"

"Yes."

He picked up the phone. "What flavor?"

"Do you think they have pralines 'n' cream?"

"If they don't, they'll get it."

When the waiter arrived, Buck asked him to set supper on the coffee table, so we could eat in front of the TV. Usually on a weekend night at six o'clock, we were at an arena or auditorium somewhere, getting ready to go onstage, so this was the first time I'd watched *Hee Haw* with Buck sitting beside me as "color man." Naturally, I was most interested in the female cast members. I recognized the ones who had been on the show for many years, but "Who's that?" I pointed out a blonde with Farrah Fawcett hair.

"Mackenzie Colt." Buck said, "I brought her to *Hee Haw*. She opened a few shows for us, and then she thought nothing would do but that I bring her along to sing on the show, so I did, and then she somehow wrangled an audition as one of the Honeys. That's what they call the girls on the show, you know."

"So, after she became one of the Honeys, she couldn't sing with you anymore?"

He mopped a bite of steak in the gravy on his plate. "As I recall, she stopped singing with us before they cast her."

"Why?"

He cut another bite of steak. "I guess it just wasn't the right fit."

Now an unfamiliar girl with long brown hair appeared on the screen, standing next to a big man in overalls, holding a pitchfork.

"Who's she?"

"That's Linda Thompson, Elvis's girlfriend."

"Elvis? He's dead."

Buck rolled his eyes. "I know that, Classy Sassy," he used the nickname he liked to call me, "I meant she was his girlfriend before he died."

"I thought his girlfriend's name was Ginger."

"Elvis had a lot of girlfriends."

"Kinda like you."

Buck cut his eyes at me. "Watch the TV."

When the show signed off with the whole gang singing, *We love the time we spend with you* . . . Buck shook his head, "Gonna be a zoo."

"What do you mean?"

"Monday, first full-cast day."

"Why do you call it a zoo?"

"Maybe one of these days you'll find out."

"In October?"

He nodded, "I'm thinking about bringing you to sing with me in October." He patted my knee. "I'm thinking about a lot of things. You just sit still, and see how it works out. There's some major changes happening."

"Like what?"

He closed his eyes and leaned his head back. "I don't want to get into it right now." He winked at me, "You'll figure it out."

*  *  *

A few weeks later, on a red-eye, winging our way across the night-sky above the fly-over states, the only passengers in first-class were Buck, Jack, Tammy Wynette, her husband-manager, George Richey, and I, so it wasn't long before everybody took advantage of the coincidence, switching their seats around to create an impromptu confab of country-music legends. If I were ever going to get free career advice, these would be the four to get it from. I made myself as inconspicuous as possible, scrunched against the window, while next to me, Buck turned sideways, looking backward, talking to George and Tammy, with Jack leaning across the aisle to join in.

I didn't recognize all the names they brought up and I wasn't familiar with some of the terminology and Nashville slang, but I caught enough to understand that the changes Buck had mentioned were indeed big, even somewhat scary. The four of them seemed concerned about the "new wave," as they called it. I didn't know what the new wave was, but apparently it didn't include them, which was why Tammy was looking for a record producer to replace Billy Sherrill, who not only discovered her, but produced and co-wrote her biggest hits, and Buck had left Capitol Records, the label he'd been with since the 1950s.

Sitting in the dimly-lit cabin, listening to these two giants from my childhood speaking in hushed, somber tones, I knew it was epic. Something important was ending, I just wasn't sure exactly what. A chill ran up my spine and I placed the little airline pillow beneath my head, trying to fall asleep. I didn't want to hear anymore.

But even while the "old guard" of the country music industry was readying itself for death in preparation for resurrection, Buck was planning his comeback. As the summer days lengthened, so did our touring schedule, and with that, came many hours of conversation, in which I learned that far from leaving his legend to smolder, Buck was making plans to rise from the ashes. Even though it wasn't apparent to me that his career was diminishing, he had felt it for quite some time, and although he spoke often of his musical partner and muse, Don Rich, he didn't date the decline of his record sales to Don's death, but to *Hee Haw*.

"It's impossible to sustain a recording career and a career on television at the same time." He never said he was planning to leave *Hee Haw*, but he must have been thinking that direction, because he was very excited about reigniting his recording career.

It can't have been accidental that these changes coincided with Buck turning fifty in August. I think it was his version of a midlife crisis, and in his case, it wasn't such a bad thing. Especially, not for me.

We were together on his birthday, August 12. It was an afternoon, outdoor concert and some of his fan club members brought a birthday cake, and took pictures, in which Buck made sad faces and joked about being a crusty old man. Right about then is when he grew a beard and switched from wearing a cowboy hat to wearing what he called "Injun" hats. He also decided to change my name to Jesse Rose McQueen.

I didn't like the beard, I didn't like the hats, and I sure didn't like the name Jesse Rose McQueen.

Actually, it was Jack McFadden who came up with the name. The original Jesse Rose was a midwife who assisted in the birth of Jack's stepdaughter. He said he'd always thought it was a great stage name, and he'd been saving it for just the right person. According to Jack, I was that person, even though to me, the name conjured the image of a singer onstage at Harlem's Cotton Club in the 1920s. I told Jack and Buck I'd have to think about it.

The next week, Buck summoned me to Bakersfield to listen to a couple of songs he was working on. One was called "The Cowboy and the Lady" and he wasn't finished with it. He got his guitar and sat in his desk chair to sing it to me. "Cowboy walked into a barroom, said I'm looking for a lady, said the lady's name was Jesse Rose; long dark hair, big bright eyes, pretty little thing, about yea high." He went through a couple more verses, singing da-di-da when he didn't have words, and at the end, "The cowboy and the lady rode away."

"That song's about me," I said when he finished.

"What makes you think that?"

"The lady in the song looks like me, and she has my name, that's what."

He widened his eyes in mock surprise. "I thought your name was Vicki." Then he said, "Oh, I almost forgot, you had to think about that, didn't you? Here's another song." He strummed an intro, talking over it, "Pay attention now, because I want you to record this one with me," and without giving me time to respond, he started singing, "Jesse loved the ladies like grandmas' love babies, and I ain't never heard no one complain . . ." finishing, "Sit down, sir, let Jesse Rob the Train."

"That's your next hit record," I said.

And that's how I became Jesse Rose McQueen.

As with the many life-altering events that had continued since that fateful collision at the Orange Show, changing my name wasn't so much a decision as it was an obvious next step in the natural progression of my career path, which, somewhere along the way, had broadened to encompass my personal life. I can't pinpoint the time or place where my relationship with Buck transitioned from business to friends to lovers, but I can say for certain that it followed the same timeline as our mutual musical respect.

From making music to making love is the most natural progression of all. My background was rock music, and so, to some extent, was Buck's. While Nashville had been ladling out the syrup of countrypolitan, Buck kept audiences dancing to the pounding beat of his trademark "freight-train" sound, with edgy high harmony and screaming Telecasters. When it came to music, we spoke the same language, and our simpatico didn't stop there.

Buck Owens was not just street-smart and business savvy, he was a scholar whose intellectual curiosity matched mine. Buck's "schooling" ended with seventh grade, but he was one of the most educated men I've

MEET JESSE ROSE McQUEEN!!!

The pretty new face in the Buck Owens Show
line-up is songstress Jesse Rose McQueen.
Jesse was born September 15, 1956 in Mobile,
Alabama and grew up in Centreville, Alabama.

Jesse's singing career started at the tender
age of four when she was a contestant in a
Shirley Temple look-a-like contest.  The
host of the show liked her singing and put
her on a weekly "Talent Showcase" show in
Birmingham.

"Send My Daddy Home" was Jesse's first
record.  She was eight when she recorded
this Christmas tear jerker.  It got quite
a bit of local airplay.  She then made some
television appearances in New York and California.

At fifteen, she started singing with a rock and roll band and then did
nightclub singing using a great variety of music in her act including country
music.

Jesse moved to Los Angeles, California in 1977.  On April 1, 1979, she was
booked at a show that Buck & the Buckaroos were also performing.  When she
was introduced to Buck, her manager told Buck that she could sing.  So Buck
took her into his dressing room and she sang "Help Me Make It Through the Night".
Buck was so pleased with her singing that he brought her out on stage that
night and she has been traveling with the gang ever since.

Jesse loves doing country music and loves to travel with Buck and the
Buckaroos.  She says they are all fun to work with and they are the most
congenial group of people she's ever worked with.

She was very excited when Buck's single "Let Jesse Rob the Train" was
released as she sang backup on the single along with the Buckaroos.  She
hopes to record more in the future.

I hope you all will welcome Jesse to our gang!!

Fan Club Article 1979, courtesy Becky Scott

ever known, entirely self-taught, and it seemed important to him that I had attended a private college, even though I counted my classroom studies a mere fraction of my education. Like Buck, I was self-taught, and our minds were magnets that drew our heads together in a never-ending conversation, becoming ever more absorbed as our intimacy deepened. He taught me to play chess, I lent him books by Ayn Rand and Albert Camus; he quizzed me on obscure English words; I spoke French to him because he liked the sound of it; and we both loved football, so he rooted for my Crimson Tide, while I cheered for his Longhorns or Cowboys. And although I didn't participate in any sports, I went along with Buck for R&R vacations to Scottsdale's Camelback Inn Resort, relaxing by the pool, while he played golf and tennis and tended to the business of his radio station, KNIX in Phoenix. On one trip, we even hooked-up with his sons Buddy and Michael to attend the first boxing match of former Dallas Cowboy, Ed "Too Tall" Jones. Then when October rolled around, I learned to like baseball when he and Jack placed their annual bet on the World Series.

October was a big month, with September providing a lead-in with a performance on the Wheeling Jamboree, America's second-oldest live country-music broadcast. Then there was an appearance on the Canadian television program, the *Tommy Hunter Show*, North America's longest-running TV music-variety series. On these stages I was stepping into spotlights that had shone on everybody from Roy Acuff to Roy Rogers, which would have taken my breath away had gradual progression not stolen the excitement I would have felt if I had looked into a crystal ball one year before, and seen what I would be doing and with whom.

Surely, I would get at least a small thrill when I finally arrived at the studio on Nashville's Music Row to record with Buck for the first time, I thought. I should have been out of mind with excitement. One of the most major of the major changes Buck was making in his career, was the decision not to use the Buckaroos on this new album, and yet, here I was, handpicked by Buck to provide vocals on his next single.

He'd explained this to me on that day in his office when I first heard "Let Jesse Rob the Train."

Leaning back in his desk chair, staring up at the ceiling, he started talking in a way that I knew would ramble around to something important.

"Here lately, I've been doing a lot of thinking, and I've realized that I've been going about things all wrong since Don Rich got killed. Don was a big part of my music. *Big part*. And ever since, I've been bumping around like a billiard ball trying to find what we had, the sound, the success. The fun. I don't know why it took me so long to realize you can't duplicate something that was unique. If I'm going to continue making the kind of music I want to make, and having the success I want to have, I've got to start completely fresh with something else unique. That's where you come in."

"Me?"

Buck nodded. I noticed it the first time you sang harmony with me on "Play Together Again, Again". You've heard my records with Don and me singing together. Our voices had an edge that cut through, you know what I mean? Well, maybe you don't know what I mean, but your voice has that same cut-through quality that makes people's ears prick up. I don't know how to explain it, but I know it when I hear it, and you'll be singing with me from now on." He raised his eyebrows. "Who knows? We might be the next big thing."

By the time I arrived at the studio to cut "Let Jesse Rob the Train," I'd had plenty of time for the astonishment to sink in, so crossing the threshold of the studio simply felt like the next step, even with the head of A&R for Warner Brothers observing from the sidelines, and Grammy-winning producer Norro Wilson at the controls in the booth.

The studio was smaller than I expected, not half the size of Buck's studio in Bakersfield, and there was no outer office or waiting area. The front door opened right into the studio, and immediately to the left of the door was a row of chairs, where Jack McFadden sat talking with Bob Doyle from Warner Brothers and a middle-aged blonde, whom he introduced as Rose Maddox. Watching me walk away, headed for my spot at the microphone, Rose leaned over to Jack and I heard her say, "Look at that little girl in those tight jeans. Her butt's not big as my thumb."

I didn't know how to take what she'd said, but it made me laugh. Later I found out that she had been a big star in the 1940s and was considered a pioneer among female country vocalists. She had even cut a few records with Buck, and later, when he played their duets for me, I heard exactly what he meant about a voice that "cut through." Rose Maddox had that kind of voice, and if I was going to sing country music, that's exactly how I wanted to sing it.

The rhythm tracks for the session had been cut earlier. Today would be the first time I heard them. I clapped the earphones onto my head, and the ringing guitar intro to "Let Jesse Rob the Train" set me dancing while I sang.

Buck hadn't told me I'd be singing on any other songs that day. Maybe he was waiting to see what Norro thought about my vocals, but if the first song had been an audition, I passed, because I also sang on two others, "Sweet Molly Brown's" and "Victim of Life's Circumstances," which would become the B-side of "Let Jesse Rob the Train."

Buck's plan for the evening was room-service dinner, and early to bed, so we could be on time and in fine fettle to do "Buck's Place" in the morning. He ordered beans and cornbread and a big glass of milk, polished off the beans, then sat on the sofa dunking cornbread in his milk, while I finished my BLT.

"Something I want to talk to you about," he said, then dunked another bite before continuing, "They're going to want you to be one of those girls."

"What girls?" I asked.

"*Hee Haw*. The girls on the show."

"That's crazy. I don't look like those girls."

"You're right about that," he nodded, "You're a whole lot prettier than any of them."

I smiled, "You think you might be a little prejudiced?"

He shook his head. "No. I'm telling you, they'll want you to be one of the Honeys, and I know you'll think that's great, but it won't be. You are a serious singer, and I think you can be a big recording artist, but you can't have a recording career and be a *Hee Haw* Honey at the same time. It'll be up to you, but I think I already know what you'll do."

If everything else to that point had seemed a natural progression, this absolutely did not. Never in my wildest dreams had I imagined myself a *Hee Haw* Honey. I had never even been elected "Class Beauty" in High School, although at graduation, I did walk away with the big trophy for "Most Outstanding Senior Girl," along with a whole bunch of academic awards, hardly the kind of credits you'd find on a *Hee Haw* girl's résumé. So far, I had never known Buck to be wrong, but he was way off the mark about this.

Even so, the idea of being one of those gorgeous *Hee Haw* glamour gals was enticing. All the more, because I'd never thought of myself that way. I hardly got a wink of sleep, because every time I closed my eyes, I saw myself dancing around *Hee Haw's* barnyard set, wearing a low-cut calico dress.

What a shock, after the hair and makeup crew got done with me the next morning, I gazed at myself in the dressing-room mirror, and looking back at me was a *Hee Haw* Honey. *No time to think about that.* I wriggled into my skinny jeans and purple satin shirt, and Buck and Jack herded me down the hall to the studio, where I took my place with the Buckaroos, at the microphone under the big Klieg lights. Then just as I was getting comfortable in my spot, a short, balding man, hurried up to where I stood and crooked his finger, beckoning. He looked like someone in charge, so I hopped off the bandstand and went to hear what he had to say.

"Hello, Jesse Rose," he offered his hand, "I'm Sam Lovullo, *Hee Haw's* producer. I want to welcome you to the show. I also want to ask you a favor."

*What on earth*? I wondered.

"Buck's hat and beard," he said. "They look terrible on camera. I've tried to reason with him about it, with no success, and Jack McFadden says you're the one Buck listens to."

*Me?*

"Would you please ask him to let somebody in makeup give him a shave, and to ditch that hat. What he wears at his live shows is his business, but *Hee Haw* is mine."

I thought about it for a few seconds. Buck was very into his new look, but I agreed with Mr. Lovullo. I walked over to where Buck sat on a stool, waiting for us to begin taping. Ducking my head beneath the brim of his brown "Injun" hat, I got close to his face, and said, "The producer doesn't like your hat and beard."

Buck's face turned to stone. "I know. He told me."

I said, "One of your best features is your thick blond hair. Not many fifty-year-old men have hair like that, and it really is a shame to cover it up."

He cut his eyes, looking into mine. "You like my hair?"

"Yes, I like your hair. You didn't know that?"

He grunted. "I guess I could take the hat off. But I won't shave my beard. And they'll have to come fix my hair before we start taping." He handed me his hat.

I kissed his scruffy cheek. "Thank you."

In the back of the studio, Mr. Lovullo was watching. He came forward and took my hand. "You may have saved Buck's relationship with *Hee Haw.*"

I had no idea what he meant, but whatever was going on, I doubted that my good deed was as epic as Mr. Lovullo made it sound. I only knew that I had done the producer a favor that allowed me to climb back onto

Buck's Injun Hat, Buck Owens Fan Club breakfast, 1980

the bandstand, while the tall, blonde hairdresser combed Buck's hair. The show must go on,

Buck didn't believe in re-takes; if we had to do a song more than once, it was due to a technical glitch of some sort, not our fault. Buck and the Buckaroos were always dead-on, and as one of them, they expected the same of me. Never mind that I'd never heard four of the seven songs we'd be doing, and there would be no run-through. Someone at Buck's office had sent me a cassette of the songs, but the titles weren't written on the label, and there was no vocal track on the tape, so all I heard was a bunch of instrumental music that I didn't recognize. When I mentioned it to Buck, he dismissed my concern with, "Ah, you'll be fine," and as usual, he was right. My ear caught the high harmony like magic, and I sailed through the musical gauntlet.

As the band unstrapped their guitars, the director, Mr. Boatman, and the producer, Mr. Lovullo, came over to talk to Buck, and each of them made it a point to compliment my vocals, and say they looked forward to seeing me tomorrow. I hadn't realized I'd be there the next day, but they seemed to be the bosses.

Leaving the studio to go have lunch with Buck and Jack, while they talked music-business, I rode in silence, assessing my first day at *Hee Haw*, waiting for a lull in their conversation, to say, "Everybody sure seemed to like me."

Buck said, "That remind you of anybody, Jack?"

I wondered who *anybody* was. Maybe Jana, or maybe Buck's girl-friend singer from long ago, Susan Raye.

Jack interrupted my musing, "Jesse Rose, I'm going to give you one of the best pieces of advice you'll ever get. When you come back to this set, you find a corner somewhere, and you stand in it until somebody asks you to do something."

The next day was full-cast, the day Buck told me would be a zoo. When we arrived, it was immediately apparent what he meant. The hall-ways were crawling with people hugging and kissing and talking and laughing. Passing the makeup room, I got my first glimpse of a real live *Hee Haw* Honey.

# Chapter 9

MISTY ROWE WAS SITTING in the chair nearest the door, while the tall hairdresser put electric curlers in her hair. As of yet, she didn't appear to have on makeup, because I noticed that she was extremely pale. When she saw me looking at her, she frowned and turned her head. I realized she probably thought me rude for staring, and I remembered Jack's advice.

But I didn't have time to find a corner, because just as I was about to move on, a small woman with short blonde hair, dressed in jeans and a white shirt, walked up to me and crooked her finger, "Come this way."

Leading me down the hall, she introduced herself as Faye Sloan, wardrobe mistress, and said she needed to get me into costume for "Pickin' and Grinnin'". This was the first I knew that I'd be on camera that day. I'd assumed I was just tagging along with Buck and Jack, but those visions of myself prancing around the set in a low-cut dress couldn't have been more wrong. The dress she took from the rack was a dark-blue calico like the one in my dreams, but this dress was never meant for one of the *Hee Haw* Honeys. This dress was more appropriate for Granny on *The Beverly Hillbillies*. Faye held it while I stepped into it, then she zipped it up and said, "What size shoe do you wear?"

"Five-and-a-half."

She handed me a pair of beige high heels. "These are six-and-a-half, but they're the smallest I have."

The best I could say was that the shoes didn't fit me any worse than the dress did. But I didn't have time to say that, or anything else, because, mumbling something about getting Buck dressed, Faye walked out the door, leaving me standing in front of the mirror, bunching up the waistline's six-inches of excess fabric, and wondering if I should ask somebody for a safety pin. Recalling Jack's advice, I decided to go on into the stu-

*Hee Haw* Cast "Pickin' and Grinnin'" with Ed McMahon (1979)

dio and find a dark corner. The way I looked in Granny's dress, I needed someplace to hide.

Buck was standing at the periphery of the set, watching crew members placing horse blankets and throw-pillows on bales of hay grouped around two microphones on stands. Walking up to him, I smiled and said, "I'm all ready."

He frowned. "What's that they've put on you?"

I pulled out the extra fabric at the waist. "It doesn't fit very well, but it's comfortable."

A rock-star-looking young man with a dark beard was standing at a tall table shuffling papers. Buck called out to him, "Gary, get Faye Sloan in here."

In a matter of seconds, Faye hurried through the doorway and over to where we stood.

Buck pointed at me. "I know you've got something better than that for her to wear."

Faye gave him a one-sided grin. "You don't expect me to waste one of my good dresses on a backup singer, do you?" She said it in a teasing manner, but I thought there was truth in her jest. "Come on," she said, motioning me to follow."

Ten minutes later, I walked back into the studio, beaming. The shoes still didn't fit, but the dress did. After a little perusing of the clothes rack in the dressing room, Faye had pulled out a red calico dress that fit me to a tee. She even completed my *Hee Haw* Honey look with a push-up bra. Passing several of the girls in the hallway, one of them remarked, "That's Barbi's dress."

Faye gave her a look, "Not anymore," and herded me through the door into the studio, where Buck was now seated in front of a microphone, surrounded by the haybales and milk cans. Faye presented me for approval.

He nodded, "Whole lot better."

Suddenly a voice filled the room, sounding like the Wizard behind the curtain, "Cast to the studio," and here they came, Minnie Pearl and Grandpa Jones; Roy Clark, Kenny Price and Junior Samples; LuLu Roman, Roni Stoneman and Cathy Baker; Archie Campbell and Gordy Tapp; Kenny Price and Gailard Sartain; the Hager Twins and the Buckaroos; Jimmy Riddle and Jackie Phelps; the Nashville Edition and the *Hee Haw* Band; and last through the door, but in no particular hurry, came a bevy of beauties who were unmistakably the *Hee Haw* Honeys: Leading the parade, a blonde I recognized as the show's Nurse Goodbody, Gunilla Hutton, was laughing at something said by the one Buck had identified as Elvis's girlfriend, Linda Thompson; then with their heads together as if telling secrets, came two of the others I remembered seeing on the show for many years,  Marilyn Monroe look-alike, Misty Rowe, and the new Mrs. Kenny Rogers, *Hee Haw's* Southern Belle, Marianne Gordon; behind them, walking as if in a trance, came the Amazonian brunette, Lisa Todd; and rushing in at the last minute, the Farrah-haired girl, Mackenzie Colt, who had originally come to the show with Buck and the Buckaroos.

The tall man with a brown mustache, who I now knew was Bob Boatman, the Director, began placing the cast, pointing to a haybale, "Minnie, you and Grandpa sit here beside Roy," or a milk can, "Roni, you over there by Buck," and on and on until everyone was seated. He'd placed me to the far right, above and behind Grandpa, in a spot that I knew would only allow me to be visible during a wide-shot, but since I hadn't expected to be in the shot at all, I was just happy to be there. As with my collision with Buck at the Orange Show, I recognized a lucky break, and would do my best to prove myself worthy of a front-row seat. Unlike the rest of the cast, who talked among themselves and only "lit up" when they knew the camera was on them, I grinned until my jaws ached, and clapped my hands like they were naughty children in need of a spanking.

Recognition came more quickly than I would have dared hope. The guest star for that particular "Pickin' and Grinnin' was Ed McMahon from the *Tonight Show*, and as I passed him when we all "took five," he stopped me and offered his hand, "Young lady, I want to compliment you on your professionalism. I've been watching you all day, and you have not missed a single cue" He circled his finger in the air. "Your energy could light this whole studio."

"Thank you," I began, but before I could introduce myself, the Producer, Sam Lovullo, rushed over and did the honors, adding that I was new to the show, which prompted Mr. McMahon to repeat his praise, this time, touting me to the "boss." It was a reference that no amount of money could buy, and I had gotten it the old-fashioned way – I earned it.

At the end of the day, when I was hurrying down the hall to meet Buck and Jack in the parking lot, a voice behind me called, "Jesse Rose," and I turned to see Mr. Lovullo.

"Have you ever done any comedy?" he asked. "Before you get out of here, we want to try you in a couple of 'Haystacks' with Buck.

*Yesss*! I restrained myself from a fist-pump. To that old saying about being at the right place at the right time, Buck would always add a third ingredient, amending it to, "Right place at the right time *with the right product*," which had just happened to me. Right place and time were the *Hee Haw* set not long after they had lost their popular little brownette, Barbi Benton, and the right product was my flair for comedy. As much as I may have dreamed of becoming a latter-day Sarah Bernhardt, the director at Town and Gown theater back home in Birmingham cast me as Sally Bowles in *Cabaret*, and my method acting coach here in L.A. insisted I was perfect for Judy Holiday's dumb-blonde character in our workshop production of *Born Yesterday*. Those roles were a lot more demanding than anything I'd ever seen on *Hee Haw*; this would be a cinch.

They put me in another of Barbi's hand-me-downs and I took my place lounging with Buck in a life-size haystack. The process would be a read-through of the joke on the cue cards, straight into take-one. Reading through the first joke, I was disappointed to see that Buck had the punchline. In fact, I had almost no lines at all:

BUCK: *Jesse Rose, do you believe in the hereafter?*
JESSE ROSE: *Yes, Buck, I do.*
BUCK: (Trying to kiss Jesse Rose) *Then you know what I'm here after.*

The next one was only slightly better, but at least I had the punchline:

> BUCK: (Trying to kiss Jesse Rose) I bet you'd let me kiss you if I was a millionaire.
> JESSE ROSE: Of course, I would. I'm crazy about millionaires.

Instead of running straight through the line, after *Of course I would,* I paused and brought one shoulder forward, leaning into the camera with a sultry wink, "I'm crrr-aazy about millionaires."

From somewhere high above us came laughter and applause. Until then I had not realized we had a studio audience. And as I was walking off the set, a man with thinning dark hair and a bushy mustache hustled over to me. "I'm Bud Wingard, and I hate to admit it, but I wrote those jokes." He extended his hand, "You sure put one over on me."

"I did?"

He motioned me into an alcove, "When they told me to find some jokes for Buck's new female vocalist, I thought, *Aw, man, some girl singer who wouldn't know a punchline if it socked her in the kisser; this will never make it onto the screen.* So, I went and dug around in my files till I came up with two of the worst old jokes I had, and I'll be darned if you didn't save them." He patted my shoulder, "Thanks."

"You're welcome," I said, "They really weren't all that bad."

He slapped his knee, "Hah," and walked away laughing.

I didn't know what I'd said that was so funny, but on a comedy show, I knew you always wanted to leave them laughing, and that's what I'd done.

*  *  *

After the snack service on our flight home from Nashville, Buck closed his eyes, seeming to nap, while I read Mary Stewart's newest Arthurian novel, *The Last Enchantment,* when Buck broke into the fantasy. "I want your opinion about something."

"Okay," I tucked the book cover into the page I was reading, marking my place, and turned my head to pay attention to Buck.

"I'm going to give you a hypothetical situation, and you tell me what you think about it," he said.

I slid my book into the envelope on the back of the seat in front of me and folded my arms, ready to listen.

Buck said, "What if somebody, a man let's say, asked somebody – a female he was involved with – to live in his house, just be there for him, you know."

"Like a wife?"

He nodded. "Yeah, and as long as she stayed there, the man agreed to pay all her expenses, and also give her a certain amount of money every year that she stayed, and it would be completely up to her how long that was. In other words, he couldn't just toss her out anytime he felt like it, but if she left she got nothing. All this would be drawn up as a legal contract. What would you think of a deal like that?"

I thought for a minute before saying, "So it's like being married, and it's a legal agreement, but the two parties are not man and wife, right?

"That's about it," he said, "and remember, she can end it anytime she wants to."

"Okay," I nodded, 'I see. Speaking hypothetically, it sounds like a pretty good deal for somebody, but if you want my personal opinion, I don't think it's the kind of situation I'd be interested in."

"Mm-hm," Buck said, "Well you might change your mind." He closed his eyes and seemed to go to sleep.

I opened my book and got lost in the liaison between Arthur and his evil half-sister, until Buck interrupted again. "I think I'm going to be in L.A. a lot from now on. Might buy a house there." He closed his eyes, and once again, appeared to go to sleep.

This time I didn't open *The Last Enchantment*, I raised the window blind, and gazed out at the sunset sky, thinking about Buck buying a place in L.A. At that very moment, several of Hollywood's most eligible bachelors were hoping to get a call from me saying I was back in town, and although Buck surely must have known I didn't sit home many nights when we weren't on the road, I got the impression he'd rather not be confronted with the fact of any other men in my life, so, we avoided the subject. I wondered how easy it would be to keep my love-life to myself, with Buck living in the 'hood. When it came to the dating scene, Los Angeles was a smaller town than you'd think.

Perhaps it was no coincidence that right about the time of that conversation, we had our first gig in L.A., when producer Nick Vanoff, scheduled Buck and the Buckaroos to appear on his new television production, *The Big Show*. This was one more instance where I didn't quite get the importance of the opportunity. Nick Vanoff had five Emmys under his belt as producer of TV shows like *The Kennedy Center Honors*, *The Julie*

*Andrews Hour, The Hollywood Palace, The Sonny and Cher Show, The To-night Show,* and others too numerous to mention. Yet, there he was, inviting me into the booth, and chatting as if I were of the same stature as Julie Andrews or Cher. Once again, whoosh, right over my head.

In addition to all his other TV series, Nick Vanoff was one of *Hee Haw's* founding fathers, so it wasn't surprising that he'd booked Buck for his new show. The surprising thing was that Buck did not take along the Buckaroos. His band for *The Big Show* would be a trio made up of Buck on guitar, Doyle Singer on bass and me on tambourine. Doyle and I would also sing harmony, as we always did, but when I questioned Buck's wisdom of depending solely on me as percussionist, he shook his head. "You play good tambourine. It'll be enough."

As usual Buck was right. The three of us performed "Let Jesse Rob the Train" so effectively that Buck decided from now on, this would be the group. No more Buckaroos, just Buck, Doyle and me, playing small venues with pick-up musicians. I wasn't sure whether I'd gotten a promotion or we'd all stepped down a notch.

Victoria dressed for Club Barrington Cabaret Show, with her poodle Caniche "Neesh" (1980). Photo courtesy of Michael Ballard

# Chapter 10

VICTORIA
*Winter 1980*

THE NEW YEAR BROUGHT major changes. For one thing, my roommate Michael and I moved from our Hollywood Hills apartment to a luxury pad in Beverly Hills, within walking distance to my manager's office
on Beverly Drive, who recommended an interior designer to update and
refresh my furnishings to match the apartment's creamy tone-on-tone
palette.

The day they delivered my white velvet sofa, and matching off-white
wing chairs, was the same day the paper hanger covered the bathroom
walls in pale silver. When all was in place, I looked around and realized
that I was literally watching my life being transformed.

Buck and I spent the last night of 1979, sipping champagne – an unusual thing for Buck – in a hotel suite in Pasadena, prior to his ride in the
New Year's Day Rose Bowl Parade. He saw the evening as the perfect time
to celebrate the "new" Buck Owens, which indeed did not include his
Buckaroos. In fact, Jack had already booked a string of one-nighters for
Buck, Doyle and me, playing with house bands in saloons. But the biggest
news was that we were also celebrating the launch of Buck's movie career,
which was what he'd meant when he told me he would be spending more
time in L.A. Come February, he'd begin shooting an ABC television movie, produced by Aaron Spelling, called *Murder Can Hurt You!* a parody of
TV detectives. Buck would have a starring role as MacSkye, a takeoff on
Dennis Weaver as *McCloud*.

Even though Buck had leaked a few hints, I hadn't expected these
sort of changes, and I wasn't at all sure I liked them, but there was no time
to think about it, because Buck's roadhouse tour was coming right up, so

almost as soon as I got home from Pasadena, I tossed my trusty tambourine into the suitcase with my stage outfits, and away we went.

To my surprise these scaled-down performances were not so different from performing with the Buckaroos. With the three of us at the front of the stage directing the pickup musicians, the music flowed, and having the crowd literally right there with us created a synergy that wasn't possible in an arena.

After the first gig, in the limo on the way to the hotel, Buck explained that these venues were not a step down; they were a step back. He wanted to get back to the roots of his music, all the way back to the time when he was a young Buck playing roadhouses like the Blackboard in Bakersfield. It seemed to me that his step back was working. Buck was more relaxed, and his stage energy was through the rafters.

Then disaster struck at a Holiday Inn, somewhere in the Northwest.

Through all my months of touring with Buck's show, Jack Mc Fadden had never once come to my hotel room, so I was surprised when someone knocked at my door, and I found myself looking straight into his big square face.

He trudged past me and sat in one of two club chairs, gripping his knees. He hadn't changed out of the business clothes he'd worn to the show that afternoon. The tweed jacket was rumpled, and his hair sprang up in silver tufts.

I transferred my Tab Cola and cigarettes from the nightstand to the table between the two chairs, and sat down.

"Buck's canceled his flight to Los Angeles tomorrow," he said, "reneged on the movie deal."

"What? Why?"

"Buck doesn't have to have a reason." He shifted his chair and leaned on his elbows, to look me in the eyes. "This is the fork in the road of his career, and if you'll talk some sense into him, I'll owe you for the rest of my life."

"Me?" Seemed like I was saying that a lot these days. Why did these old show-biz pros think I was the one to save Buck's career?

Jack nodded. "Buck will listen to you when he won't listen to anybody else."

I didn't know about that, but I did know that Buck was searching for a new direction, and that both he and Jack seemed to think this movie was it. I, on the other hand, was not so sure. Although no one else had made the comparison, turning Buck into a movie star seemed very similar to the direction Colonel Parker had steered Elvis Presley's career. If Buck thought *Hee Haw* destroyed his credibility as a recording artist, wasn't that exactly what people said about Elvis's string of silly movies? So here goes Buck doing a silly movie. But who was I, to call a movie silly when I'd never been in a movie, silly or otherwise? *Murder Can Hurt You!* was a catchy title that sounded like something I would enjoy watching, and Buck would be among a cast of seasoned actors with long lists of credits and hit shows. Jamie Farr, Gavin MacLeod and Tony Danza were on top of the ratings in *M\*A\*S\*H, Love Boat,* and *Taxi;* and Victor Buono, Burt Young, Don Adams and Mel Blanc were among the illuminati of actors, Talk about intimidating. I suspected I'd just hit on the problem. No matter how many gold records Buck Owens hung on his wall, he was a rookie actor. He'd be the greenhorn fresh off the *Hee Haw* farm, walking onto a Hollywood set, trying to keep pace with the cream of Hollywood's crop. Buck Owens had stage fright.

I smiled at Jack. "I'll do what I can."

\* \* \*

"What do you want?" Buck stalked away and flung himself onto the bed, lying propped against the headboard, staring at the TV with the sound turned off. He'd changed from the jeans and jacket he'd worn onstage, into a gray jogging suit. A few inches from his hand lay a script.

I breezed past and sat at a dinette table in front of the draperies. "I hear you've changed your mind about the movie. I thought you were excited about doing it,"

"I'm not an actor. I'm a singer and a musician."

"So am I, but I'm also an actor, and I think you can be a really fine one." I was beginning to figure out that my training in "method" acting qualified as the kind of higher education Buck revered, so I hoped he'd put some stock in my opinion. "Did you hear what I said?"

He looked at me from the corner of his eye. "You really believe that?"

"Yes. You'll be a cowboy playing a cowboy. Haven't I told you that acting is 'being' the part?"

"I don't know what you're talking about," he growled.

"Bring the script over here and I'll show you. Let's run some lines. Come on, just for fun."

He didn't answer, but slowly, he got up from the bed and dragged himself to the dinette table, sinking low into the chair across from me, like a surly teenager. "All right, if you really want to, I'll listen to you read some of it, but don't ask me to read anything." He shoved the script my direction.

"What's the name of one of the female characters?" I asked.

"I don't know. Salty, I think."

"Salty?" I riffled the script. "Oh, here she is. Salty." I read one of Salty's lines and stopped. "MacSkye has the next line. Who plays MacSkye?" I asked, although I knew.

"Me."

"So, if you won't read your part, I guess I'll have to be MacSkye, which means I'll have to get into MacSkye's character. Seems silly, but since you won't do it, I'll try my best. *Whoa, pilgrim* – "

Buck stopped me. "That line's not in the script, that's John Wayne and you don't sound a bit like him."

"No, but you do."

"Nobody's ever told me I sound like John Wayne."

"I just told you. But if you don't believe me, why don't you read this line and listen to yourself. You'll see. Start right there." I put my finger on one of MacSkye's lines.

He stared at the page.

I said, "You don't need to study it, you've probably already studied it too much. Just read."

He took a deep breath and started speaking the line, "Woah . . ." He looked up at me, "Well, what do you know, that word is in the script," then continued reading, "*You* stay *down*, now, *don't* you get *up* . . ." punching words like it was a Kornfield skit. He slammed the script shut and slid it across the table. "I don't sound a thing like John Wayne, I'm terrible."

"Let's do an exercise that we do in my workshop." I inched the script towards him. "Lots of actors find this difficult, but I think you can do it. Read it one more time, and this time, take out every drop of emotion."

"You say it's an exercise they do in that method acting group of yours?"

I nodded.

"No emotion? What's so hard about that? Yeah, I might be able to do it."

I sat perfectly quiet as he read every word in a flat monotone. When he finished, he closed the script and winked at me. "Little Classy Sassy, you're one smart cookie."

So, for the third time, I saved Buck's career, or so said Jack, and Buck checked into the Century Plaza Hotel, not far from my apartment, for the duration of the filming. My respite from the road while Buck was working on the movie gave me the opportunity to do a two-week gig performing my regular show – meaning not country – in the cabaret room of L.A.'s hottest private club, while during the day, Buck usually sent a car to drive me over to hang with him on the set.

Then came the fateful morning when he called, and I blithely said, "You don't need to send the car today, I have one."

The silence on the other end continued so long I thought he might have hung up. Then I heard "Must be something wrong with this phone, I thought I heard you say you have a car."

For the whole two years I'd lived in L.A. I had not owned a car, and Buck was determined to keep it that way. Not that he wanted me to stay at home. He happily paid for limos and cabs to take me anywhere I wanted to go. In fact, that was our deal. He would foot the bill for my transportation until his "black vision" cleared, at which time he would help me buy any kind of car I wanted, but until that time, he didn't even want to discuss it. In fact, the way he reacted when I even mentioned it, closing his eyes, moaning and going pale like he was having a migraine, was scary enough to keep me quiet on the subject. When Buck Owens said he was psychic, he wasn't joking around, he was serious, sometimes deadly serious, as in the case of my car. He refused to tell me what he saw in the "black vision" about me, but it must have been bad.

So, it's understandable that he was shocked to hear me say that I would drive myself to the studio that day.

I backtracked. "That came out wrong. I didn't buy a car. I just meant I have a car to drive."

There were a few more seconds of silence on Buck's end before he said, "Why don't you tell me what you're talking about, Jesse Rose?" His use of my stage name instead of Classy Sassy was a signal that my backtracking hadn't worked.

I plopped down on the bed, and settled in for an extended conversation, snuggling my white poodle, Neesh, on my lap, as always. "Okay, it's very simple," I began, "A friend lent me his car. Maybe not exactly a friend. Actually, I only just met him."

Buck grunted.

"You don't need to worry," I said. "I don't know him well, but people at the Club Barrington – the place I'm singing – he's a member, so lots of people there know him. I honestly believe he is a really nice guy."

"What kind of car is it?"

"Very safe. A Mercedes 450SL."

"We-e-ell," Buck said, "He must be a really nice guy because that is a really nice car to lend to someone you don't know. Just how did he come to lend you his 450SL?"

"The other night this guy, the car guy, called me over to the bar on one of my breaks and told me he had heard something about me that upset him. Of course, my mouth flew open – I couldn't imagine what he meant. Then he chuckled and said he'd heard that I'd been taking cabs to the club, and he didn't think that was safe."

"So, this complete stranger is worried about your safety. I guess he is a really nice guy."

"I told you so. And then he said he was going out of town and wouldn't need this car and he'd like for me to use it. He said he has some other cars, anyway."

Buck took a long breath and blew it into the phone. "Jesse Rose, when you get through singing tonight, I want you to get in that nice car that the nice guy loaned you and drive yourself over here to the Century Plaza Hotel. You and I are going to have breakfast and talk a little bit."

"I won't be leaving the club until two o'clock."

"I'm aware of what time you get off. I've got to be on the set real early tomorrow, so two o'clock will be perfect. Call me as you're leaving and tell me what to order for you."

Buck answered the door of his suite in a bright green velour jogging suit, not yet dressed for the studio, which meant my call from the club had been his wake-up. At the same moment that I tossed my coat onto a chair, a white-jacketed waiter rolled a table into the living room and began taking covered dishes from warming drawers beneath the long tablecloth. Buck cut his eyes at the young man then scowled through his eyebrows at my low-cut black dress. Normally, he would have lectured me about going around half-naked, but tonight there were other things on his mind. He tucked into sausage, eggs and coffee, while I sipped grapefruit juice and toyed with a cheese Danish, waiting for him to begin.

He opened with "Jesse Rose, didn't your mama ever tell you not to accept rides from strangers?" then went on for twenty minutes, warning me about the dangers of the big city, reminding me that I wasn't as sophisticated as I thought, and picking me for info about my new friend.

When the lecture ended, I assured him I'd be more careful, kissed him on the cheek, and promised to see him at the studio in a little while. He was pouring another cup of coffee when I put on my coat and tossed a wave, goodbye.

"Hey, Jesse Rose" his voice stopped me at the door.

I turned around. "Yes?"

"You know that old saying I told you, about not taking rides from strangers? Here's another one: 'Get the fur coat first.'"

I wrapped my arms around the champagne mink I was wearing and wrinkled my nose at him. "I already have a fur coat – two of them."

Buck threw his head back in the braying laugh that I loved to hear, and as I closed the door, he called out, "You be careful little Classy Sassy."

But I was not going to be careful. And Buck knew it.

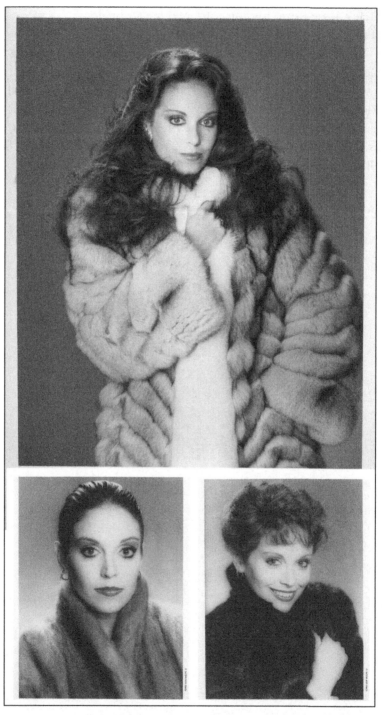

Victoria in Furs (1980s). Photos courtesy of Harry Langdon and Toris Von Wolf

# Chapter 11

THE VERY NEXT FRIDAY NIGHT was my first date with the really nice guy who lent me the car. His name was Jim.

A new beau for me was old news for my roommate, Michael. He wasn't wasting valuable minutes of his Friday night in Boys' Town, staying around to meet this latest fella, but we had houseguests that weekend, Judy, a dancer from New York City, and Eloise, another New York friend who now lived in Palm Springs, and they considered a preview peek at my date worth a later start to their girls' night out. The half-hour delay paid off in spades when Jim walked in, tall and dark with blazing blue eyes, dressed in gray flannels, navy blazer, and burgundy silk tie, so elegant he made my little black dress seem overstated. Especially since it was the dress with the drastically-cut neckline that had bothered Buck. But this was Hollywood, after all, besides which, I was heading straight from dinner to the cabaret stage at Club Barrington.

If the dress bothered Jim, he hid it well, immediately complimenting my appearance, before greeting Judy and Eloise, then small-talking his way around the apartment, remarking the updated decor, and pausing here and there to inquire about my old family things which furnished the room. Tracing the satinwood inlay of the china cabinet, he muttered, "This will be beautiful in my house."

Judy and Eloise looked at me with raised eyebrows, and I spoke up, "That was my grandmother's," hoping he got the message, *not for sale,* which apparently, he did get, because he checked the gold Piaget on his wrist, bid Judy and Eloise a good evening, and we were off to the Bistro Garden in his big white Mercedes. I recalled him saying that he had some other cars, so this must be one of them, but cars didn't impress me much. Everybody drove flashy cars around this town.

"Have you been to the Bistro Garden?" Jim asked.

"Yes."

His smile faded, so I added, "But only once, and that was for lunch."

The Bistro Garden in Beverly Hills lived up to its name, with dark paneled-walls, a mirror-backed bar and lace-curtained doors that opened onto a fragrant patio garden. Here you could spot anybody from sisters Margaux and Mariel Hemingway to Eva and ZsaZsa Gabor. From James Bond, Roger Moore; to Bond Girls, Maud Adams and Jane Seymour. I wondered if we might even run into a few of my new cast-mates. On my previous visit, *Hee Haw* Honeys Marianne Rogers and Barbi Benton were among the Hermès-clad lunch bunch enjoying chopped salads, on the patio.

This particular night, *The Odd Couple,* Jack Lemmon and Walter Matthau, dined with their wives at a table across from our banquette, next to the baby grand, which allowed them frequent song requests of the pianist, but our table, the first banquette upon entering, facing the open French doors, was undoubtedly the best in the room.

I couldn't allow myself a full meal, because I had to sing afterward, so the stone crab that Jim suggested was just right, and the Puligny Montrachet he ordered instantly became my favorite wine, until it slipped to second favorite behind the Château d'Yquem we drank for dessert. I had to admit this guy knew a thing or two about dining. Actually, he knew a thing or two about a number of things, and I was so wrapped up in our conversation that when time came to leave for the club, I hated to go.

The only consolation was that leaving the restaurant didn't mean leaving Jim. On that night, while I was onstage, he was right across the room at the bar, waiting for me to join him on my breaks. Having grown up performing in nightclubs, I was perfectly at home sitting on a barstool, cracking jokes with Jim and his friends, and the night went by too fast.

In Jim's car, riding home to my apartment, he asked why I was so quiet.

"Just winding down," I said. On a first date, it seemed absurd to admit that I was sad to be parting, even if it was the truth.

I lived in a security building, so when we got to the outside door of the lobby, Jim took the key from my hand, "That's a gentleman's job," and unlocked it for me. The next thing I expected was a goodnight kiss, but instead he asked, "May I come up?"

It wasn't the first time I'd fielded that request, but Jim had been so mannerly, it caught me off guard for a moment before I gave him my southern-belle smile and said, "No."

His response was a peck on my cheek. Then he hurried down the sidewalk to his car, and as I stepped into the elevator, he was already driving away.

I entered my apartment through the kitchen's service door, grabbed a can of Tab from the fridge, and headed into the living room.

Michael was still out, but Judy and Eloise were lying in wait on the white velvet sofa, dressed in tee-shirt nighties, their long brown manes pulled up into messy ponytails. Passing the dining table, I dropped my coat and bag onto a chair and stooped to let Neesh spring into my arms.

As I walked over to sit in the nearest of the wing chairs flanking the sofa, Eloise threw her hands in the air and squealed, "Which part of Heaven did that guy fall from?"

I peeled off my strappy heels and repositioned myself with my legs dangling over the arm of the chair. "I take it you think he's good looking."

Judy slapped her forehead. "He's Clark Gable with Paul Newman's eyes, Vicki."

Eloise laughed. "All I ask is that if you throw this one away, you toss him my direction." She looked at Judy. "Let's tell her what we've been talking about."

I pulled the ring on my can of Tab, lit a Marlboro Light, and Neesh curled himself into a ball on my lap, settling in for girl-talk.

"Did he say his name was Halper? Eloise asked.

"H-A-L-P-E-R," I spelled.

"I told you," she poked Judy's arm, "Just like Halper Lake Drive."

"Where is Halper Lake Drive?" I asked.

"You know all those streets in Rancho Mirage, or maybe it's Palm Desert? Anyway, they're all named for movie stars, Frank Sinatra Drive, Bob Hope Drive, Dinah Shore Drive, Harpo Marx Drive, but there's one right in the middle that is not named for a movie star. Halper Lake Drive."

Judy said, "Don't forget that big Halper building at Cedars-Sinai. What does Jim do?" she asked.

"I hope you two are not writing a mystery novel, because you're not very good armchair detectives." I smiled at Eloise, "No my little Yiddishe Mama, he's not a Jewish doctor, he's head of a record company, in fact, he wants to produce me, but don't be thinking he's some kind of mogul, because he's just getting started. It may even be a lie for all I know. He could have been using it as a come on."

Undeterred, Eloise pressed her point, "What about his family?"

"He didn't mention his family." I blew a stream of smoke at the ceiling. "Okay, wait. I just remembered that one of the captains at the Bistro Garden sent regards to Jim's mother, but everybody has a mother, don't they?"

Eloise waggled her eyebrows. "Not everyone has a mother whose last name is the same as the one unknown name among all those movie star streets."

'I snuffed out my cigarette. "I hate to spoil all this Nancy-Drew fun, but I'm going to the races with Jim on Sunday. Why don't I simply ask him?"

*   *   *

The Santa Anita Turf Club dazzled me with its grand staircase curving down to the Chandelier Room. Then on the terrace for our luncheon al fresco, I was too entranced by the sunlit view of the San Gabriel Mountains, to pay attention to the Hollywood legends stopping by to say hello to Jim. Cary Grant, *How are you?* Aaron Spelling, *How are you?* Desi Arnaz, *How are you?*

Even the people I didn't recognize looked like movie stars. Everybody was dressed as if they'd stepped out of an episode of *Dynasty*, but Jim was the most striking man there, in his black cashmere sport coat with a green and black striped tie. Fortunately, I had caught a sale at I. Magnin for a new tweed pencil skirt and white silk blouse, so I felt that I fit in, and Jim certainly seemed to enjoy parading me on his arm.

I hadn't planned to do any betting, so I occupied myself with people-watching, until Jim handed me a program that he'd folded open to a list of names, "Pick one of these."

The names of the horses were fun to peruse, but the numbers and abbreviations were meaningless code. I counted the races, then divided the number into the amount of money I had with me, which came out to a five-dollar bet for each race.

I looked up at Jim. "Is there a minimum bet, like in Las Vegas?"

He laughed. "When you're with me, the only time you'll need your purse is when you go to the powder room. Now for a beginner's lesson in handicapping a race: First, how much to bet is one of the trickiest things to figure, so you better let me worry about that. You pick a name you like, I place your bet, and if you win, I bring money back to you, that's how it works."

I thought about it for a second then said, "What if the horse I pick doesn't win?"

"Then I don't bring you any money. But it's a can't-lose system." He winked at me.

It didn't escape me that this can't-lose system had a flaw in it somewhere, but why worry about that when it was making Jim so happy to see me squeal and clap when he brought me my winnings. Several times, he brought me money, even though my horse lost. The first time that happened, I questioned him.

"Your horse came in third," he explained.

"That's what I don't understand. He was ahead the whole way around, and then he fell back to third, but you still brought me money."

"You bet him to *show*," Jim said, "*Show* means third place."

"Well aren't I smart?" I reached across the table and patted his head.

At the end of the day, I had won over four-hundred dollars, and was considering becoming what Jim called a "tout," but Jim must have done considerably better, because people kept coming over to ask how he had picked certain horses.

After the last race, while we were waiting for the valet to bring the car, Jim asked, "Have you ever been to Jimmy's?"

I hadn't assumed our date included dinner, but I was glad to hear it. I didn't want this day to end. Ever.

Jimmy's was yet another posh restaurant in Beverly Hills. But unlike the Bistro Garden's French coziness, Jimmy's was all shimmering sea-green glamour. We sat in a candle-lit corner booth, the perfect spot for couples who might want to do a little snuggling while they dined. Couples like us.

Both the snuggling and the dining were memorable. Jim recommended that I start with the caviar on buckwheat blinis, and heartily approved my entrée choice of pheasant in blueberry sauce.

I was sampling a plate of dessert cookies and sipping the last of my Chateau d'Yquem, when he took my hand and said, "Will you marry me?"

I laughed.

Jim didn't. He wasn't even smiling. "Well?"

I narrowed my eyes, peering at his face, "You can't be serious." *Could he*?

"Why would I ask you to marry me if I wasn't serious?"

I gave him the same southern-belle smile I'd used at my apartment door on Friday night. "I can think of one reason. It's the oldest one in the book."

He still wasn't smiling. "What if I agree not to make love to you till after we're married?"

Oh, my God. He was serious. Did he really expect yes or no right this minute?

"Shouldn't we just date, and date other people too?" I said, "take a while to get to know each other better?"

He said, "I know you as well as I need to, well enough to know that I don't want to see you while you're seeing other people. I won't do that. But you can keep dating other people as long as you want, and if at some point you decide you'd like to marry me, maybe I'll still be available."

*And maybe you won't.* Eloise was right, guys like Jim fell from Heaven, not from trees, and running all the guys I was dating through my head, I couldn't think of a one I wouldn't risk, to keep from losing this one. Of course, Buck could present a problem, but I'd never found Buck all that hard to handle, I'd worry about that later. Meanwhile, here was this fabulous man. Hadn't I been thinking that I never wanted this day to end? The truth was I never wanted this *date* to end.

But the *other* truth was that I couldn't marry Jim. I was already married.

I tapped my finger on my lips as if considering his proposal, when in fact I was calculating how long it took to get a divorce in Alabama. If my recollection was correct, even if I agreed to marry Jim, I'd have a three-month waiting period in which to change my mind.

I looked into his gorgeous blue eyes and said, "Yes."

# Part III
## Diana

DIANA GOODMAN

Diana (1980s)

Pageant '80! Front L-R Sher Patrick, Day Lipford; Back L-R Mary Bocchicchio, Phyllis Kelly, Diana Goodman, Melody Griffin (1980)

# Chapter 12

DIANA
*1980–1984*

### HOLLYWOOD, HERE I COME!

I never forgot Elvis's promise to bring me out to Hollywood to be with him, and in my grieving process after his death, that never-to-be trip was one of my favorite fantasies, as I drifted in an Elvis dream-state. Then one day, around Christmastime 1979, I snapped out of it, as if a hypnotist had clapped his hands in front of my face.

My mom was at her usual post in front of the kitchen window, swiping dishes in hot soapy water. "I think I'll give the Miss Georgia people a call," I said to her, lifting the receiver of the wall phone, "They might know somebody in Hollywood who can help me become a star."

Mama chuckled to herself and kept washing dishes. *That's okay,* I thought. *One of these days she'll see.* And it looked like that day might be sooner than either of us could have imagined. It just so happened that right that very minute, Bob Parkinson, a producer of the Miss USA Pageant, was in L.A. casting beauty queens for a new show called *Pageant '80.*

The concept was a spoof of beauty pageants, starring former state winners of Miss America. That could be a problem. I was a state winner in the Miss USA pageant, and if you don't know the difference, let me assure you that in those days there were a lot of beauty pageants, but there was only one PAGEANT, and that was Miss America. The difference was T-A-L-E-N-T, spelled in all caps, and whether it's singing an aria or twirling a baton, you can bet that every girl who makes it to Atlantic City for the granddaddy of them all is overloaded with it. Which is why I opted to enter Miss USA. But even though a lack of any discernable talent might

135

hurt my chances of becoming Miss America, I saw no reason it should hurt my chances of becoming a star.

"Can you sing or dance?" The two men in the casting office were Bob Parkinson of the Miss Universe Pageant, and composer Bernie Wayne, who wrote "There She is, Miss America." Bob was a tall, dark, handsome business type, and Bernie a pudgy middle-aged man wearing a cardigan. I looked from one to the other, knowing I was about to tell them a bold-faced lie.

"I can sing."

If my brothers and sisters had heard me say that, they would have fallen over each other, laughing. Which might not be a bad idea.

"I've been working with a comedy troupe called the L.A. Connection," I said. What I didn't say was that I'd only just met one of the guys in the group, and he'd told me they might let me do something with them sometime.

To my surprise, Bob and Bernie's eyes lit up.

*Well, whaddayaknow?* If exaggerating my talent and experience was all it took to succeed in Hollywood, I'd be a star before I'd even unpacked my suitcase.

The two men stood up, and Bob offered me his hand, ending the interview.

Okay, so maybe this star thing wasn't going to happen quite as soon as I'd hoped. And anyway, the show they were casting was in Atlantic City when I'd only just arrived in L.A. I went back to the fleabag motel I'd checked into and started unpacking my bags. I'd only taken a few items out of the suitcase when the phone rang, with a professional-sounding female on the other end telling me I'd gotten a call-back for *Pageant '80!*

Even though I knew that getting a call-back meant I was still in the running for the gig, I wasn't sure what a call-back might entail. Would I have to sing? Now I was wishing I hadn't lied to them. On the other hand, if I hadn't lied I probably wouldn't have gotten the call-back. I decided that if they asked me to sing, I'd say I had a sore throat.

Again, it was Bob and Bernie across the desk from me. Bernie said, "We've got several brunettes and a redhead that we know we want to use for the show. What we don't have is a tall curvaceous blonde, so you are exactly the type we're looking for, and I think I can write a song that will be perfect for you. A cute little comedy number. Does that sound like something you could do?"

"Yes!" I said, hoping the confidence in my voice would convince them that they didn't need to judge my vocal abilities for themselves, and sure enough, they didn't ask me to sing, but I began to doubt that was such a good thing, when they thanked me for coming, and showed me the door.

*Gosh,* I thought, *what does a girl have to do to seal the deal in this town? I've been here three whole weeks.*

Three more weeks went by with still no call from *Pageant '80!* I got to know the young couple who ran the hotel, and found out they were fellow Hollywood hopefuls, so the three of us spent our days hanging out in the lobby reading *Variety* and the *Hollywood Reporter,* penciling circles around casting calls, then trudging up and down the sidewalks, from one dead-end audition to another, so that by the time *Pageant '80!* called, I was beginning to understand that getting cast for a show in Hollywood, even if the show is not actually *in* Hollywood, is practically a miracle.

"I got it, I got it!" I danced around the lobby, hopping and twirling in circles. Karen came around the desk and wrapped me in her arms, dancing and squealing together.

When we settled down, she sat on the sofa with me, listening as I described the show.

"Wow, Caesar's Palace in Atlantic City," she said, "You've hit the big-time in no time, Diana."

Even though I still didn't fully grasp the magnitude of starring in a major casino show, I knew one thing for sure: I may not have been talented enough for the Miss America Pageant, but I'd made it to Atlantic City. In January, I would be hitting the Boardwalk as a star.

Meanwhile, I had a few more hoops to jump through. A few days after they called to tell me I'd gotten the part, Bernie Wayne called me to come to his studio, and when I got there, he handed me the sheet music for the song he'd written for me. "Do you know 'You Make Me Feel So Young?'" he asked.

"I do?"

"You do what?"

"Make you feel so young."

"Ha ha," he said, "you're pretty funny, and here's your chance to prove it. Instead of 'You Make Feel So Young,' you'll be singing 'You Make Me Feel So Old.'" He sat down at the piano, "What's your key?"

I stared at the meaningless squiggles on the sheet music, and said, "I don't think I'm familiar with this song. Could I take this music with me and work on it a little?"

"Sure, you can." Bernie got up from the piano stool. "Call me when you get comfortable with it."

*Fat chance*, I thought.

After a couple of weeks, when Bernie hadn't heard from me, I heard from *him*.

"I'm not quite ready yet, still working on it," I said, then over the next few weeks, I avoided his calls when possible, and otherwise made excuses, until finally it was time to leave for Atlantic City, and I had managed to keep the job while keeping them from finding out I couldn't sing a lick.

Still, I couldn't postpone the inevitable, and on the flight to New Jersey, I began to get nervous about what might happen when I finally had to open my mouth in front of these music pros, and let out the warble, otherwise known as my singing voice. My plan had been "fake it till you make it." But what on earth had given me the notion that I could fake a singing role, in a cast full of classically-trained vocalists who could give Beverly Sills a run for her money? Maybe once we landed I should catch the first flight home and save myself the embarrassment. Except I didn't have the money to catch a flight.

Ultimately, I decided that if I was ever going to take a gamble, Atlantic City was the place to do it. Better to roll the dice and lose than never take a shot. So, a few days later, I was sitting in a huge showroom with five other former beauty queens, each waiting to take the stage for a run-through of our solo. Spotting Bob Parkinson, I walked over and greeted him with a big smile. "Could I please go last?"

He gave me a stern look. "Your time is up, Diana."

I slunk back to my seat among the other girls, who were chatting and laughing, all excited, while I huddled in my chair with my arms wrapped around my stomach, hoping I wouldn't throw up on the front row when I sang the first note.

Bob must have taken pity on me, because he at least didn't put me first in the lineup that day, but listening to the girls who came before me only rattled my nerves that much more. Miss Louisiana, Phyllis Kelly, was an opera singer who performed an aria beautifully, note-perfect as far as I could tell; Miss New Mexico, Melody Griffin's, jazz number could have rivaled Ella; and Miss Delaware, torch-singer Day Lipford, was the first African-American to place in Miss America's Top Ten. So that removed all doubt as to how my vocal talent stacked up against the other girls. When Bob called out "Diana," I slid low down in my chair, hiding from sight while I made up my mind whether to run onto the stage or out the door.

"Diana!" he yelled.

I stood up slowly, and walked to the stage on wooden legs, sucking in gulps of air, while giving myself a mental pep talk. During those weeks in L.A. I had been practicing the song, and even though I knew I wasn't any kind of singer, I could at least carry a tune, and anyway, hadn't Bernie changed the lyrics to be funny? Once I saw the other girls, it was clear that I was the show's Marilyn Monroe stereotype, so why not take a note from the original blonde bombshell? Recalling her breathy version of 'Happy Birthday, Mr. President,' instead of trying to compete with the magnificent voices of the real singers in the show, I decided to mimic Marilyn, and make my performance as cute and sexy as I knew how.

To my astonishment, I did not throw up, and when I finished my song, the girls applauded and shouted "Bravo!" like I was one of them. And so, I was.

I may not have been the most talented performer on the stage, but I played my part, the audience loved it, and as the weeks went by, instead of getting tired of doing the same show night-after-night, my excitement grew. Coming into work every day, we passed through the casino, where women dressed in sequins and furs stood around the gambling tables with men wearing silk shirts and Rolex watches, surrounded by the sights and sounds of flashing lights and bells and whistles, so that by the time I got to the showroom, I was buzzing with the glamor and clamor of it all.

Then came the night when I got my chance to be the star of the show. Bob beckoned me into the wings beforehand, and pointed out a good-looking middle-aged man in a dark suit, sitting in the audience near the front.

"That's Buzz Aldrin," he said, "You know, the astronaut. Can you sing 'Fly Me to the Moon?'"

Good grief, I'd done well enough to manage one song; surely, they couldn't expect me to do two. "I don't know the words," I answered, assuming they'd give it to one of the others.

But Bob nodded. "Just do your regular schtick with him."

My regular schtick was to select a short, fat bald man from the audience, then bring him onstage to stroke his head and make over him while I sang "You Make Me Feel So Old." But Buzz Aldrin didn't look a bit old. How on earth was I supposed to make this tall, tan American hero blush? I shouldn't have worried. He played it like a pro and the applause meter went to "tilt."

During my stay in Atlantic City, I was handed a lot of men's business cards, most of them going straight into the trash. But when Buzz Aldrin handed me his card and asked me to call him when I got back to L.A., that was a different story. As soon as I got home, I gave him a ring, hoping he'd remember asking me to call.

"Diana!" he said, "I'm glad to hear from you. Let's get together. Want to come to my place for dinner?"

Actually, no, I really didn't want to come to his place for dinner. I wanted him to take me out to some Hollywood hot spot, so the paparazzi could take my picture on the arm of a famous astronaut. But I couldn't think of a graceful way to refuse, and it was only this one night. Surely, he'd take me out next time.

His apartment was not far from my new West Hollywood address, although in a more expensive building, and sleekly furnished in 1980s style. He greeted me warmly, remarking that he hoped I liked Chinese take-out, then seated me at the dinette table, without offering the usual pre-dinner cocktail, which I had been eagerly anticipating. *Oh, well,* I thought, *wine with dinner,* but he filled my wineglass with ice water.

Our dinner conversation was easy and light, then when we finished, he said, "Come on in the living room and let's talk awhile."

*After-dinner drinks?*

The massive coffee table was covered with a jumble of photos, magazines, clippings and all sorts of papers.

Buzz sat down beside me on the sofa. "Sorry about the mess, I'm writing a book."

I expected he would then ask what I'd like to drink, but to the contrary, the move to the sofa was his opportunity to explain that we were having dinner in because he was a recovering alcoholic, and it was easier for him not to be around others who were imbibing.

I understood what he was saying, but I wasn't happy to hear it. Might as well put a match to those paparazzi pics of me with a famous astronaut.

Even so, my respect for him grew as he went on with his story. "After the moon landing, the second I hit earth, my life changed like that." He snapped his fingers. "My every waking moment was spent glad-handing at some press event or other. Booze was everywhere, and somebody was always there to make sure I had a drink in my hand at all times. So, before I knew what was happening, I went from having it, to wanting it, to needing it. After you've been to the moon, what's next? I got discouraged, disappointed, sank into a depression, and tried to drink myself out of it." He grinned. "That didn't work so well."

He talked on, about the moon-landing and life afterward, in a way that made me understand what he'd gone through, but while I admired him, I quickly realized that the timing was not right for a romance between us. This man had been to the moon and back, in more ways than one, and I had barely set my feet on Sunset Boulevard. I didn't even want to try to climb up to his level, I was having too much fun.

But the money I'd made doing *Pageant '80!* would only pay for so many nights on the town. During the day, I was still searching *Variety* for casting calls, and finally, I got one. Even if it was only working as an extra in a made-for-TV movie, the pay wasn't bad, and the connections might be great.

A week later, I followed the directions they'd given me, and parked in front of a brick ranch-style house in West L.A. They hadn't told me anything about the movie, so what a surprise when I got to the check-in table, and at the top of the sign-in sheet was printed, *Elvis and the Beauty Queen.*

I'm not sure when or how I learned that the Beauty Queen of the title was Linda Thompson, but after a couple of days standing around with a gang of extras, being herded here and there by a young guy who treated us like cattle, because he seemed to think that's what we were, I decided I'd climbed too far up the ladder to step that far down. I left the set without ever mentioning to a soul that I was Elvis's *other* beauty queen.

Back to searching for casting calls. Several times, I had noticed an ad for work, singing telegrams, but I had never circled it, because I thought it was beneath me. Since then, my experience on *Elvis and the Beauty Queen* had changed my thinking; nothing could be more demeaning than being "cattle" in a movie about a man who had once treated me like his queen.

In an amazing coincidence, my first telegram "role" was as Daisy Mae, which allowed me to wear the polka-dot dress that I was wearing on the night I met Elvis at the Memphian theater, and the next job they got for me was playing a mermaid, floating around a pool at a party in Beverly Hills, so that wasn't so bad either, even though my skin was shriveled for a while afterwards. Then one day they called me and said that I was to deliver a seven-million-dollar check to Clint Eastwood.

*Hee Haw* Cast "Saalute" (1982)

# Chapter 13

*CLINT EASTWOOD? Seven-million dollars? This must be some kind of a joke.*

Of course, it was a joke. That's the point of a singing telegram. But the seven-million was real, and apparently, so was Clint Eastwood. Besides which, I was delivering it to him at Mr. Chow, one of the trendiest, most expensive restaurants in Beverly Hills. I'd been dying to go there, but the location presented a dilemma. What to wear? Although the singing-telegram agency hadn't specified any particular attire, I assumed they wanted me to look sexy. On the other hand, Mr. Chow was the height of ultra-modern elegance, and I didn't want to present myself as a bimbo, and risk blowing my shot at impressing one of the movie moguls who dined there, or, better yet, Clint Eastwood, since I was already fantasizing a dream date with him.

After a dozen or more tries, pulling one outfit out of the closet, only to put it back and replace it with another, I settled on a blue silk skirt-and-blouse that matched my eyes, or so my friends told me. It was long-sleeved with a demure scoop neckline, and a hem that fell just below my knees; but the bodice was perfectly fitted, and the skirt fluttered around my calves in a flirty way that I thought would strike a balance between la-dy-like and sexy. I entered the restaurant through the back, as instructed, and told the first busboy I saw why I was there. "That room," he pointed to a door down the hallway, where a man behind a desk, greeted me.

"Come on in." He got up from his chair and stepped over to a closet. "They dropped off your costume. Here it is."

He handed me a monkey suit.

I stared at the costume, in shock.

"Well, can you act like a monkey?" he asked. When I didn't answer, he said, "You know, like this." He stooped, dangling his arms below his knees, bending his elbows up and down, and making monkey noises, *eeff-eyff*.

I licked my lips. "I guess I could do that."

"Good," he said. "You can dress in the restroom across the hall. A guy will knock on the door when it's time for you to present the check, and he'll tell you exactly what to do."

When he left, I picked up the costume from the desk and held it up in front of me. *Oh, brother.* My first time to see and be seen at Mr. Chow and I'd be wearing a moth-eaten monkey suit. If I thought it couldn't get any worse than being an extra in a movie about Elvis and Linda, I was thinking again. It was at that exact moment that I found the bikini inside the costume.

If I do say so myself, I make a darned good monkey. I entered the banquet room, with my knees bent so low, my knuckles almost dragged the floor, and I was eeffing and eyffing like an ape having an asthma attack. Then the big moment came when I presented the check to Clint.

Apparently, everybody in the room except for Clint knew the amount of the check, because they burst into applause as soon as he looked at it, but with typical Eastwood cool, he just grinned a little, then peered into the eyes of the monkey head, "Okay, who's in there?" and the other men started, guessing, calling out names, "Joe, you big ape, come on outta there and have a drink with us!" "Perfect casting, Marty!" "Stop monkeying around, Hal!" all of them assuming the person in the costume was one of their cronies, playing a joke.

That's when I pulled down the zipper, and let the monkey-suit fall to the floor, leaving me standing there in all my bikini-clad glory. The hoots and whistles were deafening, and this time, Clint threw back his head in a guffaw, elbowing the man beside him, "Make room, bud." Then he looked at me and patted the man's empty chair. "Have a seat."

When I hesitated, he said, "Or maybe you'd be more comfortable having lunch with your clothes on. Why don't you get changed, and come back and join us?"

So, I'd get to wear my classy blue ensemble after all. I quickly repaired my hair and makeup, got dressed, and took my seat next to Clint. The waiter placed a plate of gourmet Chinese food in front of me, but I was too excited to notice what it was, much less eat it. Clint and I made pleasantries, then he chatted and joked with his friends, while I sat quietly, warming myself in the sexual energy that surrounded him like heat from a furnace. As the afternoon grew late, the crowd began to thin, and Clint said to me, "Looks like lunch has extended into happy hour. Want to get out of here and grab a drink somewhere else?"

*Make my day!* We rode in his pickup to Chasen's, and although it may well have been the same truck he drove in *Every Which Way but Loose,* he didn't say so, and I decided it was best to act like I'd been riding in pickups my whole life, because I had. So, heading down Beverly Boulevard, I gazed out the window with a great big smile when our unusual vehicle drew the curious stares of drivers in Bentleys and Rolls Royces. *I'd sooner travel in a truck with Clint Eastwood any day.*

Clearly, he was a regular at Chasen's. The maître d' ushered us to Clint's usual seat at the bar in the cozy mahogany-paneled lounge, where he ordered a whiskey and I sipped white wine, while he made conversation with everybody in the place, as one-by-one they came over to say hello and congratulate him on the success of *Any Which Way You Can,* the sequel to *Every Which Way but Loose,* both mega-hits co-starring Clyde the orangutan, which was the reason behind my monkey-costume delivery of the seven-million-dollar check.

After a while, Clint suggested that we move to one of the cushy red leather booths and order something to eat, but looking at the menus, we decided that neither of us was hungry enough for dinner, so we ordered a selection of appetizers to give us something to pick at while we talked. Or rather, while I talked. I soon learned that Clint's image as the strong silent type is the real thing. Not that he wasn't a good conversationalist, but his recent movies had been well-discussed at lunch, and again at the bar, so he tossed the conversational ball in my lap, asking me about my life, starting with my childhood in Georgia, and ending with my current pursuit of stardom in Hollywood. By the time I'd finished all that, it was getting late, Clint was yawning, and my dream date was coming to an end.

Considering the sexual heat, I was feeling from him, I was a little surprised that, so far, Clint hadn't made any advances toward me. Now he was taking me home, and I couldn't help wondering what would happen once we got there, and hoping that something would. He parked his pickup, then came around and opened my door, helping me down the small step to the ground, but instead of walking me to the door of my apartment building, he lingered, leaning against the hood of the truck. "Would you like to get together again, sometime – I mean, I can't say when it would be, because I'm leaving town tomorrow, and I'm not sure when I'll get back, but whenever that is, I'd like to see you."

I smiled. "Why don't you come up for a night cap?"

He shook his head. "I'm dead on my feet." Then he gave me a quick kiss, and said, "I've got your number, I'll call you." He pulled a card from his pocket and handed it to me. "Or you call me." As he climbed into the truck, he said, "If I can ever do anything to help you, let me know."

Watching him drive away in his beaten-up pickup, I giggled, thinking how funny the whole thing had turned out. I'd left my apartment that morning hoping I'd get to meet Clint Eastwood, and wound up going to dinner with him.

More importantly, I'd also wound up with his phone number, and a few days later, I dialed the number, just to see if he would answer. He did not. But I left a message, and he called me back to say that he was still out of town. So, I waited another week and tried again, with the same result, and after a couple of more tries, I decided to put away my dreams of a future as the next Mrs. Eastwood, and make myself content with the memory of my one dream date with Clint.

Anyway, there's more than one fish in the sea, and it was not long after that, when I saw an ad for *Rick Nelson in Concert.* The photo in the ad looked just as cute as I remembered, and even though it had been three years since I'd seen him, I wasn't stupid enough to lose Ricky's number. What luck! The man who answered my call remembered meeting me at Rick's show in Houston, and said he'd leave a ticket for me at the door.

The venue was not exactly a concert hall, and not exactly a nightclub either. There was no dance floor, and the long rows of tables reminded me of a cafeteria. I was on the front row, where Rick was sure to spot me, which he did, although he was not the kind to sing a song to me, the way Elvis had. Where Elvis was flamboyant, larger than life, Rick was understated, real. Both were gorgeous men, of course, and even though Rick had put on a couple of pounds, he was still looking lean and lanky in his tight jeans and plaid shirt. He seemed to be into more of a country-music vibe than he had been before, and the club was the kind of place where the entertainers could step off the stage, into the audience, which is exactly what he did when his show was over.

"Hi, Diana," he gave me a kiss on the cheek, and sat down beside me.

We chatted comfortably, catching up, but there was something different about him, and it had nothing to do with a couple of extra pounds or the cowboy clothing. He wasn't as relaxed as he had been three years before; he seemed less boyish, less innocent.

"Hey," he said, "I'm staying at my manager's place right now, and some folks are coming over for a little wind-down, if you'd like to join us."

He and his guys walked me to the parking lot, whooping with laughter when they spied my freshly painted metallic green 1950 Buick Super, and I followed them to a 1940s bungalow, where people were beginning to gather. Rick ushered me into the kitchen and poured me a glass of white wine. Then he said, "Let's go back here," and led me to a sofa in a small den.

Again, we made small talk, but I didn't seem able to pull him out of himself. Whatever connection we'd had in Houston was broken, and I was on the verge of excusing myself to go home, when a man walked in and asked, "Little something to calm your nerves?"

I lifted my glass. "I have wine."

The man grinned and put a pill on the coffee table, cutting it in two with a pocket knife. Rick swallowed one half and handed me the other.

I gazed down at the pill on my palm, recalling the all too similar situation with Dr. Nick. But Rick had gulped the pill nonchalantly, and maybe I did need something to calm my nerves, maybe if we were both calm, we'd get back the connection we'd lost.

If anything, the connection got worse. I was calm, all right, so calm that the only thing I wanted to do was put my head on Rick's shoulder and go to sleep. When I woke up, it was daylight, and Rick had disappeared – probably to his bedroom – and I tiptoed into the living room, picking my way through potato chip crumbs and sleeping party guests.

Driving home, I wished I had lost Rick's phone number. I would rather have remembered him as he'd been when we met in Houston.

They say it's darkest just before the dawn, but this dawn was the exception to the rule, because somewhere between Rick's place and mine, my trusty old Buick began to act up. It lurched along, and I'd pull to the side of the road, it would drive okay for a couple of miles, then start lurching again, until I decided to roll into the first gas station I saw, which happened to be in Hollywood, not far off Santa Monica Boulevard. After tinkering with the car, the mechanic said he could fix it, but it would take an hour or so.

That was okay with me. Spending a few hours browsing the boutiques that lined Santa Monica Boulevard was a welcome diversion. I had just pressed the pedestrian button at a crosswalk when a black Mercedes stopped at the red light and the driver rolled down his window. "If you're not a movie star, you should be," he said.

I smiled at him, "I'm trying."

"I know the perfect show for you, give me a call." He handed me his business card and drove away.

In my hurry to cross the street, I dropped the card into the bottom of my shoulder bag, and with one thing and another forgot about it until a few days later, when I was looking for my keys and came across it. *Steve Binder* was the name printed on it, and beneath that was *Producer*. I'd never heard of Steve Binder, and it hadn't taken me long in Hollywood to figure out that although a lot of people called themselves producers, very few of them actually were. Still, this guy had a mighty fine ride, and I had nothing better to do, so I gave him a call.

"Let's meet for dinner," he said.

The restaurant was a quiet little place on a side street in Beverly Hills, and I was pleasantly surprised to discover that Steve Binder truly was a producer and the meeting was strictly business. Could it be possible that someone in Hollywood was actually going to give me a break?

"When I heard your accent I immediately thought of this guy." He handed me a duplicate of the business card he'd given me that day on the street, but this time he pointed to a name and number that he'd written on the back. "This man's a friend of mine. He'll be expecting your call."

\*  \*  \*

"*Hee Haw* Show, Sam Lovullo speaking," a pleasant-sounding man answered.

Two of the girls on the show were pregnant, and that meant there might be a spot for me. I put on the blue silk outfit that had become my interview uniform, and drove to the *Hee Haw* office on Cañon Drive in Beverly Hills.

A receptionist showed me into an office where four men were waiting. A gray-haired man named Frank Peppiatt, another middle-aged man named John Aylesworth, and a short, balding man who was Sam Lovullo, introduced themselves as producers of the show. They also introduced their young dark-haired colleague as Barry Adelman, one of the writers.

Sam took my head shot and bio, and after I answered a few basic questions, they handed me a script, which consisted of two *Hee Haw* "bits." After I read the "bits," they explained that they weren't really hiring anyone, they were just seeing me out of respect for Steve Binder. But they also repeated what Sam had told me on the phone. A couple of the Honeys were expecting, and so there was a possibility of an opening. They didn't tell me which of the girls were pregnant, and I didn't really care, I just wanted the job.

They thanked me for coming and said they'd be in touch, but I was a little let down. I'd walked in thinking there was a job opening; now I felt that they'd only been doing a friend a favor.

So back to drawing circles around casting calls in the show-biz rags before hitting the sidewalks on yet another useless round of auditions. On the other hand, it wasn't always so much about the audition, as it was the connections you made waiting in line. For instance, during one interview, I met a photographer who liked my looks and was kind enough to give me the name of a talent agent, who not only agreed to see me, but recommended that we meet for dinner at Ma Maison, a cozy little place on Melrose Avenue, which was exactly the kind of spot where I could see and be seen by all the right people.

I gussied up in my tried-and-true blue silk outfit, and drove the few blocks to the restaurant, feeling a little dismayed when I saw all the Rolls Royces parked in front, thinking – fresh paint-job or not – the valet was sure to direct my old Buick to some back-alley parking lot, and me along with it. So, I couldn't believe it when he politely helped me from the car, like I was Alana Stewart or Jerry Hall, scooted into the driver's seat and wedged my Christmas-green clunker between a Ferrari and a Stutz. Looking at it parked that way, it hit me that the car looked right at home; in fact, it fit the vintage vibe of the restaurant better than any of the super-model rides surrounding it. I squared my shoulders with renewed confidence and strutted through the door of the restaurant.

BRRINGGG!! An alarm bell went off. I jumped like I was shot, and froze, waiting for someone to shout, *Hit the floor!*

Instead, the maître d' gave me an apologetic smile, "Sorry to *alarm* you, heh-heh, but whenever a beautiful woman enters, we ring a bell so that everyone can take notice and enjoy her progress through the room."

I stuck my chest out even further, following him to the table, and put an extra hitch in my get-along to make sure I gave the onlookers their money's worth.

The agent, Joan, greeted me warmly, and as usual, I ordered French fries to nibble, stopping myself just short of asking for ketchup, thinking that hollandaise would be a more impressive choice, with the added benefit of making less of a stain if I happened to drip it on my blue silk.

Whether my choice of condiment made an impression or not, at least I didn't spill any on myself, and at the end of the evening, Joan kept my headshot and resume, which in Hollywood meant absolutely nothing, but the night had been a bell-ringer anyway. Yes, I knew the bell was a gimmick. With the constant ringing throughout our dinner, I would've been deaf, blind and the dumbest blonde Miss Clairol ever created, not to know that, but in my short stroll through the dining room I'd had more pairs of important eyeballs ogling me than a whole year of trudging the boulevard, so I'd gotten a lot accomplished, even if the agent never called

But the agent did call. And although I was too excited to listen closely when she explained what the job entailed, *Las Vegas* and *Billboard ad* was all I needed to hear, so a few days later, I joined the fifteen glamour gals that Joan was shepherding to Vegas for the audition. On the flight out, we all became fast friends, chatting excitedly and wondering what the audition was all about. It was a relief to know that I wasn't the only one who was "flying blind," and I was too giddy with the prospect of a real modeling job to pay attention to any uneasiness I felt about what I was heading for. My only concern was that I was the "old lady" of the group. When I found out some of those girls were barely eighteen, I hurried to the restroom and peered in the mirror, wondering if it was time I started using a little more makeup than my routine of mascara and lip gloss.

Then we landed, and my worries disappeared like magic at sight of a long line of limos waiting to transport us to the hotel. I didn't have enough experience to understand that nothing about these proceedings was normal, and anyway, how do you define normal in Hollywood or Vegas? The other girls and I followed Joan like sheep, not bothering to remember the rest of that saying, *being led to the slaughter,* and calling myself silly when our trek through the lobby ended in a perfectly normal conference room, where Joan introduced a nice-looking middle-aged man in a dark suit and tie, whose foreign-sounding name was Greek to me, although I didn't think that was his point of origin. Maybe Joan had called him "Ad-Man." As far as I could tell, we were here to audition for an ad, so maybe that was his nickname. The rest of his name was unintelligible, but somehow it had reminded me of Yogi Bear and Merle Haggard. *Yogi from Muscogee? Ad-Man Yogi, Ad-Man Muscogee?* I decided that Ad-Man was close enough. Joan was informing us of things I probably needed to know, so I'd better start paying attention, although I didn't hear anything until she said, "owner of the hotel."

*This man? No way.* Everybody knew that Vegas hotel owners looked like Marlon Brando with cotton stuffed in his cheeks. This man didn't even look Italian. Or maybe he did. He had dark skin and dark hair, but he was no Al Pacino, who would have been my preference over Marlon Brando, but you can't have everything, and it appeared that this man would be conducting the interviews, so I'd better forget Al Pacino, and start making eyes at "Ad-Man," who was now telling us that the interviews would begin in thirty minutes. He then left the room, and we all started unzipping our garment bags and plugging in curling irons, to change into our interview outfits. With no idea what type of ad I was trying out for, I'd chosen to wear a baby blue pantsuit, figuring it would work for just about any situation. By the time I'd changed into it, and refreshed my hair and makeup, Joan was calling my name, saying that I was up next. She walked me out and pointed down the hallway. "No need to knock, just go on in."

I went left toward the door she had indicated, turned the gigantic gold knob, and stepped into a bedroom that looked like something out of an Arabian fairy tale, complete with the Sheik in a flowing bejeweled costume.

*Hee Haw*'s "All Jug Band" (1982)

# Chapter 14

"**Ad-Man**" **was standing** in the middle of the opulence, dressed in Saudi robes. He nodded in a formal way that was almost a bow, and swept his hand, offering a seat on the sofa. Then when I got my bearings enough to walk over and sit down, he handed me a glass of golden wine, and made a palm-up gesture to several lines of white powder drawn on the mirror-topped coffee table.

I shook my head, managing a hoarse "No, thank you," then proceeded to gulp wine while he questioned me.

*Where are you from? What brought you to California? How old are you? Do you have a college degree? Have you ever been married? Do you have any children?* After each question, he smiled and listened attentively to my answer, in such a charming way that I began to relax and realize that, while he was not Al Pacino, he was a very handsome man, so this time when he offered more wine and a line, I accepted. Now I was ready to talk, and it was my turn to ask the questions. First of all, what kind of billboard ad was I auditioning for?

"Well, yes," he smiled, "I am considering a new billboard ad for my hotel, but I'm really looking for new wives."

"Wives?" My first thought was that he must be casting a movie, so I widened my smile."

He nodded. "If you accept, of course."

I held up my forefinger, leaned over the coffee table, snorted another line of coke, washed away the taste with a slug of wine, cleared my throat and said, "Are you proposing to me?"

He raised his palms. "What did you think?"

"I don't know what to think. Please explain."

"Well," he shrugged, truthfully, you are a little older than I usually like, but you look young, and you've never been married, no children, so it's okay, and I'd like to offer you the opportunity, which is a very good one, and very simple. As my wife, you will receive fifty-thousand-dollars per year, plus all expenses for all your needs, no matter how extravagant, everything carte blanche, not only in this hotel, but everywhere in Las Vegas, all you do is sign your name. This of course is one-hundred-percent legally set forth in a five-year contract. So, you see, at the end of that five years, if you save your money, you would be able to set yourself up with an education or a business, whatever you decide."

I took another swig of wine. "What would my part of the deal be? Didn't you say *wives*, plural?"

"Yes," he nodded. "You would be one of many, and your only obligation is to be available whenever I am in town, here in Las Vegas, which is usually a couple of times a year. One caveat: You would not be allowed to leave the property, and certainly not the city, without permission."

"So, I would live here in Vegas?"

"Of course. What fun, yes? You will see the wives' housing tomorrow. We are conducting a tour. But meanwhile . . ." He stood up and made another of his sweeping gestures toward the massive bed. "Shall we?"

I must admit I was tempted. The silk and fur coverings on the bed looked extremely inviting, and his charm was working its spell on me, along with the wine and cocaine, so it took some willpower to decline, and I wasn't totally pleased that he took it so well. I would have liked for him to show at least a little disappointment, but he simply nodded in his gentlemanly way, smiling when I told him that I would seriously consider his proposal.

Stepping into the hallway, I came face to face with the next girl waiting to enter.

Returning to the conference room, when I confronted Joan, her eyes widened in disbelief, "Are you trying to tell me you didn't understand why you're here?" She raised an eyebrow. "I must say you're awfully naïve – especially for your age. I assume this means you don't care to see the wives' residence quarters tomorrow." She turned to walk away.

"Wait." I stopped her. "Yes," I bit my lip, wondering if I would regret saying, "I would like to see where the wives live."

Apparently, curiosity got the best of the other girls, too, because every one of us showed up for the tour. It hadn't occurred to me that we would be meeting "Ad-Man's" current wives, but each greeted us graciously, as we toured the residences, which were luxury two-bedroom apartments, with chef's kitchens, spa baths and private pools, lavish enough to tempt just about anyone, especially someone living in a cheaply-furnished one-room apartment like mine.

Joan had encouraged us to converse with the wives, saying that we were free to ask any and all questions, so as we went along, with each beautiful wife dripping in diamonds, playing the perfect hostess in her gracious home, swinging wide the doors to walk-in closets with row after row of sumptuous furs and designer gowns, the pieces of a picture-puzzle fit together, revealing a carefree existence of privilege and sophistication, with the only downside being too few visits from "Ad-Man," which surely must speak well of him. I was tempted.

All these months I'd been trudging up and down the mean streets of Hollywood, in and out of casting offices where I was told I was too tall, too fat, too southern, too old, until my ego was as tattered as the soles of those white platform heels I'd been wearing since the night I met Elvis. Now, with one stroke of a pen, I could sign my name to a life where my feet would never be shod in anything less than Manolo Blahnik, and never have to wear a single pair more than once. More importantly, at the end of five years, I'd have $250,000 to pay for acting classes, a personal trainer, a wardrobe and anything else I needed to become the star I'd set out to be. I was ready to sign on the dotted line, you bet your booty.

Then at the end of the tour, the beautiful dark-haired wife in the last apartment whispered to me, "Don't do it."

"I beg your pardon?" I stepped closer.

"It's not just five years," she said, "You will become addicted to the lifestyle, and you will never leave." She raised her liquid-brown eyes to mine, "At least, not until he tires of you."

When I told Joan that I'd decided not to sign the contract, she informed me that it would be more appropriate to tell "Ad-Man" personally, which meant another walk down the long hallway to what I now thought of as his lair. But this time he offered no wine, and there were no lines of cocaine drawn temptingly on the gilt-edged mirrored coffee table. He took my turn-down with a shrug, and to my surprise, offered me a week's stay in Vegas with carte blanche at his hotel, as well as any other.

"Really?"

"Of course." He waved a hand in his signature sweeping gesture, "Have fun," then he touched my elbow, guiding me out the door.

As soon as I hit my room, I was on the phone to my sister Crystal, who hopped on the first plane out, and for the next week the two of us hit the strip, washing down steak and lobster with Cristal and Dom Perignon, front row in showrooms watching Tom Jones, Englebert Humperdinck, and Siegfried and Roy, then shopping till we dropped, stocking up on those furs and jewelry that I wouldn't be getting since I hadn't signed the marriage contract with "Ad-man."

On the plane back to L.A. a sense of hopelessness came over me. I felt like I was flying into a dead end. What had ever made me think I could make it as an actress. So far, the only job I'd managed to get was playing myself as Miss Georgia, and beauty queens didn't have a long shelf life in Hollywood, especially not a beauty queen who was thirty-years-old in a town where twenty-five was considered over the hill.

I schlepped my bags up the stairs to my apartment and dropped them on the ratty carpet of my bedroom/living-room/kitchen. What a dump. And to think that right this minute I could be moving into one of those luxury apartments in Vegas, shimmying into a designer bikini for a dip in my own private swimming pool. I wondered if it was too late to take Ad-Man up on his offer. Probably all I had to do was call Joan. I glanced at the phone and saw that the light on my answering machine was blinking. Well, of course it would be; I'd been gone for a whole week, but there wouldn't be a message from anybody I wanted to hear from. I poked the play button and flopped down on the sofa.

"Hello, Diana," a cheerful male voice came from the machine, "This is Sam Lovullo at *Hee Haw.*"

I jumped off the sofa and ran for the phone, before I realized that it was after office hours, too late in the day to call him back. I'd have to wait until morning to hear what I hoped would be good news. It couldn't be bad news, could it? In my experience so far, producers didn't take the time and trouble to call and tell you that you didn't get the part. On the other hand, they did make it a point to tell me that they were interviewing me as a favor to Steve Binder, so maybe this was different, maybe as a courtesy to Steve, Mr. Lovullo would call me to let me know I didn't get it. The way my luck was going, it wouldn't surprise me if that was exactly what I heard when I called the next morning. And sure enough, his very first words popped my balloon.

"Both of our pregnant Honeys have decided to come back this season, so we won't need to replace them."

Even though I'd thought I wouldn't be surprised, it was still a huge letdown. "Well, I guess that's good for the show," I said, and was about to continue, "I appreciate you letting me know," when he broke in.

"But we've decided to hire some fresh faces anyway."

The fresh faces would be a Bo Duke-type *Hee Haw* Hunk named Chase Randolph: a Honey named Nancy Traylor whose dark hair would help even out the imbalance between brunettes and blondes on the show, and me, even though one of my show-biz acquaintances who was also a friend of one of the Honeys, said that when he told her about my hiring, rather than *Can't wait to meet her*, as he expected, her response was "*Hee Haw* needs another blonde like a hole in the head."

You'd think he would've had the good sense not to tell me, but he seemed to get a kick out of it, so I set off for Nashville with those words of welcome playing like a broken record in my brain. But it would take more than one snarky comment from some barnyard bimbo I'd never even met, to keep me from feeling like a movie star as I strutted my stuff into the First-Class cabin of a wide-body jet, winging my way into Music City USA, where upon arrival, I would be handed keys to the car provided for my own personal use during my stay at the Maxwell House, a brand-new luxury hotel set high on a hill overlooking the Nashville skyline.

The clerk at the reception desk was expecting me, and bowed and scraped like she was every bit as impressed with my stardom as I was. Who could blame me if I tilted my nose just the slightest bit toward the ceiling as I followed the bellhop through the lobby?

With the time difference flying west to east, when I finally got settled into the hotel room that would be my residence for the next month, it was getting close to bedtime, so I turned in early to make sure I was wide awake for my costume fitting the next morning at the home of *Hee Haw's* wardrobe mistress, Faye Sloan.

*　*　*

Faye's log cabin looked like it could have been transported from the *Hee Haw* set. Another car was parked in the driveway, which I figured belonged to some of the other Honeys who were there for costume fittings, so imagine my surprise to walk in and see Faye's assistant tape-measuring the puny chest of a woman with Marty Feldman eyes and a Leon Spinks smile.

"Hey there," she said, in a voice that was the female version of Andy Devine, "I'm Roni Stoneman."

"Hi, I'm Diana Goodman," I said, staring at her harder than I should have, trying unsuccessfully to place her among the *Hee Haw* cast. I started to ask if she was also new, then thought better of it, realizing that if she was a longtime cast member, admitting I did not recognize her would get me off on the wrong foot, so I played it shy instead, following the old saying, *It's better to remain silent and be thought a fool than to speak and remove all doubt.*

The old saying proved to be a wise one, because Roni was talkative enough for both of us, and I was more than happy to let her run on until she'd talked herself into being my new best friend. Considering the "hole

"The Dixie Twins" Diana Goodman and Roni Stoneman (1981)

in the head" comment that one of the Honeys had made when my friend in L.A. told her about me, I figured I'd need a buddy among the cast, and it might be even better if she wasn't one of the show's beauties who could consider me competition.

As it turned out, Roni and I were to play twin sisters on the show.

As the Dixie Twins, gap-toothed beanpole Pixie Dixie and blonde bombshell Trixie Dixie were a comedy sketch, which was such an obvious sight gag that it hardly needed lines. Wearing polka-dotted Daisy Mae dresses – nearly identical to the one I wore at the Memphian Theater and elsewhere – all we had to do was walk in front of the camera and say, "Hi, we're the Dixie Twins," and the audience roared with laughter. I soon found out that Roni was one of the most gifted comedic talents on the show, so working as her partner was a good way to ease a new cast member into the broad comedy that was *Hee Haw's* hallmark.

The *Hee Haw* folks were sensitive to my lack of experience on television, so they gave me the first few days to become familiar with the set and to learn how the taping schedule worked, which was nothing as I'd imagined.

When they had told me I would only be in Nashville for one month, I wondered how on earth we could shoot thirteen episodes with all those different scenes and different guest stars, in such a short length of time. But as Sam Lovullo walked me through the studio on my first day there, he showed me the Barber Shop set, and explained that, the next morning, Archie Campbell and other men on the show would be doing thirteen Barber Shop "spots," then that afternoon, Roy Clark and his band would tape all their songs for the next thirteen episodes, and Gordy Tapp and Gailard Sartain would do thirteen General Store "spots" and the days would proceed that way, until enough material for thirteen episodes was in the "can" to take back to Hollywood and edit all of it into thirteen shows that would run from September through November. In October, we would all come back to Nashville and do more material for the shows that would run December through February. Wow. Whoever thought of that system was some kind of genius.

The first *Hee Haw* Honey I met was Lisa Todd. Several days after I arrived, it was time for full-cast day, and she and I were to meet in the lobby of the hotel to ride to the studio together. I had a vague recollection of what she looked like, so I exited the elevator, keeping a sharp eye out for her, but as soon as she appeared, I realized I would have known it was Lisa, even if I'd had no idea of her description. At almost six-feet tall, with her mane of black hair and Dolly-Parton size bosom, Lisa Todd was impossible to miss, and her warm smile and friendly greeting equally impossible to reconcile with her sex-goddess appearance. On the way to the studio, she navigated the morning rush-hour traffic with easy confidence, while keeping up a running stream of conversation, giving me the ins and outs of life at *Hee Haw*. Lisa had been on the show for ten years, so I thought she'd be a good one to learn from, but I suspected fitting in with the other girls would not be as easy as she made it sound.

What I learned very quickly was that Lisa herself didn't fit in with the other girls; she didn't even try. Arriving at the Opryland Studios, she made quick work of parking the car, and then motioning me to follow, hurried into the makeup room, with me in tow.

"This is Diana Goodman, everybody," she called out, and the four women standing at the hair and makeup stations looked my direction. "That's Elizabeth," Lisa said, pointing to a pleasantly plump middle-aged woman with honey-blonde hair, brushing blush onto the prominent cheekbones of a brown-eyed blonde – Gunilla Hutton; "That's Anita," she pointed to a small gray-haired woman, powdering the nose of a fresh-faced girl with a corn-yellow page-boy, wearing denim overalls – Cathy Baker; "There's Gwen," an Amazon of a gal wearing skin-tight jeans and high-heel sneakers was putting electric rollers into the flowing mane of a petite brunette – Victoria Hallman. Then Lisa introduced the other hair-dresser, Cindy, a dark-haired beauty every bit as eye-catching as the lanky girl whose golden-brown locks she was back-combing. I gasped when I realized that the girl in Cindy's chair was none other than my old Elvis rival, Linda Thompson. Our eyes met in the mirror and each of us quickly looked away, which was how we handled the situation throughout the remainder of that June in Nashville. If I spotted her in the makeup room, I headed into wardrobe, if I was sitting on the left side during "Pickin' and Grinnin'," she seated herself far right, and on like that, avoiding any problems, beginning that very moment in the makeup room, when Linda said, "I think my hair's done, Cindy," and scooted out the door, with Gunilla popping up from Elizabeth's chair to follow.

Elizabeth waved me over, and I took Gunilla's vacant chair, watching in amazement as Elizabeth worked her magic. Then I had a turn in Gwen's chair, then on into the dressing room to get on my tee-shirt and cut-offs, before making my way into the studio to sit on a scratchy bale of hay, clapping along while Buck and Roy stood on a wagon, singing country songs that were old when my grandmother was born.

The day went more slowly than I would have expected, dragging on until it turned into evening. Yet, the bright side was that the butt-numbing hours sitting on the hay bale, surrounded by the whole cast, gave me an opportunity to meet everyone, and even though I can't say I felt immediately at home in Kornfield Kounty, I reminded myself that I was extremely lucky to be part of this iconic show, and I was one-hundred-percent determined to do my very best to fit in. So for the next little while, I spoke only when spoken to and smiled as sweetly as I could whenever anyone looked my direction – and even when they weren't looking – until one day when we took our noontime break, as Misty Rowe hurried down the hall ahead of me, hot-footing for the exit, she glanced over her shoulder and said, "Wanna go to lunch?" and without slowing pace, added, "You'll have to wear your costume, there's no time to change."

*Wear my costume?* How the heck was I supposed to eat lunch in shorts so tight they were cutting off the circulation in my thighs? Beside which, after stuffing myself, I'd be miserable the rest of the day trying to suck in my gut. But this was the first time one of the cast members had invited me to join them for anything, so I dared not refuse. I trotted to keep up with Misty, and just as the exit came into view, I spotted a pair of Junior Samples' overalls, laid on a chair. Those would surely camouflage my lunch-stuffed tummy bulge. I grabbed them up, pulling them on as I made my way into the parking lot, and from that day forward, I ate lunch in a pair of Junior's castoff overalls, and by later in the afternoon, when I had to wear the cutoffs on camera again, my lunch would have digested. The one thing I never figured out was how the other girls managed to consume platefuls of fried chicken and gravy and biscuits at lunch, then prance onto the set with their stomachs flat as an empty plate. But if it was some kind of secret among the *Hee Haw* Honeys, I would have to wait to find out, because when my first taping session in Nashville came to a close, my only friend among the girls was still the first one who'd befriended me, wacky, loud-mouthed, good ol', Roni Stoneman. It wouldn't be until my return trip to the *Hee Haw* set in October that Linda Thompson and I would face off.

*Hee Haw* Honeys Front, Cathy Baker; Bottom Row, L-R Victoria Hallman, Misty Rowe, Lisa Todd, Roni Stoneman, Linda Thompson; Standing, L-R Irlene Mandrell, Jackie Waddell, Diana Goodman, Gunilla Hutton, Minnie Pearl, LuLu Roman (1983)

# Chapter 15

EVEN THOUGH ALL THE FEMALE cast members shared the same small dressing room, it was easy enough for Linda and me to avoid each other. With that many women in the same room there was always somewhere else to look, other than at each other, but working together, day in, day out, it was inevitable that the time would arrive when we came face-to-face, with no escape.

For some reason, on that day, I was all alone in the dressing room when Linda walked in. I was on one side, putting on my Honey dress for the afternoon, so she took her dress off the rack and went to the other side of the room, while I hurried, zipping my dress and fastening my shoes, trying to exit as quickly as possible.

Then, very quietly, she said, "You know I remember you."

I looked up from fastening my shoe, "Really?"

She tilted her head, appraising me. "I'm surprised Elvis dated you. He usually preferred small-breasted women."

I'd heard some good left-handed compliments, but that won the prize. I had no idea how to respond, which was her intention.

She said, "I'm married now, to Bruce Jenner, and we have a beautiful baby boy. Elvis was a special part of my life, but I've moved on." Then she smiled, "Welcome to the show," and walked out.

I released the breath I'd been holding. Thank God. Things were going to be all right. Even so, we never mentioned it again, and neither of us ever told any of the other cast members, although not long after our dressing-room encounter, when we both returned to Hollywood, she called and offered to fix me up on a couples' date with Bruce's manager, George Wallach. She explained that Bruce and Merlin Olsen were performing on a Bob Hope Special, which was a variety dinner show, where we would all be guests. I'd met George Wallach previously, and not been particularly attracted, but it sounded like a fun event, and I was eager to strengthen the truce with Linda, so I said yes.

We went as three couples, and on the way to the venue, I learned that Merlin, Bruce and Bob Hope would be performing a spoof of the Mandrell Sisters, with Bob as Barbara, Merlin as Irlene and Bruce as Louise. This, of course required them to wear dresses, which seems downright spooky, given what we now know was going on inside Bruce at the time. But, if he was a woman, I must say I would never have guessed, because even playing Louise Mandrell, wearing a chiffon evening gown, every six-feet-two-inches of Bruce Jenner looked like a man.

There was one odd moment though, which might have been a clue. Walking into the event center, Merlin was carrying the dress he was going to wear, and Linda was carrying Bruce's. The event was a black-tie affair, and Linda and I were all gussied up in cocktail attire and spike heels, not exactly appropriate for her to be hauling Bruce's wardrobe, so after a while, she tried to hand the dress to him. "Could you please carry this?"

He refused, adamantly.

"Okay, then," Linda retorted, "Maybe Merlin will carry it." Then she sing-songed, "Merlin's secu-ure."

None of that held any deeper meaning at the time, so I shrugged it off as Bruce being a spoiled man, who preferred not to carry his own stuff, and Linda made a joke of it, so we all proceeded to have a fun-filled evening, with Bruce, Bob and Merlin bringing the house down, spoofing the Mandrell Sisters. I had such a good time, that when George invited me to his house for a barbecue, I was pleased to accept, especially since he said I could bring along my little sis Crystal, and when the party turned out almost as much fun as the Bob Hope event, I began to wonder if I might develop a sincere interest in this guy. Then, to my everlasting astonishment, a few weeks later, Linda called to tell me that George had sent Bruce a bill for my dinner at the benefit show, and that was the end of that.

So, what if my love life wasn't all you'd expect from a former Miss Georgia and current *Hee Haw* Honey? I'd moved to Hollywood hoping to be an actress and a comedienne, and that's exactly what I had become. Part of me was still that star-struck kid whose bedroom walls were plastered with pictures out of movie magazines, and now I was on a TV show that was "plastered" with the real thing. Each *Hee Haw* episode featured three guest stars, and if you multiply three times twenty-six episodes per year, it adds up to seventy-eight stars that I got to work with each season that I was on the show, which included literally every star in country mu-

*Hee Haw* Honeys in the Kornfield with Glen Campbell and Jonathan Winters (1983)

Victoria's Birthday L-R Douglas Jencks, Victoria Hallman, Diana Goodman,
LeRoy (1983)

sic, from Dolly Parton to Johnny and June Cash to Garth Brooks, but also
athletes like Mickey Mantle and Richard Petty, Broadway and Hollywood
legends like Ethel Merman and Sammy Davis, Jr. Even Big Bird from *Ses-
ame Street.* For a star-struck kid from Georgia, *Hee Haw's* Kornfield was
my personal little piece of Paradise.

I even got to the point where it didn't bother me so much that the
other Honeys didn't seem inclined to welcome me into their tight little
clique. I still had Roni, and Lulu was always kind to me. Then in September of 1983, I opened my mailbox to find the fanciest invitation I'd ever
seen, inviting me to Victoria Hallman's birthday party, to be held at the
Bistro Garden in Beverly Hills. I clasped the invitation against my chest,
dancing around the room, wondering if I dared view it as an invitation
into the Honeys "inner circle."

The Bistro Garden was a classy spot for the Beverly Hills A-list, and
the invitation specified dinner and dancing, so I bought a white satin
jumpsuit, and took along my handsome blond cousin LeRoy, who just
happened to have a white suit that matched my outfit, which I hoped

would help us make the right impression, but if I expected follow-up invitations from the Honeys, I was disappointed. During the October taping, the girls treated me with as much disdain as ever.

On November 14 of that year, *Hee Haw's* beloved funny fat man, Junior Samples, died of a heart attack at his home in Cumming, Georgia. I was the only *Hee Haw* Honey to attend his funeral, but even for that, I couldn't get credit. In bestselling author Lewis Grizzard's coverage, he

"Fit as a Fiddle" *Hee Haw* Promo Poster (1983)

wrote that Misty Rowe was there, with her frizzy blonde hair and her too-short skirt. Maybe I shouldn't have minded being mistaken for Misty, but even with the frizzy hair and short skirt comment, I would have appreciated the mention.

I never even knew if Misty found out about the unflattering mix-up, because by the time I saw her again, four months later, Junior's funeral was old news, and as usual, none of the Honeys seemed interested in hearing anything I might have to say, anyway. We had all flown to Nashville, where the Honeys would be featured on *Glen Campbell's Country Comes Home,* a network special, shot at the Opry House, and it didn't matter one whit whether the girls spoke to me or not. I was performing on the stage of the Grand Ole Opry!

That was a busy spring. Gunilla Hutton had become engaged, and on the flight home from the Glen Campbell special, the first-class cabin was buzzing with the Honeys making plans to attend the wedding shower that Victoria Hallman was hosting at the Bistro Garden, the same restaurant where I had attended her birthday bash. I thought they were rude to talk about it in front of me, since I clearly would not be included in the celebration, so I stuck my nose in a *People* magazine, pretending not hear.

What a surprise – what a *thrill* – to get home and find an invitation to the shower in my mailbox. I immediately went shopping and bought Gunilla a silk gown and robe that was more expensive than anything I'd ever bought for myself. It was worth every penny just to see her surprise and delight when she opened the gift, although I considered myself the one who'd gotten the gift. I'd been to many showers in my time, but never to one anywhere close to the banquet room of the top restaurant in Beverly Hills, with fifty or more guests dining on the chef's finest, and drinking ourselves silly on vintage French champagne. To top it off, Victoria had been kind enough to seat me next to Lori Saunders, who played Gunilla's little sister Bobbie Jo Bradley on *Petticoat Junction.* Being one of three "country" sisters, myself, I had always identified with the Bradley girls, so eating lunch elbow-to-elbow with one of them was a special honor that I never expected. I left the Bistro Garden that day feeling not only like one of the "inner circle" Honeys, but like a Hollywood insider, too.

Something told me my star was on the rise. As far as actual camera time on *Hee Haw,* they had cut the two spots that featured me, but they were sending me on more PR trips, usually star-studded celebrity golf tournaments, which seemed more like play than work, and they always included some sort of live concert, which gave me the opportunity to appear onstage beside legends like the Gatlin Brothers, Debbie Reynolds, or *Hee Haw's* own Roy Clark. At one event, they even let me have five minutes onstage to try out my brand new stand-up comedy routine. My pulse was racing like a heart-attack, but I managed to get through it, and the audience gave me a nice round of applause, so I congratulated myself on a successful debut, and Debbie Reynolds congratulated me, as well.

Then there was the time when pro football player Ed Marinaro was one of my fellow celebs at a tournament, and you can be sure I couldn't take my eyes of him. Apparently, he was casting some looks my way too, because after the tournament he invited me to a romantic dinner at his beautiful home in L.A., then followed up with a few nights on the town, before our conflicting schedules got in the way, and our budding romance wilted.

Too bad about that. My age was creeping into the mid-thirties, and our *Hee Haw* producer, Sam Lovullo was so persistent in telling me I need-ed a husband, that I'd begun to think he was right. Three years in a row, I

Michael Jordan and Diana. (1982)

had attended Michael Jordan's celebrity tournament, and as a thank-you gift, Michael had given me a gold nugget, which I intended to have made into a wedding band for my husband. Assuming I ever caught one.

Until then, I would keep myself happy by being the perfect *Hee Haw* Honey. Except, for some reason, fate seemed to have other ideas. Things started going wrong for me at *Hee Haw*. Nothing big, or at least I didn't think so. One time, there was confusion about who was supposed to turn in the rental car, and I got blamed; then I played a silly joke, snatching a floral arrangement out of a hotel hallway, and returning it to another floor. Rumor was that I stole it. Good grief. Then the worst thing was when I gave Victoria's husband a ride to a cast barbecue. That's all it was, just a ride, but the timing was bad. They were separated, although he was in Nashville to see Victoria, which I didn't quite understand, so everyone assumed the worst, as they always did where I was concerned, and Sam and Barry Adelman called me into the office for a "chat." They quizzed me about any problems I might be having with other cast members, or anything else, and said they couldn't understand what had happened to the sparkle they'd seen in my eyes when I auditioned for the show. I answered their questions as best I could, and walked out of Sam's office thinking all was well, never suspecting that I was making my final exit from *Hee Haw*.

*   *   *

Roger's Caddy (1984)

They always say that when God closes a door he opens a window. After that October taping of 1984, I hung around Nashville for a few days, visiting with friends I'd made during my biannual stays in Music City, one of whom was Skull Shulman. Skull's face suited his nickname, but he was one of the warmest, sweetest men I'd ever met. He was also somewhat of a regular on *Hee Haw*. Although he was not a member of the cast, everyone at the show loved him so much, they'd put him in overalls and let him sit with the gang at the edge of the camera shot, so I hope this explains what I was doing in Skull's Rainbow, which was a strip joint.

On that October night, Skull beckoned me to where he was sitting at the bar with a good-looking dark-haired man that I didn't recognize as one of the regular music-biz patrons. This guy was dressed in Khakis and a sweater, for god's sake. Preppy didn't fit this joint, and it didn't fit me.

"Want you to meet a friend of mine," Skull said, offering me his seat by the man in the khakis. "Diana Goodman, this is Roger McDaniel."

Although there were other people in the room that I would rather have spent time with, I said hello politely, and before I knew it, Roger and I were talking. It turned out that he was a musician-turned-banker, which sounded to me like a good combination, but I didn't have time to find out much more, because it was getting late and the friend I was with started bugging me that it was time to go.

"I'll walk out with you," Roger said.

As with most of the tourist-type places, Skull always made sure to park the fanciest cars right by the door, but this night he'd found one that outdid all the rest. This was a white Cadillac El Dorado custom-trimmed with so much chrome, that if Elvis had ever gotten the chance to see it, he would have bought it on the spot.

I clapped my hands and squealed, "Whose car is this?"

"Mine."

"Yours?" I whirled around to face Roger. "Ohhh-whee! Can we go for a ride?"

He wasn't Elvis and he wasn't Rick Nelson, he wasn't anybody famous at all. But Roger McDaniel was the one. I got into his car that night and rode with him into forever.

Mr. and Mrs. Roger McDaniel

# Part IV
# Victoria

Portrait of Victoria (1984). Photo Courtesy of Harry Langdon)

Victoria and Jim Halper in the Recording Studio, Hollywood (1980)

# Chapter 16

## VICTORIA
*1980–1985*

**TELLING MY HUSBAND** that I was engaged to marry another man was one thing, telling Buck Owens was quite another. Johnny, my husband of five years, had moved back to Alabama almost two years before, so we already considered ourselves divorced, all it took was signing the papers. My situation with Buck was just the opposite. Although there would be no papers to sign, the relationship was complicated. But I was too busy falling head-over-heels in love to worry about that, so as usual I followed the wisdom of my role model Scarlett O'Hara and put it off until another day, which came on Good Friday 1980.

Jim insisted on asking my father for my hand, and my annual Easter visit to Alabama provided the perfect opportunity. Everybody fell in love with my fiancé as quickly as I had, so on that Friday afternoon, he and Daddy had gone for a ride to let Jim see Bibb County, where our Hallman forefathers had been among the First Families of Bibb to settle before statehood. Since Jim had never set foot in the South – except for Miami, which doesn't count – it was as good an introduction to the Heart of Dixie as he was likely to get.

That left me at my parents' house watching TV in the den, with Mother and my fourteen-year-old sister, Valerie, who I claimed was my twin born eleven years later. We were chatting about my forthcoming marriage, and eventually got around to *Hee Haw*. "How does Buck feel about you getting married?" Mother asked.

"I haven't told him."

Valerie snickered. "When were you planning to give him the good news?"

Alabama Family Home, Victoria's sisters Valerie and Robin, Victoria and Jim

"I guess now, while I've got you here for backup." I rubbed my knuckles on her head, and reluctantly got up from my comfy spot on the old brown leather sofa, heading to the kitchen phone.

"Hello-oo, Classy Sassy," Buck said when he heard my voice.

"Hey, I hope you're sitting down, because I've got big news."

"What's that?"

"I'm getting married."

He grunted like somebody had punched him in the gut. Then he said, "You won't be married long," and hung up.

I walked back into the den making a sour face.

Valerie shrugged, "At least it was quick."

The phone rang. "I'll get it," I said, "It's probably Buck calling back."

But it wasn't Buck. He had wasted no time getting his manager involved to straighten out the situation, and Jack McFadden had wasted no time calling me to do just that. "Jesse Rose, what do you think you're doing?" he said.

"Getting married."

Jack heaved a sigh. I could see him sitting at his desk, wagging his big head back and forth, like a father weighted with the burden of a problem child. "Do you understand that you've got it any way you want it with Buck Owens?"

"I already have it the way I want it."

Jack said, "Whatever it takes to make you happy is what we'll do." He sounded snappish, as if what he really wanted to say was *Stop this nonsense.*

"I want to marry Jim."

There was a long silence before he said, "All right then, Jesse Rose My-Queen."

I walked back into the den, "Jack McFadden."

Mother lowered the volume on the remote. "Is he mad?"

I dropped onto the sofa, laying my head on Valerie's lap. "He's not happy."

Uh-oh," she said, "Do you think they'll fire you?"

I shrugged. "Who knows?"

I had never intended to be a country singer, anyway, and surely not a *Hee Haw* Honey. Where all the other girls had auditioned, I had landed in the Kornfield by mere chance, so if suddenly, I was no longer a resident of Kornfield Kounty, I would consider it just one more in a long list of fun gigs. My career as a singer and actress would continue as it had since I was three-years-old, with or without Buck Owens and *Hee Haw.*

As soon as we got back to L.A. I jumped into a new project, co-producing my own recording session – something I'd never done before – with a dream team of musicians, including several of L.A.'s legendary "Wrecking Crew," who played on records by everyone from the Beach Boys to Bob Dylan to Frank Sinatra. Also on my dream team were members of Emmy Lou Harris's Hot Band, as well as James Burton, Hall of Fame guitarist for Elvis Presley, and Rick Nelson. Funny things can happen when you put musicians of that rank in the studio with a couple of rookie producers. Just one example was the first interaction between James Burton and my co-producer Leo La Branche.

Leo was a rock musician/song-writer/producer, who may have been somewhat out of his depth on this first attempt at producing country music. First up on the song list for the session that day was my female version of Merle Haggard's classic, "Mama Tried." The session players were in place to record the rhythm track, and Leo went out into the studio, to pass around charts, and stopped with James Burton, explaining how to play the signature guitar lick on the song.

James listened politely for a minute, then said, "Are you saying you want me to play that guitar lick exactly like it was played on Merle Haggard's original cut?"

Leo nodded, "That's it."

James said, "Well, that won't be any problem, since I was on that session, and that was me playing that original guitar lick on "Mama Tried. You want me to copy my own signature lick?'

Leo gave him a wry smile. "Play it any way you want to."

This stratospherically expensive session was of course courtesy of my new fiancé, who imagined himself a music promoter, producer, manager, or whatever title fit the project that took his interest from one day to the next. At the end of the session, we had three fabulous cuts, with very little idea what to do with them. Maybe I needed Buck Owens after all. The June taping of *Hee Haw* was coming up and I was slated to appear, so I could only assume Buck wasn't mad enough to fire me.

*   *   *

Since I had been married before, and Jim seemed in a hurry to get the ring on my finger, instead of a big wedding, we were planning a civil ceremony beside the Swan Lake at the Hotel Bel Air, L.A.'s most romantic wedding venue for celebrity couples, from Sophia Loren and Carlo Ponti, to Elizabeth Taylor and Nicky Hilton. Even my groom-to-be had been married there, and to a celebrity, which he was forced to confess, when it slipped out one afternoon while we were having cocktails on one of the hotel's shady terraces.

"Linda Cristal and I were married for less than a year," he rolled his eyes.

I took a few seconds to place the familiar name. *Wasn't Linda Cristal the beautiful blonde on The Big Valley? No, that was Linda Evans; Linda Cristal was the beautiful brunette on The High Chaparral.*

"How long ago were you married to her?" I asked.

"Three years, or so. I try not to remember."

"Are you claiming that you forgot to tell me?"

"No, I was afraid if I told you, you'd change your mind."

"That's silly. I have an ex too, you know."

He reached across the bistro table and took my chin in his hand, "But you don't love me as much as I love you."

Jim stood by his promise to postpone intimacy until after we were married. It was I who broke it, or rather, seduced him into breaking it, but I at least waited until we made the engagement official. On the Tuesday night after he proposed on Sunday, while I was onstage at the Club

Barrington, I saw him sit down at a table with a dark-haired man I didn't recognize. When I finished my set, I strolled over.

Both men bolted up from their chairs and Jim planted a kiss on my mouth, "Hey, honey, sit down and meet my jeweler, Yossi. He's brought some designs for your engagement ring." He handed me a piece of paper with sketches on it. "Do you prefer diamonds or colored stones?"

"Neither," I turned the piece of paper face-down. "A simple wedding band will do."

Jim shook his head. "My wife must have the most beautiful ring in Beverly Hills. A diamond."

"Cut?" Yossi asked.

"Emerald cut." Jim stroked my cheek. "Classic, like she is."

I folded my arms. "A simple gold band."

Yossi tossed his pencil on the table, laughing, "You are ruining my business, could we at least make it platinum?"

My problem had nothing to do with a distaste for diamonds, I simply didn't think an engagement ring would be appropriate when I was still officially married to someone else. But I hadn't been surprised when Jim stated that his wife must have the most beautiful ring in Beverly Hills. One of the first things he'd done after my "yes" to his proposal, was go into my closet and throw out all my clothes.

"What will I wear?" I wailed.

He patted me on my bottom. "Those cute little jeans you've got on, but only for about another –" He checked his wristwatch, "another half-hour because we're heading for Rodeo Drive right this minute. By the end of the day, you'll have a whole new wardrobe.

From Gucci to Hermès to Giorgio, in and out of stores we went, buying one ensemble after another, each coordinated with matching accessories, spending so much, I began to brace for the embarrassment I feared would come when Jim's credit card was declined. That was before I noticed that he wasn't using a credit card. I never saw him sign anything at all, nor did we take any packages with us.

When I questioned him, he shook his head and laughed. "They all know me." Then touching the tip of my nose, he said. "And now they all know you."

That evening, when we got home, Jim's bedroom was piled almost to the ceiling with packages that had been delivered. Even considering the room-size en-suite walk-in closet, given Jim's considerable wardrobe, I wondered where we would find room for mine.

The way he threw money around concerned me. I'd been in Hollywood long enough to know that spending like a rich man didn't make you one, and I worried that Jim was going overboard trying to impress me, which was totally unnecessary, and another reason I'd argued against an engagement ring.

I should have known better. One day, after I'd moved into Jim's quintessential, though oxymoronic, Beverly Hills "English cottage" on Coldwater Canyon Drive, I was luxuriating in the garden-style bathtub of our master suite, when I heard, "Honey I'm home."

He came into the bathroom, leaned over the tub to give me a kiss, then walked out, saying, "I'll be by the pool."

When I reached for the soap, a tiny black box was sitting in its place. It contained a slender platinum band with a four-prong setting holding a flawless four-carat emerald-cut solitaire. I leaped from the tub and ran for the patio, streaming soapy water on the hand-pegged plank floors as I went. "Jim!"

He was waiting for me at a table beside the pool. Naked and wet, I landed on his lap, smothering him in kisses and soaking his silk shirt with bathwater.

It all happened like magic, the ring on my finger, the wedding scheduled. Only the honeymoon was left to plan, which turned out to be as simple as Jim walking into the bedroom one day and saying, "Dinah Shore is putting together a tour of the Holy Land – Israel, Egypt – with a bunch of old Hollywood high rollers, Frank Sinatra, George Burns, Jan Murray, the usual crowd."

*Usual crowd?*

"We will be recognized on the floor of the Knesset and at some banquet or other. Do you have any interest in going?"

I was seated at my dressing table, getting ready to go out for dinner, so I adjusted the carved swans holding the mirror, to share it with Jim while he knotted his tie.

"What's the Knesset?" I asked.

"The Knesset is Israel's legislature."

"And they're recognizing you and me?"

"Technically, they're recognizing the Halper Foundation, but I'm head of the foundation and by then, you will be my wife."

"When would we be leaving?"

"End of June, first of July. I'll have to check the exact date."

"That would be perfect timing for our honeymoon."

He frowned. "Israel doesn't strike me as a romantic destination."

"Why not? We are entering Holy Matrimony, aren't we? Holy matrimony, Holy Land. Sounds right to me."

He put his hands on my shoulders, gazing at me in the mirror. "Holy Land, Holy matrimony. Consider it done."

But before that, came *Hee Haw*.

Just as in October, I would be flying into Nashville the second week of June to tape thirteen episodes as Buck's backing vocalist, but that did not mean things were back to normal. Since my phone call to him announcing my engagement, communication between Buck and me had come to a standstill, as had everything with Buck. Progress on his new album had ceased, along with all bookings for live performances.

Jim had a business meeting that delayed his joining me until the weekend. As soon as I settled into my room at Spence Manor, there was a knock at my door.

Buck was standing there. "Hey, Classy Sassy."

He followed me into the living room and sank into a club chair. I sat on the end of the sofa nearest him and he stared at me for a moment with his eyelids lowered and his mouth turned down. "I don't want things to be bad between us," he said.

"Something bad between us?" I asked.

He shook his head, "I don't guess so. What's the wedding date?"

"June 21st."

He leaned his head against the back of the chair, staring out the window at the tops of buildings on Music Row." I hear you cut a couple of songs with some pretty good musicians. Why didn't you let me hear them?"

"Oh!" I jumped up from the sofa, "I almost forgot. They're in the other room. Hang on."

I went into the bedroom, and brought back the cassette player. "I'd like your opinion."

The first song was my version of Buck's "Under the Influence of Love." On the last note, he winked at me, "Real good," then nodded his approval of "Mama Tried," before listening intently to "Close Enough for Me," a ballad written for me by Nashville songwriter, Darrell Clanton. When the tape ended, he said, "The ballad's your single, but I don't like the mix. Your vocal's the best part. Need to bring it forward. Can you get hold of the master right quick?"

"I think so."

Victoria with nephew Hallman Eady, niece Alex Eady, and Gunilla Hutton

His gaze wandered beyond the window again. "I'll call Owen Bradley. He'll probably do it for you."

So that's how I wound up at Nashville's famed Quonset Hut sitting in the dark studio working on my recordings, with one of the architects of the "Nashville Sound," in exactly the same spot where he'd done the same thing with Patsy Cline, Kitty Wells, Brenda Lee, Loretta Lynn, and just about every other female country legend you could think of.

When we finished "Close Enough for Me," he said, "Buck tells me you've got a couple of other cuts that could use some help, and I can do that for you, if you don't mind waiting a little bit. I'd have to look at my schedule, but I should have some time right about last week of the month."

"What an unfortunate coincidence. I'm getting married June 21, so . . ." I shook my head, having no idea the greatness I was shaking off. To me, Owen Bradley was just an old buddy of Buck's who happened to be very good at a mixing console. *Very* good.

The next day at *Hee Haw*, Buck was more somber than usual, but as always, he was the consummate professional. We zipped through the season's "Buck's Place," songs in the morning, and made short work of the cast songs in the afternoon.

The rest of the week also went smoothly. The cast seemed to remember me from my October visit, and the Honeys welcomed me back politely.

Gunilla Hutton even went out of her way to tell me that her ex-husband had heard me when I performed at the Club Barrington, and that he'd said I was very good, which meant a lot, both that he thought I was good, and that she would pass along the compliment. Still, although the cast was warming to me, and Buck and I had broken the ice enough for him to take me along to his fan club's annual breakfast during Fan Fair, I was counting the hours until Jim's arrival on Friday night.

Then, on Friday evening, as I was freshening up to greet Jim, the phone rang in my suite, and to my surprise, it was *Hee Haw's* producer, Sam Lovullo calling.

"Hi, Jesse Rose," he said. "Listen, I've just come out of a production meeting, and we've decided that we'd like to use you in more of the spots with the other girls, 'Moonshiners,' 'Jug Band,' those kinds of things, and we might even get you in the Kornfield, so I hope you'll be able to stay in town for a couple more weeks."

Yet another unfortunate coincidence of timing. Suddenly, everybody in Nashville was handing me a golden opportunity that conflicted with my wedding date. But, although I may not have comprehended the importance of many things that were happening to me, I understood that my answer to Sam Lovullo's question could be the tipping point of my life.

"Yes," I said, "Thank you, Mr. Lovullo."

Mr. and Mrs. James Halper (1980)

# Chapter 17

AT LEAST I WOULDN'T HAVE very long to dread breaking the news to Jim. In less than an hour he'd be standing at the door.

For once, his plane was right on time, and he must have paid the limo driver big bucks to break the speed limit, because he showed up even sooner than I'd expected. Quickly stuffing a fistful of bills into the bellman's hand and closing the door behind him, he scooped me into his arms, "Come here, you," and after a lengthy hello kiss, "Where's the bedroom?"

I paused, making a split-second decision that it would be better to break it to him before bed, rather than after, "I have something important to tell you."

"Right this second?"

"I nodded.

He sat down on the sofa, lighting a Marlboro. "This better be important."

"It is." I grimaced.

Frowning, he pressed the room-service button. "Please bring me a Harvey's, neat, or if possible, a bottle for my room."

When I started to speak, he touched his forefinger to my lips, and shook his head, "I've got a feeling I'm going to need that drink before I hear what you have to say."

I sat in silence, watching his jaw muscles flex rhythmically with the clinching of his teeth, so that by the time his drink arrived, I was as nervous as he was, and blurted out, "We need to cancel the wedding."

"I knew it!" he jumped to his feet, glaring down at me.

"Sit down, please." I patted the sofa. "I don't mean cancel forever, I just mean postpone it."

"No."

"If you'll calm down and listen, you may agree with me." I turned my eyes up to his.

He slumped onto the sofa, sipping his Harvey's while I explained. When I finished, he kissed the tip of my nose, "Why didn't you tell me that in the first place? I couldn't live with myself if I caused you to miss out on this opportunity, but I will not agree to postponing the wedding." He tapped my chest. "Not. By. One. Single. Day." He stood, pulling me up from the sofa with him. Then he gave me a quick kiss and walked out.

He had been so eager to get me in bed, now just like that, he was gone. I didn't know what to make of it. So, when he was back in ten minutes, whistling a little tune, as if nothing had ever happened, I didn't even mind that he refused to tell me what he'd gone to "take care of," until after we took care of business in bed.

He lit two cigarettes, passed one to me, and I snuggled into the crook of his arm. "What were you up to, running off like that?"

"'If the mountain won't come to Mohammed, Mohammed will go to the mountain,' or do you prefer 'Have your cake and eat it, too?' Why cancel the wedding, when all we need to do is move it to Nashville?"

\*   \*   \*

I never knew Mrs. Bloodworth's exact job description, but whatever the Spence Manor paid her wasn't enough. In one week's time, the matronly steel magnolia had taken care of every wedding detail, including flowers, cake, harpist, judge, photographer, seated reception dinner, and an appointment for me with her personal shopper, who helped me select a rosy-beige tea-length silk-organza dress, perfect for a second-time bride, so that on the evening of Saturday, the twenty-first of June, 1980, friends and family from Alabama were seated on white chairs in a banquet room at Spence Manor, quietly talking among themselves as the strains of harp music and the fragrance of pale peach roses filled the air, while Mrs. Bloodworth was down the hall assisting the bride, who really needed no assistance, which left the stalwart steel magnolia to the all-important task of manning her post by the phone in the living room, waiting for me to give the go-ahead to let the harpist know to begin "Here Comes the Bride."

I peeked around the bedroom door, calling out, "Mrs. Bloodworth," and she dutifully dialed the phone, at which moment, down the hall, the harpist began the tune for my grand entrance. Jim and his best man, my brother-in-law Al, took their places in front of the judge, and my sister Robin proceeded down the aisle, carrying her matron of honor bouquet, followed by her three-year-old daughter, my niece Alex, scattering petals, before taking their places at the altar.

The harp music swelled, the judge lifted his hands, and the guests rose from their seats, looking towards the open door, expecting to see me walk in. Again, the harp music swelled, announcing my entrance. And again. And again.

When the harpist tried the fifth time with no bride appearing, she wisely reverted to a selection of romantic light classical, and the guests took their seats, amidst a hum of conversation and nervous titters that devolved into jokes about the bride getting cold feet, which the groom did not find humorous. As my friends and kin stole glances at the door, thinking *Vicki's late as usual* or *Vicki always makes a dramatic entrance*, Jim was becoming more certain that his worst fears had been realized, and I had changed my mind.

If he thought I'd gotten a case of wedding-day nerves, he was right, but my feet were not the least bit cold. If anything, from head-to-toe, I was uncomfortably warm. While my wedding guests were making lame jokes about "runaway bride," I was gripping the bathroom countertop, doing my best to hold still, as Mrs. Bloodworth struggled with my zipper, which was caught in the delicate silk of my dress.

Then finally, *Zzzip.* "Got it!" she exclaimed, thrusting my bouquet into my hand. Then she hurried to the phone. "The bride is on her way!" And this time I really was.

After a joyous reception, with our nearest and dearest dining on Steak Diane, and toasting our union with vintage Taittinger Comte de Champagne, we retired to our suite, where our first lovemaking as man and wife was as sweet as any bride could wish.

Afterward, lying in each other's arms, Jim said, "When you were so late coming in, I honestly thought you had backed out."

I raised myself on my elbows, and stroked his thick dark hair. "Well, that's one thing you don't have to worry about anymore."

He shook his head. "I'll never stop worrying about losing you. You don't know everything about me."

I smiled, "Not yet."

He nodded, "You're probably smart to find out gradually, but there's one thing I've been saving to tell you tonight." He reached for a cigarette and lit it." I never want you to have to discuss money."

I had no idea what was coming, but it wouldn't have surprised me to hear that he was deep in debt, or rather, *we* were deep in debt.

"You are now in the top one-tenth of one-percent of wealthiest people in the U.S," he said.

After several seconds trying to calculate whether those percentages made me rich, poor or somewhere in between, I said, "Is this a test?"

"Yes, and you made an A-plus." He kissed my cheek and switched off the lamp, then switched it back on. "While I'm at it, I may as well tell you that you are also now the owner of a casino." He switched off the lamp. "Goodnight, Mrs. Halper."

\*   \*   \*

Our honeymoon trip to the middle-east began in New York City with a party hosted by Dinah Shore at El Morocco, which had been New York's most glamorous nightclub during the era of Cole Porter and F. Scott Fitzgerald, and although, by 1980, it had become an event venue, on that night, doing the rumba with Jim surrounded by the club's iconic white palm trees and zebra-striped banquettes, I could easily have imagined myself to be Ava Gardner dancing with Clark Gable on the set of *Mogambo*.

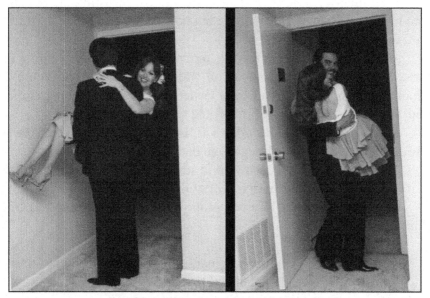

Victoria and Jim Over the Threshold (1980)

Victoria wearing amethyst honeymoon ring. (1984)

Even though we spent our wedding night at the Spence Manor, this was our official honeymoon, so we checked into the bridal suite at the Drake Hotel, another legendary haunt of stars such as Muhammed Ali and Judy Garland, so fabulous that I could have been tempted to spend the rest of our honeymoon right there, snuggling with my hubby and ordering room service, if I had not been overawed at the thought of seeing the Holy Land. When Dinah's caravan took off the next day, we were on board.

Jim's shopping spree started as soon as we landed at Ben Gurion International Airport. I had come to Jerusalem to walk in the footsteps of

Jesus, but I soon learned that Jim had come to buy jewelry, and there was plenty to be had. The souvenir stands in the airport looked like Tiffany kiosks.

"That one." Jim pointed to a ring with a huge deep-purple amethyst surrounded by three rows of diamonds.

The man behind the counter removed it from the case and slipped it onto my finger, reciting, "A Siberian amethyst of forty-three carats, surrounded by two carats of diamonds, set in eighteen-karat gold."

"Can you size it before we leave?"

The salesman measured my finger, and later that afternoon the ring showed up at the door of our suite at the David Citadel Hotel.

The next morning, Jim let me sleep in, while he went downstairs to breakfast with some of the others on the tour. I found him waiting for me when I stepped off the elevator into the lobby.

"This way," he guided me to a jewelry boutique in the hotel's shopping "mall," where the piece that he had pre-selected was out of the glass case, displayed on the counter.

"Welcome back!" the store owner greeted Jim, then clasped his hands, smiling at me, "You are right, it does match her eyes," he opened his palms toward the black-velvet stand on the countertop, which held an emerald ring featuring a five-carat marquise-cut stone set at an oblique angle, surrounded by diamonds in a modernistic free-form design. Both the store owner and Jim beamed proudly as I tried on the ring, examining it this way and that, finally deciding that even though it was not the type of thing I would normally choose, it was a stunning piece, and if Jim liked it, I liked it. The Jeweler said he would have it sized and ready for me to wear to dinner that evening, and Jim and I headed out to climb aboard a bus tour of Jerusalem.

The next morning's scenario was identical, except this time, Jim guided me to the shop that sold antiquities, where we selected several two-thousand-year-old clay lamps, as souvenir gifts for friends back home, a tear bottle of the same age for me to cry into whenever I was away from Jim, a fifteen-hundred-year-old bronze elephant, and a sieve that was more than three-thousand-years-old, which I chose, thinking what a kick it would be to host a spaghetti supper and let the guests drain their own pasta in a strainer that had belonged to a middle-eastern housewife three millennia before.

Another morning's shopping excursion completed, we climbed into a limo, for a private guided tour of the Christian sites of Jerusalem, and for the rest of the day, Jim walked reverently by my side, following the footsteps of Jesus, through the Old City; up the Via Dolorosa; on up to the Mount of Olives, the Temple Mount, Mount Zion, Calvary; kneeling in the Church of the Holy Sepulchre and the Tomb of the Virgin Mary; finally arriving back at the hotel where he collapsed on the bed, proclaiming he was too exhausted to dress for dinner. All he wanted to do was don a bathrobe and order room service.

Considering his saintly indulgence on the tour that day, I could hardly complain, and truthfully, a hot bath and room service sounded good to me, too. What neither of us mentioned was that thus far, the dining-out options in Jerusalem hadn't been much to write home about – literally. We lay side-by-side in bed, studying the room-service menu, unable to decide, until Jim slapped it shut, saying, "I'm ordering a turkey sandwich and a glass of cold milk."

"Make that a double," I agreed.

The service was prompt, and as soon as the waiter left, we sat down in our bathrobes, at the linen-covered room-service table, and lifted the silver domes from our plates, eager to sink our teeth into a juicy combo of turkey and Swiss on Rye.

Jim took one bite and slung his sandwich at the wall. "I've had it!"

"A little dry," I nodded.

"Not just dry, there's grit in it. I'm not eating a turkey and dirt sandwich."

I lifted the top slice of Rye and checked inside. There was something brownish and coarsely-ground. "I think it's pepper."

"It's dirt! I'm calling Sol."

Sol was Jim's travel agent, so I thought I knew what that meant. We'd be going home, and I really hated it because the next stop on the caravan was Egypt. "I'd like to see the Pyramids."

"No," Jim said. Then he spoke into the phone. "Hey, Sol, get us out of here." He listened for a moment, before saying, "How soon can we leave?"

I sighed. We'd only been gone five days. Not much of a honeymoon. Jim was still talking to Sol, but I had stopped listening. Then I heard him saying, "Vicki. Vicki?"

I looked up. "Huh?"

"You want to go to Athens?"

"Greece?"

"Unless you'd rather go to Athens, Georgia."

I hopped onto his lap. "Greece!"

On the flight to Athens the next day, it began to dawn on me what it meant to be rich. If you didn't like your turkey sandwich, you just jetted off to another country where the food was better. *So that's why they call it the "Jet Set."*

Next stop, the Athens Hilton, a fantastically mid-century-modern hotel, where we did not have the Bridal Suite. We had the Presidential Suite, which was a twenty-five-hundred-square-foot luxury apartment, with marble floors and walls, complete with a separate living room, a dining room that seated ten, full kitchen, and its own sauna, which I intended to try that very day, right before a bubble bath à deux in the sunken whirlpool of the marble spa-bathroom, then a relaxing glass of wine with my hubby on the enormous balcony, taking in the sweeping view of the Acropolis. The whole thing was so luxurious, and the reputation of the hotel cuisine such that we decided to spend a hedonistic evening indulging ourselves and each other.

Dirty turkey was a thing of the past, and an inside joke forever after. Jim felt so pampered by our romantic evening in, that he sweetly agreed to my suggestion that we book a tour guide for the next day, who took us on the rounds of all the must-see sites, until the climb up the Acropolis dealt the coup de grace, with Jim declaring he'd seen enough ancient ruins to last him the rest of his life.

The next day, we took a day trip to a beautiful little island, where we whiled away the afternoon on the terrace of a charming hotel, sipping Retsina and feeding each other spanakopita, dolma, grape leaves, and every other Greek appetizer imaginable, with Jim telling the waiter to keep them coming as long as we sat there watching the sailboats skimming across the sparkling Aegean, which took us through a bright red sunset during dinner, and into nightfall, when we returned to the hotel, already discussing various diversions for the following day.

Stopping in the lobby, Jim asked the concierge for suggestions.

"Do you like to gamble?" asked the man behind the desk, "Roulette, Baccarat?"

"Yes." I declared.

Jim's mouth crooked up at one corner. "Apparently so." The concierge recommended the Casino Mont Parnes, atop Mount Parnitha in the Athens National Forest. He would book a driver to take us tomorrow evening, and during the day, I could enjoy the hotel spa, while Jim went shopping.

The next afternoon, getting in from the spa, I was surprised to find Jim already returned from his shopping excursion, sitting in the living room of the suite, dressed in coat and tie, ready to leave for the casino.

"It's only six o'clock," I said.

"I know. I ordered the car to come early."

\* \* \*

The irony of a casino owner gambling in someone else's "joint" did not escape me, and Jim had made it clear that this evening was strictly for me, as he would be sitting on the sidelines, signaling the "house" to replenish my stack of chips. In other words, he assumed I would lose, and since he seemed to know so much about it, I decided it was time he explained his mysterious wedding-night comment about me being the new owner of a casino. The way he'd flung it out and so quickly turned off the lamp, made me suspect it was more of a riddle than a statement of fact, maybe even a joke, so I had waited for him to bring it up again, and when he didn't, I became even more sure that he'd been joking. Weren't casinos owned by big conglomerates? One person – or two if you included me – couldn't own a casino, could they?

With Jim comfortably settled in the back of the limo, I came at the subject sideways. "Do you think the casino we're going to is anything like *your* casino?"

The Nevada Club Casino (1950s

The trick question didn't faze him one bit. "I'm sure there are similarities."

"Where is your casino?"

"Reno."

"What's it called?"

"The Nevada Club."

"Oh. I've seen that one. Very cool retro marquee. Close to Harrah's, isn't it?"

"Next door."

"How long have you owned it?"

"Most of my life. I inherited it."

I leaned forward and closed the privacy glass between front and back seats. "Are you in the mafia?" I whispered.

"If I tell you, I'll have to kill you." He laughed, "Then I'd have to kill myself because I wouldn't want to live without you."

"So, you are a partner in the Nevada Club with your cousins or somebody?"

"No, just me, but there are more people involved. I lease it out, and sometimes the people I lease it to lease it to somebody, so it can get complicated. The ownership has been layered from the beginning."

"Tell me."

"Well, since I was three-years-old when the Nevada Club opened in 1946, I wasn't in on every detail, but basically, my father had his fingers in a lot of pies, and he didn't necessarily want his name on the front of every building."

"I think you just mixed several metaphors," I said.

Jim nodded, "Appropriately so. My father put up the money for the casino, and he was the actual owner, but he brought in my mother's brothers, Harry and Ed Robbin, and called the casino Robbin's Nevada Club, stipulating that when Uncle Ed and Uncle Harry died, ownership would come to me. Obviously, in the past thirty-five years, there have been other partners and all kinds of deals made, but if you dig down through all the partnerships and leases, here I am."

"Headed to a casino in Greece," I laughed, "when we could be in Reno losing money to ourselves."

Jim grinned. "That's about the size of it, so you'll understand if I don't do any betting." He put his arm around me, and patted my shoulder. "It will be fun to watch you at the tables."

As we were talking, the limousine took a turn, and a mountain came into view. "Wow," I said, "I didn't know Greece had such tall mountains."

Jim opened the window between the driver and us. "How tall is Mount Parnitha?"

"Forty-six-hundred feet," came the answer, as we rolled into a parking lot and pulled up in front of a square modern building.

"Not much of a casino," I remarked.

"This is not the casino," the driver said, "The casino is up there." He pointed to the mountain, and I saw that at its summit was a building, barely discernable through the sunset clouds.

"Okay, so here we are," he said.

Jim gazed out the window at the mountaintop. "If that's the casino up there, what are we doing down here?"

The driver shook his head, "I am sorry, I thought you knew. This is the gondola terminal. Cable car, you call it?"

Jim's eyes followed a gondola suspended half-a-mile above our heads, slowly traveling an almost invisible wire to the tip-top of the mountain. "No" was all he said.

I was very aware of Jim's acrophobia, and although I had no fear of heights, I wasn't eager to get on that gondola. "Isn't there a road to the casino?"

"Yes," said the driver, "but it is too dangerous. Believe me, the gondola is better."

Jim pulled a wad of bills from his pocket. "How much?"

Again, the driver shook his head. "I am sorry, but no. There's a taxi over there, maybe he's crazy enough to take you."

Jim got out of the car and walked over to the rattle-trap cab. In a few minutes he came back and opened my door. "He'll take us."

We'd only gone a few feet up Mount Parnitha when I started begging the cabbie to turn around. I'd been on some scary mountain roads, but this was nothing more than a goat path. I could hear the edge of the cliff crumbling beneath the taxi's tires. Our driver seemed to think the best way to beat the mountain curves was by surprise attack, gunning the engine as he roared up to it, then skidding around it on two wheels. With every hairpin turn, I screamed in terror, until finally Jim put his hand over my eyes, murmuring reassurances, and when, by some miracle, we arrived safe and sound at the casino, he crossed himself and handed our driver a tip that would allow the man to retire, assuming he survived the drive back down the mountain, which would be a solo journey, since the passengers he'd brought up the hill would be taking the gondola.

In the 1980s, with television audiences mimicking the lavish lifestyles of *Dallas* and *Dynasty*, while breathlessly awaiting the splendor of the upcoming royal wedding, casino attire had regained its rhinestone image from the Rat-Pack era. Jim and I were not the only couple in the casino dressed to the nines. Jim suggested Chemin de Fer. I'd never played the game, but I liked the French sophistication of it, and with Jim telling me how to bet, I did rather well, although not well enough to keep me from the blackjack tables. As a teenage rock singer in Birmingham, Alabama, I'd grown up, playing "21" in the Magic City's after-hours, and perfectly illegal, casinos, so I understood the rules of this game, even when they were spoken in Greek. The only problem was that at the end of the evening, when I cashed in my chips, they paid me in drachmas, and I had no idea how much I'd won.

Arriving back at the suite, heading from the living room down the hallway to our bedroom, I glanced here and there, then said to Jim, "Did you have everything shipped?"

He hung his suit in the closet, and pulled on his bathrobe, walking into the bedroom. "What did I have shipped?"

"Your packages, where are they?"

"What packages?"

"You went shopping today, remember?"

"Oh, yes." He walked to the closet and took out a bag. "Here it is." He brought forth a doll. "For Alex," he said. My three-year-old niece had a serious crush on her one-and-only uncle, and the feeling was more than mutual.

"It's beautiful, let me see it." I took the ten-inch doll, examining her red-skirted Greek costume, trimmed with golden coins. "Is this all you bought?"

Jim was now lying in bed, reading the *Los Angeles Times* he'd bought that afternoon. "That's all. This is not a shopping city."

Slipping the doll back into the bag, I added, "But the food makes up for it."

Jim lowered the newspaper to his chest. "Greece is not the only country with good food."

The next afternoon, we were on our way to Rome.

\* \* \*

So far, each hotel had been better than the last, but nothing could top the Hassler. Its location at the top of Rome's famed Spanish Steps was only one of many reasons I knew I would never want to leave. From the sincere warmth of the manager's welcome, to the sophisticated mix of contemporary and antique furnishings, the atmosphere was that of a palatial residence rather than the five-star hotel that it was. Nothing about the Hassler seemed to be "trying too hard." Its grace and refinement were effortless.

Wandering the spaces off the lobby, while our luggage disappeared to our suite, Jim and I came upon the Palm Court, and couldn't bear to leave until we'd stopped for Bellinis at one of the wrought iron tables within the ancient, ivied walls. *Heaven on earth*, I thought.

Our suite did not fall short.

"On such quick notice, Sol couldn't get us a city view, but we can switch rooms if one comes available," Jim apologized.

"Never!" I flung open the French doors to the Juliet balcony overlooking the gardens. "I feel like a princess in a fairytale."

Jim took me in his arms. "You are a princess in a fairytale."

I melted against his chest, sighing, and he led me to the bed.

One thrill after another. We dined that night at the Roof restaurant, with a panoramic view of Rome. As the waiter poured our Italian bubbly, the maître d' pointed out the Campidoligio, Piazza Navona, the Parthenon, and on and on, across the Eternal City spread before us.

With the sun going down, and the lights of the city coming up, while the pianist played "Three Coins in the Fountain," it was heady to the point of dizziness as I gazed across at my husband who looked like every tall dark handsome leading man rolled into one. If at El Morocco, I'd felt like Ava Gardner dancing with Clark Gable on the set of *Mogambo*; tonight, I

Hassler Hotel Palm Court (1980)

was Audrey Hepburn dining with Gregory Peck during the filming of *Roman Holiday*. Very likely, the co-stars had been here. Perhaps they'd even dined on carpaccio, caviar, foie gras and lobster, as we did.

Even though the rooftop "tour" provided by the maître d' had given us a literal bird's-eye view, Jim and I still felt obliged to take a guided tour. However, we also felt we could postpone it, at least until we'd had time to explore the Via Condotti, which was literally at the foot of the steps to our hotel.

Via Condotti is Rome's version of Rodeo Drive, but the way Jim tore through the designer boutiques, you would never have thought that we had our own Gucci, Krizia, and Missoni right down the street from our house in Beverly Hills When I pointed out that between our first Rodeo Drive excursion to buy my replacement wardrobe and the equally exhaustive shopping for my trousseau, I had more clothes than I could wear in a year's time, Jim waved it away. "Those are summer clothes. Italy is the place to shop for winter."

At the end of the day, we had purchased enough fine Italian knits and sleek leather sweaters, skirts, jackets, bags, boots and shoes to keep me warm through every winter for the rest of my life, as well as a few things to wear while in Rome. My favorite was a pair of cobalt blue patent-leather, stiletto-heeled sandals, with hot-pink polka-dotted bows. They murdered my feet, but it was worth it. I was never on my feet for long, anyway. Each time we stepped out of a boutique, we stepped into a sidewalk caffe for cappuccino, pinot grigio or our daily snack of prosciutto and fresher-than-fresh melon.

We did, of course, go to the must-see sites – the Pantheon, the Trevi Fountain, the Vatican, and so on – but most days we simply wandered the streets, ducking into shops, exploring. After covering the designer mecca of the Via Condotti, we widened our route to discover the kind of dusty little antique shops we both loved.

One day we happened upon a tiny store that specialized in vintage hardware, but it wasn't the gilt doorknobs and cabinet pulls that caught Jim's eye. He pointed to a painting leaning against the wall behind the counter. "What is that?"

The shopkeeper looked around as if he had no idea what Jim was referring to, before his eye fell on the painting. "Oh, yes," he shrugged, "I don't know. It was here when I came in this morning."

"May I see it?" Jim asked.

The man picked up the unframed painting and passed it across the counter. I stepped closer, to look while Jim inspected the obviously old, and apparently unsigned, oil painting of the Madonna and Child. There was no need to ask what Jim thought; I knew he loved it as much as I did, so I walked away, poking through the hardware in the bins, while he dickered with the clerk.

There were also the afternoons when Jim roamed on his own while I leisurely prepared for the evening out. Stepping into the bathroom of our suite was like stepping back in time to a Roman bath of the ancient age, surrounded by a mosaic mural depicting women in togas lifting tall vases and urns, from which mysterious liquids spilled into the bathwater. I lay back, closed my eyes and sipped my prosecco, imagining the women coming to life to pamper and soothe me with their fragrant oils.

One afternoon, while I was floating in the tub, Jim came in from a solo shopping trip, and as he had in Athens, pulled a doll out of a bag, this one dressed in Italian silk. "For Alex's collection."

"Ahh, lovely," I said.

Jim held out the doll, admiring it. "She was in a store window. Lucky find."

When he walked out to put the doll away, I glanced to my left and saw that, once again, he'd done the ring-box-on-the-bathtub sleight of hand. This time there were two boxes. Inside, the first was a Victorian gold ring with a rose-red ruby surrounded by diamonds set in a silver filigree oval that stretched to my knuckle. The box next to that one held a pair of ruby ear studs.

Jim peeked around the door and winked. I winked back, crooking my finger, and he walked to the tub, untying his robe, then lowered himself into the water, sliding in behind me, so that I lay against his chest. Even with the magnificence of Rome literally laid at our feet, our most memorable moments were right there in the Hotel Hassler. It didn't take long for our suite to feel like home, as if it were our own apartment in an Italian villa, and after a couple of weeks, we got into a routine, beginning in the morning with Jim showering and heading downstairs to the Palm Court for breakfast, while I woke slowly, donned my cream silk kimono, and began my day with breakfast beside the Juliet balcony, with the fragrance of the summer garden wafting through the open doors. While my morning repast had always been extremely light, sometimes toast and tea sans toast, on one of our first mornings in Rome, Jim breakfasted with me in the room, and to my surprise, asked the waiter to recommend a fish dish.

I never knew what type of fish, just that it was very mild and lightly sautéed in butter, to a perfection that I still count as one of the best meals of my life, so that from that day on, for the rest of our stay, I dined on that buttery, white delicacy every morning. But if the breakfast fish was my most memorable meal, Jim's was the Spaghetti alle Vongole Veraci – pasta with sweet baby clams in the shell – which we discovered on a late-after-noon stroll through the labyrinthine medieval alleyways of Trastevere, when we happened into Sabatini's, a classic Italian ristorante, which for ninety years had remained a favorite with locals as well as savvy tourists, such as we. Jim and I quickly became regulars. Dining al fresco at Sabatini's, beneath the amber glow cast by strings of Edison bulbs, with the Italian-tenor owner serenading his guests, was the quintessential Rome experience.

The days and nights of our *Roman Holiday* honeymoon melted into each other so sweetly that we began to fantasize about making the move permanent, which might have happened if my heartstrings hadn't been firmly tethered to that little white poodle back in Beverly Hills, who was impatiently waiting for Mommy, to come home.

# Chapter 18

I HAD BECOME A CARD-CARRYING member of the Real Wives of Beverly Hills, and even though my life seemed a fairy tale, my husband was eager to embrace the reality of family life, by introducing me to his mother, who hadn't the slightest clue her only son had given her a new daughter-in-law.

It was no secret that Jim dreaded breaking the news to her, even though he never gave a reason, except to say, "Trust me, it's better if we tell her after the fact." With the months going by without so much as a glimpse of *Mother*, my imagination turned her into a cross between Cruella DeVille and the Witch-Queen from *Snow White and the Seven Dwarfs*.

What a surprise when she turned out to be an eighty-four-year-old little doll with perfectly coifed beige-blonde hair, wearing a couture floral-print silk suit, and triple-strand pearls. When we arrived to pick her up at her Tudor-style mansion in Beverly Hills, I switched from front to backseat, leaving her the seat of honor next to Jim, and watching Jim assist her along the stone path to the porte cochere, I detected no rancor between them. They each smiled and conversed, as they made slow progress toward the car. Then when Jim opened the door to help her in, she giggled, "Somebody get the hoist."

Once she was comfortably settled into the front seat, Jim slid behind the wheel, and made the formal introduction.

"How do you do, Mrs. Halper?" I said.

She simpered, "Well, you don't have to be so formal, calling me Mrs. Halper. I am your mother-in-law."

"What would you like me to call you?" I asked.

"How about Mom?" She twisted in her seat to face me. "I don't understand why he kept us apart for so long." Glowering at Jim, she scolded, "Not inviting your own mother to your wedding, the very idea."

During the conversation, Jim had been steering us to the Bistro Garden. He kept his eyes on the street when he answered, "Your doctor would not have let you fly to Nashville, Mother."

She pursed her lips. "You could have at least invited me." That was the last she said about it, and at the restaurant, we eased into a companionable dinner, chatting amiably.

Deciding what to order, Mom quipped, "I'd like to have that skinny-angel spaghetti with tomato sauce, but I'll be wearing it by the time we leave."

Victoria wearing Holly Harp gown (1984). Photo courtesy of Harry Langdon

Jim said, "That's what dry cleaners are for, Mother." He took the menu from her, handing it to our captain, José, "Have them make her a small order of capellini with finely chopped fresh tomato and basil."

I ordered Schnitzel à la Holstein – fried breaded veal cutlets topped with an egg, sunny-side up – and when the entrees arrived, Mom ogled my plate with a sigh, "I wish I could still eat like that. My doctor won't let me eat anything." She lowered her eyes, "I had a heart attack."

Jim gave me a meaningful look. "She almost died."

Now I understood why he had delayed the news of our marriage, wisely waiting until it could be handled with no muss, no fuss, as it was.

Mom ignored him, continuing the food conversation. "How do you eat like that and keep your figure? I hardly eat a thing, and look at me." She patted her plump midriff. "Every time I go for a check-up I've gained another pound."

"It is harder for petite women like us, isn't it?" I said.

She did a Mae-West eye roll. "You said a mouthful, honey."

Laughing at her quick-witted pun, I loved my new mom already. Now it was time for me to meet my step-daughter.

*   *   *

I had known of Robbin Rae Halper's existence since early June when Jim told me that he'd be leaving me home alone one night because he had to go to his daughter's high school graduation, which necessitated the revelation of his first wife, Jerri, a girl he'd met at Beverly Hills High, who got pregnant on their honeymoon, a few days before he left for the army. According to his account, Jerri and Jim had divorced amicably as soon as he returned, and Jerri's second husband became more of a father to Robbin than he was.

I felt mixed emotions about meeting her. At eighteen, Robbin was three years older than my youngest sister, not an appropriate age to be my daughter, had I wanted a daughter, which I did not. But I did want her daddy, and it was looking like a package deal, so one evening about dusk, Jim and I pulled up to a neat white cottage in the Valley, and down the walk came an extravagantly tall, beautiful California blonde, sliding into the back seat, and flashing a brilliant smile. "Hi, I'm Robbin."

She might not be the right age to be my daughter, but she was the perfect age to be my friend, and as we got to know each other during girl-talk lunches and family dinners, I realized that if I ever did have a daughter, I'd want Robbin to be her role-model.

\*  \*  \*

Once I'd gotten to know Mom and Robbin, there were only one aunt and a couple of cousins left to meet in Jim's family, then he set about introducing my family and his. My mother and my youngest sister, Valerie, flew in for a visit, almost as soon as we returned from our honeymoon, and the first thing we did was get them together with Mom and Robbin for dinner, and with the six of us around the table at Romeo and Juliet, Mom's favorite Italian place, the vibe among us had the big happy family feeling that Italians do so well.

For the trip, I had planned that Mother and Valerie would each have a special outing. First came Mother's, a day at the races, which turned into one of the highlights of her life, when she came face-to-face with Bette Davis in the ladies' room.

Valerie's big day was a trip to Allen Edwards' salon on Rodeo Drive, where my personal stylist cut and permed her waist-length stick-straight locks into the head-full of shoulder-sweeping waves she'd dreamed of. Then came the most thrilling day for us all.

Mother, Valerie and I had returned home from a picnic lunch at the beach, cut short when Valerie declared the ocean breeze too chilly, saying she'd rather picnic by the pool at our house, which changed our course in a way that seemed eerily fortuitous, when just as Mother and I were gathering plates and utensils to take outside to the pool, the telephone rang.

I handed the plates in my hands to my housemaid, Maribel, and stepped into the breakfast room to take the call.

"I won the Pick Six," Jim said.

"Oh, good," I said. "We're getting ready to have deli takeout by the pool. Want to come join us?"

For most people, winning the Pick Six at Hollywood Park Racetrack would be a big deal on any day, but Jim won it so often, for me, it was literally just another day at the park. To explain, the Pick Six always pays off well, because winning it means you picked the winning horse in six consecutive races, which is no mean feat, but the purse is split between all the bettors who chose those six winning horses, so obviously, if the favorite wins every race, lots of people split the Pick Six, which means each winner might only get a few thousand dollars. On the other hand, if it's that rare day when long-shots are winning, the Pick Six might go to only one person, in which case, that person could win several hundred thousand dollars.

On the day that I answered his call with Mother and Valerie waiting for lunch by the pool, the one Pick Six winner was Jim.

"Two-hundred-and-fifty-thousand," he said.

"Jim just won two-hundred-and-fifty-thousand-dollars!" I screamed.

Standing in the doorway, Valerie froze with her jaw locked open and Mother dropped into a chair at the breakfast-room table.

On the other end of the line, Jim was laughing. "I suggest you forget lunch and take your mother and sister shopping."

What Mother and Valerie didn't know was that I had won big, too. Jim's generous deal with me was that whenever he won the Pick Six, I got the consolation money, which meant I was one of the winners of the pool set aside for bettors who chose five out of the six winning horses, and since Jim always put in multiple tickets, totaling around $20, 000, whenever he won the Pick Six, I won a share of the consolation pool, many times over.

"Let's go to Holly Harp," I said, placing my fingertip beneath Valerie's soft little chin, "She's even smaller than we are and some of her things are very youthful, perfect for you, and we'll buy something for Robin, too.

Holly was my favorite fashion designer, whose atelier was in Sunset Plaza, a few minutes' drive up Sunset Boulevard from our house. On my first day in L.A., after moving from Alabama, my friend Doug Jencks, who had recently relocated from Birmingham to West Hollywood, was giving me a tour of the hot-spots, and when we passed the Holly Harp boutique, I remarked, "Someday I'll wear her clothes."

Doug never forgot that comment and reminded me of it frequently, after I married Jim and learned that he and Holly were friends. The first clothes Jim chose for me were Holly's designs, another fairy-tale wish come true.

*　*　*

The week after Mother and Valerie left for home, more Alabamians arrived. Bobby Daye, owner of the Bachelors' Showboat, where I performed for five years, came for a visit with his glamorous wife, my dear friend, Mary Rose. For the first few days, the four of us ate and shopped our way around Beverly Hills, then on the weekend, headed down to La Costa Resort, where Jim always leased a house for the Del Mar racing season. This was the highlight of Bobby and Mary Rose's visit. If you want to see stars, the Del Mar Turf Club is a good spot. Mary Rose had always been unabashedly star-struck, so Bobby kept an eye peeled and would say to her, sotto voce, "Glen Campbell and Tanya Tucker at that table… Burt Bacharach down there… Patrick Wayne coming this way…

Mary Rose and I ordered Monte Cristo sandwiches for lunch and the guys had steaks. We drank a few cocktails, won a few races, and a good time was had by all. Then came the moment for the Pick Six announcement. The big screen flashed $90,000. Jim got up from the table. "I'll be right back."

A few minutes later he walked up to the table and said, "It was me."

"What?" Bobby asked.

Jim grinned, "I won it."

I said, "The whole thing?"

"Yep."

Bobby stretched his eyes, blinking, as if trying to clear his vision. "You mean you just won ninety-thousand dollars?"

Jim nodded.

Still in disbelief, Bobby fell back in his chair, "I'll be damned."

Mary Rose was speechless.

For me it was just another day at the park.

And another and another, each as blissful as the one before, so that as summer wound down to fall, and the time for *Hee Haw's* October taping neared, I wondered why I was bothering to go to Nashville, at all. I certainly didn't need the paycheck, and I'd never been motivated by money anyway. Pursuit of fame? No, I'd learned that fame wasn't all that appealing once you'd seen it up close and personal, and my relationship with Buck Owens was about as up close and personal as you could get.

So, if I wasn't doing it for the money or the fame, then why leave my fairytale life for three weeks to swap my Gucci for gingham and tell corny jokes sitting on a haybale that made me itch?

When I posed the question to Jim, he said, "Because it's your career. Besides, I want to meet Buck."

*Meet Buck*? It had to happen sooner or later.

*Hee Haw* Set (1980)

Denver Fairmont Hotel performance Poster (1980)

# Chapter 19

**JIM AND I WALKED OVER** to the "Buck's Place" set, where he was sitting on a barrel behind a microphone, holding his red, white and blue guitar.

"Buck, this is my husband, Jim," I said.

Buck stood up, offering his hand, "Hello, Jim, glad to meet you."

Then came Jack McFadden and, one-by-one, the Buckaroos, then Bob Boatman and Sam Lovullo, welcoming my husband to the *Hee Haw* family, while Jim poured on the charm, and said all the right things, fitting in with such ease that everyone began congratulating me for marrying this great guy. And to think I had assumed they would be congratulating him on catching *me*.

The first full-cast day was the same. Jim achieved instant male-bonding with the men, and struck the right balance with the girls, friendly without flirtation. I still wasn't sure that Buck and Jim would ever be friends, but at least the hardest part was over, and they wouldn't be seeing each other often. Buck wasn't making any personal appearances, which meant my Buckaroo gig was now limited to *Hee Haw*. Fortunately, my solo career was taking off. Immediately after finishing the October taping, I was flying into Denver for a two-week engagement opening for Tex Williams in the showroom at the Fairmont Hotel.

Then it was back to my fairy-tale life in Beverly Hills, and I realized that I really could have my cake and eat it, too. Like several other *Hee Haw* Honeys, I would learn to play on both sides of the fence between hillbilly and Hollywood.

The first week of December, Buck called and asked me to come to Bakersfield. This would be the first time I'd made the drive. Ignoring Buck's "black vision" about me owning a car, Jim had surprised me with a damson-red Jaguar XJS as an engagement gift, so I was no longer dependent on public transportation. Far from it. Had I not wanted to drive myself,

Victoria with Buck Owens' guitar. (2003)

our chauffeur, Marco, could have taken me in the limo, but I was eager to get my new Jag on the freeway for its first road trip.

I had no idea why Buck had beckoned, but I was used to his mysterious ways, and they usually turned out well. When I walked into his office, his trademark red-white-and-blue guitar was beside his desk chair, so I assumed he meant to play something for me.

"You finished my song!" I clapped my hands with glee.

Picking up our old conversational gambit, he said, "What song's that?"

"Stop it, Buck, you know which song."

"I gave up on that one." He reached for the guitar, "No, I just wanted to give you your Christmas present."

"I wish you'd told me," I fumbled, "I didn't bring yours." Buck and I both knew I hadn't given one thought to a present for him.

"You don't need to get me anything." He took a marker from the pencil cup on his desk and wrote on the guitar: *To Jesse Rose, Merry Christmas 1980, Buck.*

"I just wanted you to have this." His face looked sad when he handed me the guitar, and my heart felt heavy taking it.

\* \* \*

During the three Decembers I had lived in L.A., I'd never bothered to put up a Christmas tree. My Christmas was back home in Alabama, but while Jim had every intention of being part of my family's southern-style celebration, he wanted to start our own Christmas tradition at our home in Beverly Hills.

"I've always thought the bay window in the living room would be a perfect spot for a beautifully decorated tree," he said, "It could be seen from the road, and would brighten the rush hour for drivers stuck in traffic on Coldwater Canyon."

I threw my arms around him. "Oh, goody! Michael and Judy can help decorate, and I'll bake cookies. Raisin oatmeal, so the house will smell like Christmas spice."

The next day, I went on a whirlwind Christmas jaunt, up and down the streets of Beverly Hills, loading my Jaguar with enough ornaments to decorate the tree in Rockefeller Center. I also stopped at Francis-Orr Stationery to order custom-engraved Christmas cards and stockings embroidered, *Jim, Vicki* and *Neesh.*

The next night, getting home from the office, Jim came in the front door with his arms full of beautifully wrapped packages, singing "Deck the halls with gifts from Holly," meaning, Holly Harp, of course. "Gotta have presents to put under the tree."

Michael and his new roommate Judy, who had made the move from New York, would arrive shortly, and I had just put the oatmeal cookies in to bake.

"You were right," Jim said, "The whole house smells like Christmas. Mm-mm, an oven-fresh oatmeal cookie with a cold glass of milk, what could be better?" He winked at me, "I love my wife."

Despite its sunshine-and-palm-trees reputation, Los Angeles gets chilly on winter nights, so Jim built a roaring blaze in the fireplace, and between hanging ornaments on the shimmering tree, we warmed ourselves, sitting on the brick hearth, munching cookies, feeding Neesh the crumbs, as cozy and Christmassy as a Bing Crosby movie.

The following week we hung the stockings on the mantel, mailed the Christmas cards and made travel arrangements for our trip to Alabama, which would start in Birmingham, shopping for my family, and climax with a "progressive" celebration on Christmas Eve, beginning with my mother's side of the family at a storybook candlelit gathering at my Pickett grandparents' Victorian home, then move on to my father's family at his sister, my Aunt Nell's, house for a rip-roaring time with cousins of all ages, ending with everyone donning outdoor gear to gather in the front yard for our annual fireworks display.

Then it was time for Jim and me to pile into our rental car for the drive back to Birmingham, and a red-eye flight home to Los Angeles, for Christmas Dinner at our house with Mom and Robbin. Mom brought the fruitcake, I roasted the turkey, and never was there a more perfect Christmas.

On New Year's Eve we celebrated with friends at Club Barrington, wearing party hats, tooting horns and drinking too much champagne, while I snuck admiring glances at the diamond art-deco wristwatch Jim had slipped under the tree for me. Enjoying my pleasure, every ten minutes he'd wink and ask, "Is it midnight?" giving me an excuse to make a show of lifting my wrist to check the time. "Nope, can't kiss me yet," I'd repeat, which of course, he would do anyway.

On New Year's Day we recovered from the night before, sitting at the Stickley table in our breakfast room, wearing terrycloth robes, swilling coffee while we watched football games. During commercials, Jim read the *Los Angeles Times*, commenting on this and that, at one point saying, "You need to go to I. Magnin tomorrow."

"I do?"

"Mm-hm. I. Magnin has a top-notch fur salon and they've got a sale ad in the newspaper. It gets cold sitting outside in the Turf Club at Santa Anita. Go get a full-length mink."

"Don't you want to come with me?"

"Can't. First day back at the office, crammed calendar. Get whatever you want, just don't get it altered." He grinned. "If I don't like it, I'll take it back."

It wasn't as simple as that. The next day, surrounded, wall-to-wall, by luxurious furs, after grueling hours of trying on coats, I still couldn't make a selection, only managing to narrow it down to three: the black, the brown or the white? Doing her best to help, the sales-lady pointed out the merits of each, further confusing me, until I finally broke down and called Jim for his opinion. "The black mink is a Karl Lagerfeld for Chloe, obviously very beautiful, but the white one is extremely plush – I think the sales-lady said it's sable – and I just love the color of the brown one, Autumn Haze. Could you please, *please*, run over here and help me decide?"

"Get all three," he said.

* * *

From the first time Jim set foot in Alabama, he'd been looking for a house to buy. Every time we visited, which was quite often, he and Daddy headed out on a search for our "house in the country," never turning up the perfect place.

Then one day, Mother called. "I've found it."

According to her story, she'd braved a rainstorm to attend a wedding just across the county line, in Maplesville, and on the highway to the church, suddenly, through the pouring rain, appeared this beautiful old house with white columns, set far back from the road, in a field of daffodils surrounded by hundred-year-old oaks.

As a child, I frequently visited my friend Sheila, who lived in Maplesville, and I didn't remember such a house, but it sounded worth checking out, so during our Easter visit, on Sunday afternoon, I suggested we go take a look. Unfortunately, everybody had eaten too much of a good thing at lunch, and begged off, so it ended up being just Daddy and I on the hunt for the mystery house, which shouldn't be hard to find, since Maplesville was a one-street town.

The house was even more beautiful than Mother had described, and it was completely abandoned, the double French doors leading from the veranda, wide open. I stepped into the center hall and said, "I want it."

A month later, we were sitting in the front yard of the house, in a big tent with a multitude of bidders. For support and advice, we'd brought along the former president of People's Bank of Centreville, C.E. Hornsby, and his southern-belle wife, Emily.

When the furious bidding began, Miss Emily turned to me and whispered, "I'm scay-ahd to blink my eyes."

I was scared, too. People were shouting out and hands going up so fast, that when the whole thing was over, I had no idea whether we'd gotten the house, or not. I clutched Jim's leg, "What happened?"

He chuckled and kissed my forehead. "It's yours."

I immediately ran onto the porch and into the hallway, flattening myself against the wall, hugging the house. Then I ran from room to room, with the residents of Maplesville joining me in a group happy-dance, while Jim trailed behind with the Hornsbys, checking the house in earnest. There was much to be done.

Twin Oaks in the Grove, Maplesville, Alabama (1981)

Arriving back at my parents' house to share the good news, Daddy happily agreed to be project manager and general overseer, hiring local contractors, making payments, keeping records, with the goal of having the house in livable shape for Jim and me, after the *Hee Haw* taping in June, which was coming right up.

\* \* \*

This time, Jim suggested that instead of staying at Spence Manor, we stay at the Maxwell House Hotel, with the rest of the *Hee Haw* gang. Besides being a friendly gesture, he welcomed the opportunity to stay in Nashville's newest luxury hotel, complete with a gourmet restaurant, VIP lounge, spa, and other amenities.

Jim was correct on all counts. The VIP lounge was a private sanctuary for *Hee Haw's* cast and guest stars, the rooftop restaurant lived up to its gourmet hype, and the spa's whirlpool and steam room provided the perfect wind-down before going to bed. But the biggest benefit of all was the proximity to the other *Hee Haw* Honeys.

As would become our habit, I flew into Nashville for *Hee Haw's* first work week, then Jim joined me on Friday for a long weekend, continuing the routine throughout my three-week stay. June of 1981 was my first time at the Maxwell House among the other girls. One afternoon, when we'd finished up early at the studio, I answered a knock at my door, and there stood Mackenzie Colt, dressed for the afternoon off, in khakis and a white man-tailored shirt. She flipped her Farrah-Fawcett locks, "Hi, what are you up to?"

Mackenzie had a naturally friendly way, so earlier that day, when she'd joked around with me during the taping of "Cast Songs" I'd put it down to our placement beside the Hager Twins, whose jovial spirit infected anyone who came within their orbit. But seeing Mackenzie's brilliant smile at my door, I thought perhaps I had given myself short shrift, maybe she genuinely enjoyed our playfulness on the set, and wanted to get to know me better.

Sitting down at the dinette table in my room, she began to chat by asking me all about my singing career, which was a common bond, then she told me about herself. I was shocked to learn that she'd married and had a child while she was still in high school, which was impossible to reconcile with the ambitious young woman she appeared to be.

"My body matured earlier than my judgment," she explained, pointing to her breasts. "I had these boobs when I was fourteen, so you can imagine."

Mackenzie and I shared stories and became friends.

A few minutes after she left, I heard another knock at my door and there stood Cathy Baker. "Hi, want some company?"

Cathy was even easier to talk to than Mackenzie, although I didn't need to do much talking. Cathy could keep up a long and entertaining conversation all by herself. Now I had two pals. Or as Cathy charmingly put it, we were "chums."

Next was Gunilla Hutton. Knock-knock-knock. "Hi. Want to go grab some dinner?" Make that three pals.

After an evening of giggles and girl-talk over dinner with Gunilla, I headed back to my room to call Jim with the full report. "I think I just went through *Hee Haw* Honey sorority rush."

"Did you get a bid?"

Despite a core group of cast-members who were the heart of the *Hee Haw* family, each season, others would come and go. That summer of '81, we got three new cast members, two Honeys – a buxom blonde named Diana Goodman and a leggy brunette named Nancy Traylor – and a Bo Duke-type *Hee Haw* Hunk, Chase Randolph. But although this was intended as a PR ploy, any hype surrounding their hiring was lost on the

*Hee Haw* Honeys Cheerleaders, L-R Lisa Todd, Linda Thompson, Misty Rowe, Victoria Hallman, Gunilla Hutton, Jackie Waddell (1984)

cast, particularly the Honeys. We were too busy gossiping and making lunch and dinner plans to notice a few new faces among the group, and I was too newly-inducted to worry about them. I had waited my turn, now they could wait theirs.

Then one day, I had to go to the studio on a Saturday, and whom should I run into but our new brunette, Nancy Traylor, walking in carrying a boom box.

"Hi, Nancy, are you here for wardrobe, too?"

"No, Charlie McCoy is helping me with some songs to do on the show. I'm a singer. Didn't you know?"

I didn't know she was a singer, and I knew she'd be better off not to let anyone else know either. Most of the girls on the show fancied themselves singers whether they could sing or not, so competition for solos was fierce, and the producers didn't like it one bit. Even Barbi Benton, who had a gold record under her belt, worked her way out of a gig on *Hee Haw*, by demanding too many song spots. How lucky I'd been to have Jack McFadden's advice about standing in the corner until called upon. Too bad Nancy didn't have somebody like Jack. I feared for her job. As it turned out, Nancy was gone from the show so quickly, none of us ever got to hear her sing.

The way the calendar fell that June was fortunate, since my three weeks at *Hee Haw* began on Monday, June 1, and ended on Friday, June 19, getting me home in time for our first wedding anniversary, which fell on a Sunday.

I was proud to have found a gift I knew Jim would like. One day while shopping in Gucci, I'd heard him remark favorably on a navy double-breasted blazer, after which, I immediately rushed to the store to have it wrapped and hidden in my closet, waiting for June 21.

As soon as we got in from the airport on Friday night, Jim set a small beribboned white box on my dressing table. "Our anniversary is not until Sunday," I said.

He smirked. "You know I'm not good at delaying gratification."

"Okay, then." I went to the closet and pulled out the Gucci shopping bag, handing it to him. "You first."

He exclaimed over the blazer as if he'd never seen one before, trying it on, looking at himself in the full-length brass mirror, pointing out the alterations he'd have done on Monday, then he said, "Your turn."

My small box held a pair of art deco diamond earrings, and I couldn't stop looking in my dressing table mirror, shaking my head, making them dance, entranced by their sparkle in the light of the vanity lamps. "We must go somewhere fancy tomorrow night, so I can wear these."

When I opened my eyes the next morning, another beribboned box was on the marble top of my nightstand. Lying beside me, Jim's eyes were open, and he was smiling, as if he'd been waiting for me to wake up.

I stroked his bare shoulder. "I don't have another present for you."

He pulled me close. "My present is the privilege of looking at my gorgeous wife wearing the things I give to her and knowing that she belongs to me. Are you going to open it?"

I untied the ribbon, lifted the top of the velvet case, and caught my breath. The bracelet inside was a deco circlet of diamonds set in platinum. Jim fastened it on my wrist. "This will be beautiful with your diamond watch."

"We'd better go somewhere very *very* fancy tonight," I said.

Jim chose L'Orangerie, L.A.'s bastion of haute French cuisine, which, secretly, was my favorite, and as they say, when in France . . . I would wear my new black-silk strapless Chloé chemise, with the rhinestone lightning embroidered down the front, très chic. Sitting at my dressing table, putting the finishing touches on my hair, Jim walked up behind me, reaching both arms around my neck. I leaned my head back to look up at him, about to say, "Don't muss my hair," when I felt a tickle at my nape, and heard a tiny click. The diamond necklace he had fastened around my neck matched the bracelet I'd opened that morning. I ran my fingers around the strand, staring in the mirror with my mouth open.

Jim brushed his hands together. "Now you have no gifts to open on our anniversary tomorrow, but I couldn't wait.

On Sunday morning, Michael dropped by with an anniversary card for us. First, he came into the bedroom to see my "loot," then he went into the breakfast room, and put his hand on Jim's shoulder. "So, you gave her diamond earrings, bracelet and necklace from Frances Klein on Rodeo, and she gave you a navy blazer. Hm," he patted Jim's shoulder, "You made out like a bandit as usual, bud."

Even on the other side of the house, in my bedroom, I could hear them laughing. I tied my kimono and walked into the breakfast room. "What's so funny?"

*   *   *

Later that day, driving home from the racetrack, Jim admitted that he did have another anniversary gift for me. "Sort of." We were being honored at a "big deal" banquet on November 14 at the Beverly Hilton, and I could invite whichever guests I pleased, to sit at our table.

"The Honeys!" I exclaimed.

During October's taping of *Hee Haw*, my friendship with the other girls had deepened. Once Mackenzie, Cathy and Gunilla welcomed me into the magic circle, Linda Thompson and LuLu Roman, the remaining members of the "clique," were a cinch. As soon as they stopped calling me Jesse Rose, and switched to Victoria, or even more so, Vicki, I knew I was in. Putting together a table of beautiful people for a Beverly Hills black-tie affair, who better to invite than the Honeys? I'd invite Gunilla and her latest flame Jim McDonough, Linda Thompson and her new hubby Bruce Jenner, Mackenzie Colt, and Michael could be her date, and Doug and Sasha Jencks.

With that instant decision made, I asked Jim, "What kind of awards banquet?"

"We're accepting a Scopus Award on behalf of the Foundation."

"What is a Scopus Award and what did we do to deserve it?"

"Humanitarian endeavors. They're awarded by the American Friends of the Hebrew University, but we won't be in the spotlight, because Nancy Reagan is getting one the same night."

Victoria wearing anniversary gift art deco diamond earrings (1984)
Photo courtesy of Harry Langdon

When I called to invite Linda Thompson, she said reverently, "Victoria. Are you telling me you're getting a Scopus Award?" Apparently, she was more informed than I.

Johnny Carson was the emcee. Frank Sinatra and Luciano Pavarotti were the entertainment. The ballroom was abloom with Reagan-red roses, and hearing Sinatra sing "Nancy with the Smiling Face" to the First Lady was unforgettable. Then Pavarotti took the stage and the magnificence of his voice filled the room, but even that could not compare with the tears that sprang to my eyes, seeing the pride on my husband's face when Frank Sinatra introduced Jim's father's best friend, Jim's trustee Harry Silbert, calling him "the leader, the general, of the American Friends of the Hebrew University."

And so, on behalf of the Halper Foundation, which was founded by Jim's parents, we accepted the Scopus Award, and although I still didn't quite comprehend it, I knew that something very important was happening in that room on that night.

Victoria performing on the *Grand Ole Opry* (1984)

# Chapter 20

OUR COUNTRY PLACE IN MAPLESVILLE, Twin Oaks in the Grove, as we called it, was taking more renovation than anticipated, and the estimated move-in date had passed June by six-months. Jim shrugged it off. "I'd rather move in at Christmastime, it'll be more memorable."

"Moving in" was stretching it, but by December we did have all new plumbing, wiring, alarm system, and the two units required to heat a five-thousand-square-foot house, with twelve-foot ceilings. We also had a functioning bath and three rooms that were beginning to show the promise of what the house would become – flowing taffeta draperies in the master bedroom perfectly matched the pale blue walls; the floors and paneling in the library were refinished to a gleaming patina; and the kitchen had custom cabinets painted cobalt blue, with countertops of hand-made Portuguese tiles featuring fruits, vegetables and farm animals; but for the moment, our only furnishings were family cast-offs and a few pieces that we'd wisely picked up at an antique auction a few months back. This state of "work in progress" only made us love the house more, and on our first morning after arrival, Jim walked into the kitchen and declared, "We need a little Christmas."

Since, along with the house, we'd bought forty acres, that afternoon, Jim and Daddy trudged out into the woods and cut a tree from our own property, then we gathered friends and family to string popcorn garlands, while the kids cut out construction-paper ornaments, all very merry, indeed.

The next morning, I saw the ghost.

Before the ink had dried on our deed to the house, we began hearing rumors that it was haunted, and these were not just ghost stories handed down through generations. Only a few months before our Christmas visit, the exterminator we'd hired fled the house, telling his co-workers that he heard voices when no one was there, and my father, who firmly did not believe in ghosts, admitted he'd walked into the hall one day and heard someone say, "Get out." Then he'd waved away his silliness. "Aw, probably just a bullfrog croaking in the basement."

*Ha.* My daddy had lived his whole life on the banks of the Cahaba River that split the town of Centreville in two. He'd heard a lot of bullfrogs, and he'd never heard one say, "Get out."

While Jim and I found the ghost-talk interesting, none of it scared us. There was, however, one thing that disturbed us. Literally. Every morning, precisely at six a.m., the TV and clock radio in our bedroom came on.

So, when I first saw the apparition in the hall, I convinced myself that it had something to do with my earlier than usual wake-up. For a moment, I stood there, staring at the blue-gray misty shape of a human head and shoulders, blinking, trying to clear the sleep from my eyes, struggling to make sense of what I was seeing, until it finally hit me that even though the alarm was turned off, the infra-red was still covering the hall. Of course. The apparition was floating directly in the beam of the infra-red; it was nothing more than a distortion of the light. Silly me, imagining I'd seen a ghost. I rambled on into the kitchen to make coffee.

That afternoon we drove to Centreville for a visit with our friends Buster and Roselynn Pittman. Knowing that ghosts were something of a hobby for Roselynn, I laughingly recounted my ghost incident, finishing with my solution of distorted light from the infra-red.

Roselynn nodded, "It was the infra-red, all right. Don't you know that infra-red cameras are what they use to photograph ghosts? Ghosts are visible in infra-red light. That's why you were able to see it."

"Oh."

Jim said, "I'm glad we've got a ghost. People will be afraid to come around the house when we're not there."

Ghost or not, our first Christmas in the house was as memorable as Jim predicted, but neither of us could have predicted the surprise I received upon return to L.A.

For the past year, not only had I been performing with the Buckaroos, on *Hee Haw*, but in concert, as well. They had decided that just because Buck no longer wanted to "gig," didn't mean they had to quit, which was fine with me, and apparently fine with Buck, because as soon as I got back from Alabama, he called and asked me to come to Bakersfield to get my Christmas gift.

* * *

"I hope it's another guitar" I said, giving him a hug as I walked into his office.

"Nope," he said. "Better than that."

I clapped my hands. "You finished my song!"

He sank into his chair, and closed his eyes, rolling his head side-to-side. "Get over it, Jesse Rose."

I flounced into the chair that was my familiar place beside his desk. "What, then?"

"You know Mackenzie Colt worked with us for a little while, several years back."

"Mm-hm," I nodded.

"And we cut a couple of demos on her."

"Mm-hm."

"Well, the past few days, one of those songs has been playing in my head, and I think we ought to cut it on you. In fact, I think we ought to cut a whole album."

Jack McFadden once told me that there were only two people in the world he could never second-guess; Buck was one, I was the other. Sitting there, staring at Buck staring at me, I knew exactly what Jack meant. Here I was, thinking my career had settled into a comfortable routine, and along comes Buck with a swift kick in the pants.

"When do we start?"

"Now." He got up and pressed "play" on the tape machine next to his desk, and Mackenzie's voice sang, "You're my favorite song, every day and night long, I play you over and over again . . ."

"I still think it's a hit song, but that's not a hit record. We'll do it different this time. I'll produce, Jim Shaw will co-produce. We've got some other good songs."

"I might have some, too." I said.

"Great, bring 'em in. I thought we'd get started first part of the year, so Merry Christmas, Little Classy Sassy."

He hadn't called me that in a long time.

* * *

"Buck Owens and Jim Shaw producing Jesse Rose McQueen at Buck Owens Recording Studio in Bakersfield Calif." – *Billboard*, February 27, 1982

When *Billboard* deems your recording session worthy of announcement in the hallowed pages of their magazine, you can be sure it's a big deal. But as usual, it went right over my head. I can just hear Buck muttering to Jack, his oft-repeated, "I'll get her attention one of these days."

This would not be the day. I was interested, but not as excited as I should have been, which did nothing to shorten the process. Jim Shaw or Buck would come up with a song, call me to come to Bakersfield, the three of us would attempt to coordinate our calendars, finally settling on a date, then we'd start cutting the song, which might take several trips, then I'd find a song that I liked and the whole process would start over. Our goal was ten songs. By June, we'd finished five, and Buck decided to preview it to some of his pals, first of all, Buddy Killen, owner of Tree International, the largest country-music publisher in the world. Not a bad place to start. Buddy liked it. He thought the songs were good and he thought I sang them well, but he didn't think we had a hit single – yet.

Buck was pleased. He patted my hand, "Don't worry, we'll get it."

Jack McFadden agreed. Over lunch at the Maxwell House coffee shop, he told me, "It can take a long time to find a hit song, and believe me, it's all about the song, not the production, not the singer, the song." Then he launched into a story.

"Kenny Rogers used to hang around *Hee Haw* all the time. I'm talking about when he was down on his luck, after his rock-and-roll thing with the *First Edition* but before he made it in country music. He was always pushing some new project, and I'd always listen, never heard anything that got me excited. Then one day, he took me over into a corner with a little cassette player and when he pressed the button, out came 'You Picked a Fine Time to Leave Me, Lucille.' I slapped him on the back and said, 'Congratulations, my man. That's your next number-one.' It's like that, you know it when you hear it." He stirred his ice-tea. "Just like I knew it the first time I heard you." He waved his hand, "Naw, naw, I knew it before I heard you, I knew it the minute I laid eyes on you."

"Funny, that's what Buck said."

"Jesse Rose, when you've been in this business as long as Buck and I have, that's all it takes to tell if somebody's got it, one look."

"How did you know I could sing, just by looking at me?"

"I didn't, but I knew you'd be great onstage and even greater on camera. Videos are the wave of the future in the music industry, and that will be your medium."

George Lindsey and Victoria "*Hee Haw* Honkytonk" segment. (1983)

I wondered how long it would be before country music caught onto the video craze.

I was enjoying *Hee Haw* more with every taping. Among my besties, I now counted members of the *Hee Haw* cast who lived in Los Angeles – Gunilla and I kept a regular power-walk schedule, Misty and I lunched at trendy spots, Linda and I spent lazy afternoons by her pool in Malibu, and even Jim had found a *Hee Haw* buddy in George Lindsey – but I also looked forward to the semi-annual reunions with the rest of the cast and crew: *LuLu, Cathy, group hug! Gailard, come here and make me laugh.*

Then there were the guest stars, hundreds of them, but if I had to name one who impressed me most, it would be Ray Charles. You see – where Ray didn't – *Hee Haw* worked with cue cards, but obviously, that did not work for Ray. *Hee Haw* cast members never got a script ahead of time, we simply read whatever was on the giant card they popped up in front of us, and guest stars were only given the script for a short read-through before doing it on camera, so even with that head-start it usually took several takes for them to get the hang of it. With Ray Charles unable to do a read-through of his material for "Pickin' 'n' Grinnin'," we all wondered how it would go.

In my eleven years on the show, Ray Charles is the only guest star I recall, who got every one of his lines exactly right the first time, with no retakes.

Most fun guest star? That's harder, but the group *Alabama* comes to mind.

Jeff Cook kept us laughing in the makeup room all day. Then later that afternoon when the cast was released, as usual, we were all gunning our engines, heading for the hotel as fast as we could get out of there, when suddenly, the car ahead of me screeched to a halt, and I slammed on the brakes, causing a chain reaction in the line-up behind me. *What the frick?*

Jeff Cook got out of the car that had stopped traffic, and ran back to mine, motioning me to roll down my window. He stuck his head in. "Got one more joke I forgot to tell you."

Sweetest guest star? I'd have to say Kathy Mattea, who ended up being my wonderful next-door neighbor for thirteen years, but I would also nominate Naomi Judd. As the *Judds*, Wynonna and Naomi appeared on *Hee Haw* more than once, but I particularly recall a visit when they were absolutely at the zenith of their stardom, and some up-and-coming wannabe took so much time getting his act together that after waiting the whole day and much of the night, Sam Lovullo was forced to apologize to the *Judds*, and tell them there was no time left for their performance. I didn't hear the conversation, but I can imagine how sheepishly he must have asked, "Can you possibly come back tomorrow?"

Most acts would have left hours before it came to that, but astonishingly, the *Judds* agreed to come back, which they did. But that's not the end of the story.

Victoria with George Strait, Kathy Mattea, T. Graham Brown, Randy Owen,
Jeff Cook (1980s). photo courtesy of Kathy Mattea, personal collection

At the time, Gwen our hairstylist was big pregnant, and Naomi arrived the next day, carrying a package, which she handed to Gwen. "I couldn't come back without bringing you a baby gift."

Cutest guest star? Mmm, I have two cute stories about John Schneider.

The *Hee Haw* Honeys were infamous for our revealing costumes, but what the audience didn't know was that we would have much preferred more covering, especially since the median temperature of the studio must have been somewhere around thirty-three degrees. So, one day, I was walking onto the set wearing my extremely low cut, indecently short costume, when from behind, I felt a very warm wool-tweed jacket draped around my shoulders, and turned to see John Schneider standing there.

"You've got to be freezing in here," he said.

"Thank you very much," I replied. "You are so sweet." He was wearing jeans and a cotton shirt. "But won't you be cold, now? You've got to sing, your songs are coming up next, your throat needs to be warm."

He shook his head. "I'm fine," and continued chatting, asking me where I lived, how long I'd been on the show, the usual, until the stage manager finally yelled out, "John! We're waiting for you!"

John yelled back, "Sorry, but I'm talking to Victoria right now." The studio audience, who had been watching from above, burst into applause.

Another time, when John was guest-starring, my mother and her Aunt Martha were visiting the set, so when my turn came to be in the Kornfield with John, they stood nearby, paying close attention.

As was the routine, our cue-card "tech" showed us the joke, then John and I sat down side-by-side on the apple crates hidden behind the cornstalks, then popped up on cue, read our lines perfectly and exited the Kornfield. Two professionals, one take, in and out under three minutes.

When I got over to Mother and Martha, where they'd been watching John and me do our thing, instead of the proud smiles I expected, Martha gave me a disgusted look. "If I were you," she said, "I believe I would've messed that up a few times."

For every star and every day on the *Hee Haw* set, there's a great story, but that June taping of 1982 was special because Jim and I would be in Nashville for our second wedding anniversary, and Jim decided to throw a party. Since the Maxwell House was a high-end hotel, all it took was giving the event manager carte blanche, and putting out the word to cast and crew, *Y'all come!* The mountains of shrimp on ice, the carving stations – the open bar – but most memorable for me, were the egg rolls from Joy Young in Birmingham, which my cousin Donna Wyatt just happened to know were my favorite food, and therefore, she and her husband came in ahead of party time, delivering a load of them to the Maxwell House kitchen, for a special anniversary treat.

Jim waited until bedtime to give me my gift, an art deco diamond watch.

When I reminded him that I already had a diamond watch, he said, "You think I don't know that? What's wrong with having two? This one's an Audemars Piguet, the finest in the world." He kissed the top of my head. "And you deserve the finest."

Perhaps it was a portent of the summer that was about to begin, which was one of our best, beginning with the day that Jim came in from the office and announced, "We need another house."

What he really meant was that we needed a *bigger* house, except that wasn't really true either. The truth was, *he,* not we, *wanted* a bigger house, which ended up being across the street a few blocks up, on a promontory overlooking the Canyon. Sandra Dee was the former owner and Charlton Heston was our next-door neighbor, meaning he lived on the next promontory up the hill. This was the more expensive side of the street because the view was spectacular, and not only was the house larger, it was also newer. But that didn't mean I liked it more.

Our first house had been warm and cozy, like the house in the movie *The Enchanted Cottage*. The new house was a two-story Tudor style, of stucco, brick and rough-hewn beams, surrounded by a gated wall constructed of the same stucco, brick and beams, none of which looked genuinely Tudor, but what was the point of building a Tudor house in Los Angeles, anyway? The living room was spacious and beigely inoffensive, but I immediately replaced the garish dining-room wallpaper with ivory watered silk; the breakfast room had a wide glass slider that led to a covered patio and pool overlooking the canyon, so that got a thumbs-up, and I liked the cheerful yellow Mexican-tile counter-tops in the kitchen. The den rated three plus-marks for its glass slider, wet bar and fireplace, which would be a snuggly spot for Jim and me to watch *Cheers, M\*A\*S\*H, Dallas, Dynasty*, and our other favorite shows, then, upstairs was the master suite, luxuriously large by any standards, with its adjoining sitting room and two-room spa bath. Beyond all that, were other rooms – guest quarters, maid's, laundry, etc. – which I would rarely enter, so I decided to fall in love with our jaw-dropping view and add character to the house with our antique furnishings.

Jim and I loved entertaining houseguests and were pleased when so many wanted to visit. That summer we welcomed my sister Robin, with our niece and nephew, Alex and Hall, who were almost as wonderstruck by the ride to Disneyland in the limo as they were by the park itself.

Then later, my "pet" little sister, Valerie, also visited, which required another trip to Disneyland, a shopping spree, and many game-nights with Michael, playing a Sherlock Holmes board game, turning our silly solutions of the mysteries into giggle fits. My favorite was the one when I declared the murderer was a "monkey with a shotgun," when the actual solution was "pygmy with a blowgun." Forever after, anytime I started acting like I thought I was smart, Valerie would say, "Okay, 'monkey with a shotgun.'"

Next came my cousins Donna and Tom from Birmingham with mutual friends Cindy and Dick Scott, who delighted in the Hollywood aspect of dinner out with Jim's buddy Vince Edwards of *Ben Casey* fame, and if that weren't enough, the following day, the guys went golfing with George Lindsey, who brought along his pal Ernest Borgnine, all of them making fast friends, Tom and Dick coming home calling Ernest "Ernie."

\* \* \*

1983 brought four big events. Jim turned forty, I turned thirty, my little sister Valerie graduated high school, and I received star billing on *Hee Haw*.

In June, during the summer taping, producer Sam Lovullo called me into his office and informed me, "We've decided to change your billing on the show. Not that we're trying to take you away from Buck," he chuckled, "but it's high-time we took you out of the Buckaroos billing slot and gave you one of your own, as a *Hee Haw* Honey. You've been doing all the Honey spots for years now, so what do you think?"

I thought "Yes," and it never occurred to me that someone should have at least mentioned it to Buck before making the change. It was one of many considerations I overlooked where Buck was concerned.

Soon it was September, my birthday month, which meant my best birthday bash ever, when Jim hosted a black-tie dinner-dance in the banquet room at the Bistro Garden.

Victoria Hallman *Hee Haw Billing Shot* (1983)

For the occasion, I bought a bright-blue bugle-beaded Halston jump-suit and tunic that sparkled like melted sapphires, and our guests were equally glamorous, the *Hee Haw* gang as splendidly turned-out as always.

In my exuberance, I had even invited Diana Goodman, thinking that, as one of the Honeys, it was time she was included, and when any-one rolled their eyes at the matching white outfits she and her date were wearing, I shrugged it off, "This is Hollywood."

The chef outdid himself with filet mignon and Coquilles Saint-Jacques, we drank oceans of my favorite Taittinger Champagne, the band played on, and we danced the night away. Then with a fanfare, they rolled out the birthday cake, revealing my gift from Jim, in the form of an Eiffel Tower cake-topper, my clever husband's way of telling me that a trip to Paris was in the offing.

*   *   *

Heaven seemed determined to make 1983 the most celebratory year of all for Jim and me. Christmas brought the most fabulous gifts, the brightest Christmas tree, and the merriest celebrations with friends and family. Then, to top it off, the Bistro Garden decided to pull out all the stops for a grand New Year's Eve event, complete with a big-band dance in their new ballroom. Of course, we had to be there. The Niklas family, owners of the Bistro and Bistro Garden, were not just our favorite res-taurateurs, they were our friends. The family scion, Chris Niklas and his girlfriend Ellen, frequently joined us for couples' nights out, and were our houseguests at La Costa for the Del Mar race meet.

On New Year's Eve, between courses, and turns around the dance floor, vivacious with frequent champagne toasts, everyone table-hopped with abandon, until eventually, Niklas daughter Carolyn and Chris's girl-friend Ellen wound up tête-à-tête with me.

Carolyn's honey-colored hair swung forward as she leaned in. "We're enrolling in Wolfgang Puck and Patrick Terrail's cooking school," she said, keeping her voice low, which made sense, as Puck was the chef at Patrick Terrail's Ma Maison, a competitor of her family's A-list gathering spots. "It was my father's suggestion," she explained.

Ellen tucked her preppy blonde pageboy behind her ears, lowering her head into our huddle, "The point is, we need a friend to complete our three-person kitchenette, because if we don't get someone, they will put just anybody with us."

They narrowed their eyes, raising their brows, as if I should understand, which I did.

Ellen shrugged. "You like to cook, and Jim likes good food.

Carolyn added, "Jim *knows* good food, and he says he'd love for you to enroll with us."

"Count me in." We raised our glasses in a toast to the New Year and new adventures.

The only consideration I ignored was that I had just re-enrolled in my actors' workshop, forsaken when Jim and I married. These were nightclasses, so between acting and cooking, I'd be leaving my husband alone three evenings per week.

What, me worry? Jim loved me to distraction. Our marriage was as solid as a rock. So, what if he'd been married a few times before. Five, to be exact, which I had discovered gradually, as he recommended would be best. Each of these marriages had been merely incidental, four of them lasting less than a year, where we'd be married four years come June. Four blissful years. Those previous marriages had nothing to do with ours.

Jim Halper and Victoria at the Palomino nightclub in Los Angeles (1983)

# Chapter 21

**AFTER A FEW WEEKS** of classes at Ma Cuisine, one night I walked in to find Ellen and Carolyn whispering together in our kitchenette. As I got closer, they glanced up and I overheard Ellen say, "I think we should tell her."

I stepped into the kitchenette. "Are you talking about me?"

They exchanged glances and Ellen said, "We're worried about you and Jim."

"What? That's ridiculous. Jim and I are great."

Another look passed between them, tossing the ball to Carolyn. "Well. He goes to dinner by himself a lot, as I'm sure you know, and the other night, some of us were at a table near his, and somebody called out, 'Looks like you're going to have to join our family,' and Jim said, 'That may happen sooner than you think.'"

I rolled my eyes, "What is that supposed to mean? He was just joking around."

"Okay," Carolyn got busy boning her squab.

In a small voice, Ellen said, "We tried."

\* \* \*

Early in 1984, the *Hee Haw* Honeys received word that we'd been invited to appear on a network special called *Country Comes Home*, hosted by Glen Campbell and Charlie Pride, to be taped at the Grand Ole Opry in March. Since I had a car and driver, it had become customary for me to pick up Gunilla on the way to LAX, when we were jetting off on Honey business. Sometimes the other girls would also be on our flight, and this time, our first-class cabin mates were Linda Thompson and Diana Goodman, so we turned the four-hour flight to Nashville into a girl-talk gab fest, with many oohs and aahs over pictures and funny stories about

Linda's little boys and much excitement, discussing arrangements for Gunilla's upcoming wedding to Jim McDonough.

*Country Comes Home* turned out to be an easy gig, with the Honeys simply doing a pageant-like stroll down the catwalk – to uproarious applause from the Opry audience, I might add – then each of us telling a corny joke, such as my line, *There's only one thing I don't like about my boyfriend – and that's his wife.* Ba-da-bum.

As always, I used my short stay in Nashville as an excuse to drive down to Twin Oaks for a visit with friends and family in Alabama. Work on the house was proceeding well, and on this stay, my sister Robin and I were planning a day trip to an antique "mall" recommended by a friend, although upon finding our way there through trial and error along winding country roads, we discovered that this was not a mall, but several malls, if old barns and other types of farm sheds can be called that. The buildings had been arranged in order of the perceived value of the items contained. In the high-end barn, I found a mahogany mirrored vanity with matching side table that would have looked perfect in Scarlett O'Hara's boudoir, and an unusual set of Windsor chairs with spear-shaped splats, which would dress up our kitchen table, and several other things, which completed the basic furnishing of our three "must-have" rooms. I could hardly wait to tell Jim when he called that night.

"It all sounds beautiful," he said. "Wish I were there to give you a big kiss of congratulations."

"You can kiss me tomorrow when I get home."

"I'll be right here waiting. You know how much I love you, don't you?"

"Mm, how much?" I lay down on the bed and snuggled in for some pillow talk.

"I won't bother telling you how much I love the way you look, because I've told you a million times that you've got the most beautiful face I've ever seen, but more than that I love your heart." He paused for a second before continuing, "Do you realize how hard it is to live with someone as sweet and good as you are? It can make a person feel pretty rotten by comparison."

"Jim. Stop that. If you were rotten I wouldn't love you."

"That's what I'm talking about. You always see the good. Do you know that I worry that God will take you too soon? Only the good die young."

"I don't like this talk, let's go back to all the things you love about me."

He chuckled. "I love the way you make love, the way you kiss, the way you sing; I love the way you laugh at my silly jokes and the way you laugh at your own silly jokes, the way you cry in sad movies; I love your fried chicken and milk gravy…"

"Fried chicken?" I said, but he went on, listing everything he could think of, until I finally told him I needed to go to bed to be up early for my flight to L.A. and he made kissy noises into the phone, "Goodnight, honey, see you tomorrow."

The next morning, as I was putting the last few things in my suitcase, the phone rang, and Jim said, "Are you alone?"

"Yes," I said, "but mother and Valerie are on their way over to see me off."

"Are you sitting down?"

"No." I sat down on the bed. "But I am now." I was starting to tremble. "What's the matter?"

"You know that you're the only woman I will ever love, don't you? And you know I want to be married to you for the rest of my life?

I paused, wondering what could possibly be coming. "Yes."

"Okay, I want you to keep all of that in mind when I tell you that I've moved out."

Thank God, he had told me to sit down, because I would have fainted.

"Don't worry," he said. "I will be here when you get home."

"What are you saying? You've left me?" I was panting now, unable to catch my breath.

He said, "We are not getting a divorce. Do you hear me?"

"No, I don't."

"Then I'll say it again. No divorce. In fact, if you try to divorce me, you won't be able to find me to serve papers."

"What are you talking about? I don't want to divorce you, I love you." Now the tears were coming.

"And I love you. Nobody else. Please remember that, and try not to overreact. I'm only telling you so it won't be such a shock when you walk into the house and find some things gone. I'm not going to talk about it anymore right now. We will talk when you get home."

"You'll be there, you promise?"

"Yes. I love you. Bye."

I sat there, holding the dead receiver in my lap. Then I looked at the clock and realized I needed to get my bags in the car. The sooner I got to L.A., the sooner I'd be with Jim and talk him out of whatever foolish thing he'd done.

I zipped my carry-on and grabbed the keys to the rental car, running for the kitchen door. As I stepped outside, the keys slipped from my hand,

and dropped into the crack between the top step and the threshold of the back porch. "Oh, my God," I wailed. The steps were poured concrete and the keys were now between the back of that solid block and the brick foundation of the house, irretrievable.

Mother and Valerie pulled into the back driveway, stepping out of the car, their faces expressing shock at the tears streaming down my face.

"Vicki," Valerie put her arms around me.

"What's wrong, honey?" Mother brushed the wet strands of my bangs out of my eyes.

I couldn't bear repeating my conversation with Jim, so I said, "I've lost the keys to the rental car. Down there." I pointed to the crack between steps and foundation. "I can't get them out; I'll miss my plane, I don't know what to do."

Mother's blue eyes searched mine. "Don't cry, it'll be all right. You and Valerie go inside and wash your face and get something cold to drink, while I run down to the filling station and find somebody to get the keys out of the crack."

\* \* \*

I was crying so hard I could barely see to drive. In the VIP room at the airport, I wore sunglasses and held a hankie to my face, hunched in my chair, as if I weren't feeling well, which was certainly the truth. On the plane, when the flight attendant gently asked if I needed anything, I apologized, telling her that I'd had some bad news about a member of my family, which, again, was the truth. Mercifully, there was no one in the seat beside me, and I was able to huddle, facing the window, hoping my sunglasses hid the tears that would not stop.

As usual, Marco picked me up at LAX, and when we pulled into the drive on Coldwater Canyon, Jim was standing in the doorway. I burst into fresh tears and he put his arm around me, ushering me into the foyer. "Stop crying, honey. Come in here and let me try to explain." He took my sunglasses from my face and slid them into his pocket, steering me toward the den, but not quickly enough to keep me from glancing into the living room and dining room, both of which were stripped bare. I tore myself away from him and ran into the living room, standing in the middle of the emptiness, wailing.

He pointed to the painting of the Madonna and Child that we'd bought on our honeymoon. "I know you love this one, so . . ." He walked into the dining room, and laid his hand on the antique French hutch. "Since we have two of these, I thought I'd take one and leave the other."

I barely heard what he was saying. All I could do was stand there looking around at the bare walls, mouth-breathing.

"Come on." He gripped my shoulders, moving me down the hallway into the den, where he seated me on the sofa and took his regular easy chair and ottoman. At least he'd left this room intact. "Where's Neesh?" I asked.

"He's boarded for tonight. I thought it was best." He looked at his watch. "But there's plenty of time for me to pick him up, if you want."

I nodded, then raised my hand. "But not right now." I curled up in the corner of the sofa, staring at him. "Jim . . ."

"I just need some space," he said. "I'm not ending our marriage, I'm saving it. Nothing is changing except that I will be living somewhere else."

"That's a pretty big change."

"Not really. I still want to see you, I still want us to do everything we've ever done. You'll still be my wife, I just want to live separately for a while."

I took a deep breath. "How long?"

"I don't know."

"Where are you living?"

"I've rented a house over in the Valley."

"But moving out while I was gone, why?"

"If you had been here, I wouldn't have been able to leave you."

"That should tell you something." I hugged myself, suddenly shivering with cold. A numbness that was probably shock crept over my body. "I want Neesh," I said.

"Okay," he got up from his chair and kissed the top of my head. "I'll be back."

But he did not come back that day. Our assistant, Ellen, brought Neesh. She sat with me on the sofa while I cuddled my "baby boy."

"I have no idea what happened," she said. "One week he was saying, 'Make dinner reservations at the Bistro for me and my bride,' and the next week he's telling me to order a moving van. I was stunned."

When Ellen left, I called Michael, but he didn't answer, which meant I might not reach him until morning.

I considered calling other friends, but couldn't face trying to explain what had happened, when I didn't understand it, myself, so I sat on the loveseat in the den, stroking Neesh and watching the sunset over the canyon, until it grew dark, bringing the California night-chill, and I turned on the gas logs in the fireplace, gazing into the flickering flames, trying to make sense of what had happened.

Jim said the separation was temporary, that nothing would change. I didn't believe a word of it. For a long time, I sat there in the dark, thinking nothing, because I had no idea what to think. Then the phone rang.

"Vicki, this is David. I hear you've split from your husband."

Bad news traveled like chain lightning in this town. Except, to my old boyfriend this wasn't bad news.

"David. Hi," I said. "I don't really know what's going on. I just got home, and my husband's moved out. How did you know?"

"Where do you live?"

I gave him our address.

"Okay, I'm leaving the Playboy Mansion right now. I'll be there in ten minutes."

Michael had always said that if I hadn't married Jim I would have married David, and it was true that David and I had gotten along without so much as a cross word for two years. Then one night in the Club Barrington, following my head-spinning betrothal, while everyone else was stopping by our table to offer congratulations, I had spotted David's best friend eyeing me from his barstool, and a few minutes later he walked over. Without a glance at Jim, he said, "Hey, Vic, congratulations on your engagement." He leaned on the table, looking me dead in the eye. "Thought you might want to know that David's been in a skiing accident. He's in intensive care." He stood up and rapped his knuckles on the table, "See ya," and walked away.

Michael was with us that night. I turned to him. "Guess I should let David know I'm getting married."

Michael said, "Might want to wait until he's out of intensive care." He made a face. "Unless you want to kill him off."

Now, four years later, here came David, to my rescue. I sighed. Was it possible I had chosen the wrong man?

I went to the powder room and looked at myself in the mirror. What a wreck, and I didn't have the energy or time to do much about it. David could take me as I was, or leave it. I was past caring.

"God, you are beautiful," were his first words when I opened the door.

I burst into laughter then collapsed on his chest, sobbing.

"I'm sorry, I'm ruining your nice starched shirt," I said, touching the damp spots on the button-down collar. He was as nattily dressed as ever in gray flannels, with a yellow Sea Island sweater tied casually around his shoulders.

"If you'll invite me in, I'll hold you while you cry until you soak the whole damn shirt." He grinned, and his eyes crinkled in the way that had made all my friends swear Richard Gere must be David's kid brother. His dark hair had gray highlights now, but he still had the boyish charm that had attracted me in the first place. That and his brains. David was the cliché Philadelphia lawyer who'd possessed the business savvy to invest wisely enough to leave his practice at age forty, and move to LaLa Land, living the good life.

Neesh was scrabbling at his ankles, as if he remembered this former friend. David stooped and patted his tiny head, "Hi, there, little buddy."

"Come on in the den," I said, "No place else to sit."

Passing the living room, he stopped, staring into the empty space. "I'll be damned. You came home to this?"

In the den, he went to the bar and mixed a G&T for himself and poured a glass of Chablis for me. After several hours of talking and completing the soaking of his shirtfront, he said, "You must be exhausted, we need to get to bed."

"No," I shook my head. "I appreciate you coming, and I'm truly glad to see you, but I'm not ready for that."

He patted my arm, and then pressed his hand to his wet shirt, plastering it to his chest. "Uh, no, I wasn't under the impression that hot sex was on the agenda, but you don't need to sleep alone tonight. I'll hold you till you fall asleep."

"I don't think sleep is on the agenda either," I said.

He reached into his pants pocket and pulled out a pill bottle. "A present from Zeke."

David's older brother was a neurosurgeon, and whatever magic pills he'd sent worked, because I slept for ten hours, and might not have awakened then, if David hadn't been standing beside the bed, repeating, "Vicki, Vicki, time to wake up."

The horror of the day before immediately swept through me, but just as quickly, David smiled and set a tray on the nightstand. "Your maid helped me with breakfast." He fluffed the pillows for me to sit up, then set the tray on my lap.

I couldn't even look at the waffles, but I sipped the cup of Earl Grey.

"Does Neesh need to go out?" David asked.

"Yes, just take him in the backyard, but stay with him until he finishes." Coyotes ate Gunilla's little dog.

Picking Neesh up from the bed, he handed me a pill.

"What is this?"

"It'll make you feel better, and you need to get up and dressed. I'm taking you to my place in Palm Springs."

"No, I can't leave." What I meant was that I couldn't bear to be any further from Jim than I already was.

"Yes, you can leave," David said. "I don't know what's going on with your husband, but you hanging around being miserable is not going to improve the situation. Believe me. I'm a guy. I know these things."

I knew those things, too. The smartest move I could make was to disappear with another man, and let Jim wonder, so that's exactly what I did.

Victoria Hallman, Buck Owens and Gunilla Hutton (1984)

# Chapter 22

EVEN IF JIM DIDN'T FEEL A TWINGE of jealousy at my getaway with my former flame, he would be stung by my choice of location. Once upon a time, Palm Springs had been his second home. On the night of my first date with Jim, when I had gotten back to my apartment and encountered the interrogation of my houseguests, Eloise and Judy, and Eloise suspected that Halper Lake Drive in Rancho Mirage had something to do with Jim's family, she'd been right.

Back in the 1950s, a group of Hollywood's A-list known as the "Golden 65", such as George Burns, Danny Kaye, the Marx Brothers, Frank Sinatra, and Jim's father Lou Halper, were close friends who became founders of Rancho Mirage when they purchased neighboring homes surrounding Tamarisk Country Club, where they were all members. Tamarisk Country Club, as well as those homes, the legendary Tamarisk Ranchos, were all built by Jim's father's company, Devon Construction. To say Jim's roots ran deep in the Palm Springs desert would not be speaking metaphorically.

Due to this lifelong connection, Palm Springs was an obvious choice whenever Jim felt the urge to get out of L.A. for a few days, so the area held many fond memories of stays in our favorite villa at the Ingleside Inn, where Clark Gable and Carole Lombard spent their honeymoon, and where local luminaries from Hollywood's "Golden Age" still gathered for cocktails at the bar in Melvyn's Restaurant, with Jim and me frequently among the group.

Since David was now a certified local. it's likely that we also joined the Melvyn's crowd during my stay at his palatial desert home, but I was so "calmed" by tranquilizers and whatever else Zeke prescribed to make me feel better, I don't remember a single thing about that week, or maybe two weeks. I have no idea how long, but I must have made phone calls to my friends back in L.A., to let them know where I was and what was going on, because when I returned home, they all checked on me frequently, expressing their death-wishes for Jim, and lauding me for riding off into the desert with another man. In their opinion, I had come back too soon. I should have stayed in Palm Springs until I forgot Jim Halper existed. Buck even suggested that I should have gone Jim one better by taking everything he'd left in the house, including my clothes, and let him come home and find it *completely* empty.

Undoubtedly, they were right. Turn-about is fair play, but I still had hope, and Jim and I were seeing each other regularly for date nights, sometimes having dinner at one of our usual haunts, a day at the races, or an evening at home grilling steaks and watching TV. We even took a couple of long weekends away, so lovey-dovey that anyone seeing us together would have thought we were on our honeymoon, which only made things worse. Dating my own husband drove me crazier than I already was, so I followed every piece of advice anyone offered, trying various prescription meds that were supposed to make me feel better, but only made me feel nothing at all. I even considered my GP's suggestion that I try male hormones. Then, somehow, Gunilla's fiancé talked Jim into couples' counseling with a new-age psychologist he and Gunilla admired.

When the day of our counseling appointment arrived, I was ready fifteen minutes early, pacing the living room, with Neesh following my every step, so when he ran to the front door, it could only mean one thing. I peeked out the window to see Jim getting out of his sun-yellow 350SL, dressed in his California business-casual uniform of blue blazer and jeans, as always, looking like he'd just stepped out of *GQ*.

Coming through the door, he scooped up Neesh, nuzzling his top-knot.

I walked into the foyer, and stood on tip-toe to offer my cheek for a kiss.

"New dress," he said, "Holly Harp?"

"Nope, Valentino from Giorgio."

I did a double-pivot, showing off the red and black strapless silk, which rated a wolf whistle from my husband.

These were the kind of things that made our situation so difficult to understand. My friends were beginning to roll their eyes at the idea that Jim and I were over. "What kind of separation is it when you're spending romantic weekends together in Palm Springs and Tahoe?"

But I'd reply, "What kind of *marriage* is it when you no longer live in the same house?"

"Nutty" was the answer to both questions, so maybe Gunilla's Dr. Bravin was exactly the one to sort it out.

His office looked perfectly normal and his doctorly appearance matched his reputation as a respected middle-aged psychologist.

"Call me Marty. Everyone does," he said, then began talking about something called *A Course in Miracles*. At the end of the session, he looked Jim in the eye and said, "I want your word that you will accompany Victoria to Gunilla's wedding."

I tried to conceal my excitement, but Jim knew me too well. Driving home, he shook his finger at me. "I don't want you getting your hopes up."

After that one session, Jim declared Bravin's new-age approach hogwash, putting an end to our couples' counseling, where after, Dr. Bravin turned his attention to improving my outlook for a future without Jim, which included regular visits to a psychic, who told me that Jim and I had known each other in a former lifetime. I had been an artist and he was my brother, who was also the agent who represented my paintings. I was not an art aficionado, but the brother-agent scenario sounded very much like something I'd seen in a movie about Vincent van Gogh, and although it was fun to imagine myself as van Gogh, I didn't like the part about cutting off my ear. I eased off on trips to the psychic.

Now, Gunilla's wedding was mere weeks away, and while I wanted to be joyful for her, the paradox between our situations was like a rom-com script, except this was dark humor, and I was the com instead of the rom, planning a bridal luncheon for my friend, while my own marriage was crumbling like stale wedding cake.

When the day for the luncheon arrived, as guests entered the banquet room of the Bistro Garden, I greeted them dressed in my Gucci silk floral-print sheath, my face stretched into an over-bright smile of welcome. Bittersweet though it might be for me, this was Gunilla's party, and I would play the perfect hostess.

Chris Niklas and I had planned the menu to please the palates of our "ladies-who-lunch," and I was gratified to see that everyone chatted companionably, sipping Puligny-Montrachet while enjoying their Bistro Garden Chicken Cobb Salads, so that when the waiters began pouring Taittinger Comtes de Champagne, no one was shy in lifting a glass to the bride.

Even I was feeling rather relaxed. An Ativan and champagne cocktail will do that. So, by the time second glasses of champagne came around, I was tête-a-tête with my lunch companion to my left, *Hee Haw* Associate Producer, Marcia Minor. Marcia called the Honeys her "girls," and having been with *Hee Haw* from the first episode in 1969, Marcia was in every sense the big sister of our sisterhood, and if ever I needed Big Sis, this was the day. With

Marcia's sorrowful eyes gazing into mine, I poured out my heartache, and that very night, my phone began to ring with calls from members of my *Hee Haw* family, who were mad as hell and wanted answers. Jim had gone from being the sister-Honeys' favorite brother-in-law to – paraphrasing Scarlett O'Hara – *can't think of anything bad enough to call that lying, cheating skunk.*

But as much as I agreed with their feelings about my husband, I still had hope for our marriage. Gunilla's wedding was getting closer by the day, and I continued to remind Jim of Dr. Bravin's dictum that he accompany me, although he never actually agreed to go, then I knew he'd decided in our favor, when out of the blue, our assistant Ellen called me with the news that for the wedding weekend she had booked us into the most romantic suite at the Santa Barbara Biltmore. "Not one, but two balconies overlooking the Pacific," she said, "and those Santa Barbara beach nights get chilly, so you and Jim will have to cuddle-up in front of *your very own fireplace.*"

I hung up the phone and lay back, luxuriating in the sexy softness of my sitting room's white velvet sofa, and despite Jim's warning not to get my hopes up, I let them soar. The ceremony would bring back sweet memories of our own wedding, then we would toast the happy couple and later there would be more champagne while we sat on our balcony listening to the pounding surf, after which we would snuggle into the warmth of a soft rug beside the roaring fireplace, and then – oh then – to bed, and the next morning the dream would continue, and after a weekend like that Jim would come back home and wonder why he ever left.

For now, I only needed to count the days, passing each in various Rodeo Drive salons being creamed, clipped, curled and conditioned into a perfection of loveliness worthy of the occasion.

Then there was my dress. Holly Harp designed a scoop-necked sheath with poet sleeves, in taupe silk embroidered with tiny pink rosebuds.

I had just returned from my final fitting, when the phone rang. It was Jim.

"Hey, handsome," I flirted.

"I'm not going to Santa Barbara."

I dropped onto the bed. "No, you have to go. You promised Dr. Bravin."

"I'll see you when you get back."

"Can't you at least tell me why?"

"It's a wedding. It would turn into an emotional mess."

"It won't, it will be wonderful. Ellen's booked us into the ultimate suite."

"I know. Who do you think told her to do it? I've changed my mind, and I'm hanging up now. I'll see you when you get back. I promise."

The phone rang again immediately. "I'm so sorry," Ellen said.

"Me, too," My voice crumpled into tears. "You'll have to cancel that beautiful suite."

"I will not. You are going to that wedding and you are going to have a fabulous weekend. Anyway, who knows? As often as Jim changes his mind, maybe he'll decide to go, after all."

Not knowing which way to turn, I called Dr. Bravin, who took me through some deep-breathing exercises and reminded me to do the meditations he had given me.

Then Gunilla called. "Are you okay? We just talked to Bravin. I could kill Jim Halper. You are still coming to the wedding, right? Bravin thinks it's important for you to come, and it's important to me. I love you, Vicki. Get some sleep, okay? I'll talk to you tomorrow."

"No," I said, "Tomorrow is the day before your wedding. You have too much to do to be worrying about me."

But the next morning, Ellen and Gunilla each called again, making sure I was planning to go to Santa Barbara, which I told them I was, even though I wasn't.

An hour later, Ellen showed up, bossing Maribel around, getting my bags packed. Now the gorgeous Nazareno Gabrielli luggage we'd bought for our honeymoon stood ready and waiting in the downstairs hall to go on a trip that I had no intention of taking. Before she left, Ellen pulled back the wide expanse of beige silk from the window-wall – *whoosh* – flooding my bedroom with sunlight, causing me to pull the covers over my head. Ellen pulled them off. "I need to check-list a few things with you. Sit up, now."

Her round, rosy cheeks and bright smile weren't the worst face to wake up to. I plumped the pillows and sat up to listen.

She handed me a list, verbally ticking the items. "Number One: Marco will pick you up at noon to get you to the Biltmore by 2:30, for your hair and makeup appointment in the salon, which is Number Two. Number Three: Michael will be staying here, taking care of Neesh until you return. Number Four: I will personally give you a wake-up call at 10:00, so please don't turn off your phone, because if you don't answer, I will come over."

The next morning, I was awake before she called. Even in my drugged state, I couldn't ignore Neesh's yapping, and I could hear voices coming from downstairs, which was unusual because Maribel and the other household staff knew better than to make a sound before I was up and about.

Then it hit me. Jim! Ellen had been right, he had decided to go to the wedding after all. I vaulted out of bed and grabbed my silk kimono from the vanity bench, tying it as I stumbled down the staircase.

Jim was standing in the foyer, but it wasn't my Jim, it was Gunilla's. "Hi, Vic," he said.

"Jimmy." I raked my fingers through my sleep-tossed hair. "What are you doing here, why aren't you in Santa Barbara? Am I confused? Isn't your wedding this afternoon?"

"Oh, yeah, yeah." Jimmy waved his hands when he talked, typical Boston Irish. "Gunilla's worried that you're not going to show up, so she sent me over to bring you these." He handed me a small sack. "Meditation tapes from the Bodhi Tree. Bravin gave them to me awhile back and Gunilla thinks they'll help you. If you've got a little cassette player, you might want to listen on the way to Santa Barbara." He pointed to the luggage. "Looks like you're all set, so I'll tell Gunilla no worry. Right? Hey, it's going to be a great time." He grabbed me in a quick hug. "You take care, Vic. We'll see you later. Give us a call when you get to the hotel."

I pulled him back, for a real hug. "Thank you, Jimmy. I wouldn't miss your wedding for the world."

*   *   *

Could anything be more stereotypically LaLa Land than a starlet-cum-Beverly Hills housewife wearing Chanel sunglasses, riding in the back of a chauffeur-driven limo, with a trunk full of Italian designer luggage, and a Gucci handbag full of pills, listening to meditation tapes from her personal guru, on her way to Santa Barbara with tears streaming down her face because she's so miserable?

Believe me, I knew there was something wrong with this picture, but I must say the meditation tapes were soothing, and would have helped even more had they been strong enough to penetrate the prescription fog in my head. At least they got me from L.A. to S.B. without incident. A couple of hours later we arrived in paradise.

Picture a 1930s movie about socialites vacationing at a California resort, mountains in the background, palm trees surrounding lounge chairs by a pool in a lush tropical garden, beautiful debutantes in strapless gowns, tycoons in white dinner jackets, sipping martinis on a terrace overlooking the ocean, and that's the Santa Barbara Biltmore. Poor me. My rooms were every inch of Spanish-Colonial luxury Jim's money could buy, but without Jim, these sumptuous surroundings were merely the proverbial place to hang my hat.

In normal circumstances, I would never have dreamed of disturbing the bride on the day of her wedding, but since the groom had personally delivered the request, I dutifully rang the Honeymoon Suite. Thirty seconds later, Gunilla appeared at my door with a welcoming hug, waltzing around my suite, peeking into the other rooms and exclaiming, "Wow, this is huge!"

"Too much space for one person," I said, "I don't need this big room."

Gunilla placed her hands on my shoulders. "No, you don't need it, but you need to enjoy it. Look at the view." She pulled me over to the French doors that opened onto the balcony. Below was a tropical garden, and beyond that, the Pacific Ocean.

Never was there a more beautiful bride than Gunilla Hutton in her ivory linen tea gown, with a garland of flowers in her hair; never a more beautiful setting than that garden in Santa Barbara by the sea; and never a more romantic reception than in the Biltmore banquet hall, with the ocean breeze wafting through open French doors. I sat at the table with Linda and Bruce, attempting to keep a stiff upper lip, determined to see the celebration through to the final toast and last dance, but when I went from dabbing my eyes with a lace hankie, to desperately seeking a box of Kleenex, it was time for me to go.

Linda walked with me to the door. "Honey, are you going to be okay?" She looked doubtful.

I'd barely had time to get out of my Holly Harp dress, when I answered a knock at my door to find Linda and Bruce standing there, with Bruce holding a napkin-covered plate.

"Did we wake you?" Linda asked.

I knotted the belt of my robe. "Goodness no, it's early. Come in. Is the reception already over?"

They stepped into the room. Linda said, "Gorgeous suite, bless your little heart. At least you can still afford nice digs." She pointed her finger at me. "And you deserve it."

Bruce frowned. "Linda."

Linda rolled her eyes.

"Have a seat," I said. "There's a bottle of Taittinger in that silver cooler in the dining room. Apparently, somebody around here knows it's my favorite."

"I'll open it." Bruce set down the plate he was holding, and headed for the champagne.

"Wait, Bruce," Linda said, "I'm not sure that's a good idea. Victoria, aren't you on medication? Wouldn't you rather have wedding cake?" She sat down on the sofa and lifted the napkin from the plate. "Come sit here beside me and eat this. We need to put some meat on those spindly little legs of yours."

Bruce sprawled in a club chair, flipping through a magazine.

Linda said, "You're skin and bones, Victoria, and I'm concerned about the pills."

"I'm not Elvis, Linda," I said. "I only take one if I need it."

She patted my hand. "I know you're not abusing drugs, but I don't think they're doing you any good, either.

I held up my forefinger. "Gunilla and Jim gave me some meditation tapes, so maybe I'll try those tonight."

She squeezed my hand. "That's a great idea."

* * *

The newlyweds were headed to Lake Tahoe for their honeymoon and they'd invited Jim and me along. In fact, they'd invited a whole cast of their friends to appear in a TV special featuring celebrities competing in snow games such as toboggan, snow-mobile, and downhill ski races. Lori Saunders, who played Gunilla's sister Bobbie Jo, on *Petticoat Junction*, would be one of us, as would Martin Kove of *Karate Kid* and *Cagney and Lacey* fame, along with several well-known athletes. To my delight, Jim agreed to go, but of course he had also agreed to go to the wedding in Santa Barbara, and we know how that turned out.

L-R Victoria and Leslie Nielsen; Victoria, Brenda McClain, Bill Clinton (Little Rock, (1984); Victoria and Jim Halper (Harrah's Lake Tahoe (1984)

# Chapter 23

MAYBE IT WAS THE OPPORTUNITY to combine business with pleasure, with a Tahoe-to-Reno run for facetime at the Nevada Club; maybe because he was a fan of the Los Angeles Raiders and wanted to hang with Marcus Allen and other players, who were appearing on the show; maybe he felt badly about reneging on the wedding weekend in Santa Barbara; or as I'd like to have thought, he looked forward to a romantic getaway with me; but whatever his reason, Jim went. He even pulled strings – Bill Harrah had been a family friend, after all – and got us our usual penthouse at Harrah's, instead of staying in the perfectly nice room the producers of the show were providing.

Surrounded by the romantic luxury of our creamy-plush suite with a panoramic view of the sparkling snowcapped mountains, my expectations of a reconciliation were high, and indeed the trip started off with a bang.

I was an Alabama native transplanted to sunny southern California, so my experience with snow was limited, to say the least. To say the most, I had never set foot on a ski, nor had my bottom ever touched the seat of a toboggan. I'd never even seen one. Until that day. The first event was the toboggan race.

Toboggan Number One: they called out Marcus Allen, three of his L.A. Raiders teammates, and me. *Me?*

"Victoria, you're in front," the producer said, and the four Raiders squeezed in behind. We were off! Wheeeee! Then, zigzagzigzag, *thump*, and we vaulted into the air, and down. *Crash*, the toboggan tumbled, catapulting us into the snow, with four NFL football players landing on top of me. A pile-up like that could put a two-hundred pound running back in football padding out of the game. I weighed ninety-eight pounds and was wearing a powder-suit. A siren blared and here came the snow-mobile with the red cross on its side. The Raiders got up laughing. I lay on the hard-packed snow, struggling to breathe.

Marcus Allen squatted beside me. "Are you okay?"

A medic joined him, telling me to lie still while he checked me over to see if all my moving parts still moved. Confirming that I was in working order, the two men stood up, and Marcus offered me his hand, pulling me to my feet.

"I guess this means we didn't win?" I laughed.

Next up, three-wheelers in the snow, and although I didn't win that one either, I didn't have a wreck, and finished, ready and eager for the next event, which was the slalom.

"Do you ski, Victoria?" the producer asked.

"Yes," I answered, which wasn't a lie; I could water-ski, and what was the difference?

I soon found out. At the top of the run, I locked my boots onto my skis and stood up. My left ski went into an unstoppable slide to the left and my right ski to the right. Thanks to years of dance classes, I was able to do the splits, even on skis, but I very quickly realized that the slalom was beyond my capabilities.

Bruce Jenner to the rescue. He and Linda weren't participating in the show, but they owned a house in Tahoe, and decided to come up and have fun with us while we were there.

"I'm ready to head down the mountain anyway," Bruce told me, "Hop on." He bent over and pointed to his back.

I looked down the mountain. Way down. "You're going to carry me that far?"

"Sure. Come on, let's go."

So, I climbed onto his back, and away we went, flying like the wind through the nose-biting air, Lois Lane hitching a ride on Superman's cape.

The rest of the trip went as expected, but not as I would have wished. Even though Jim and I wined and dined with the rest of the group, and had plenty of romantic alone time between the sumptuous silk sheets of the king-size bed in our penthouse, the sadness I carried weighed too much for me to rise above the reality of our separation, so these away-days, which should have been carefree and fun-filled, were anything but. We returned to L.A. still in limbo, with me dating my own husband, as well as a former beau, who no longer interested me.

Jim also came for his regular visit to the *Hee Haw* taping in June. The difference was that he preferred we stay at the Opryland Hotel, rather than the Maxwell House with the rest of the gang. I could only assume he had romantic reasons for wanting privacy, but also, he wished to avoid facing my *Hee Haw* family, whose opinion of him had reached a new low. If I hadn't given up on Jim, they had, and if I wasn't going to do anything to lift myself out of the doldrums of my failing marriage, they would.

Two of our honorary *Hee Haw* "sisters" were Anna Wilkins and Brenda McClain. Anna was a long-time member of the *Hee Haw* family, via friendship with the Hager Twins, while Brenda was a newcomer, through acquaintance with Roy Clark's backing vocalist, Sherri Baker, who was from Little Rock, Brenda's hometown, where it just so happened that a big horse show fundraiser was coming up, with celebrities in attendance to add star-power.

So far, the celebrity participants were Arkansas Governor, Bill Clinton and actor Leslie Nielsen, who was a great pal of Anna Wilkins.

Anna said, "I'm going to Little Rock for that horse show, Victoria. Why don't you come? It'll be fun. That young governor's a doll."

I knew it was a plot among the *Hee Haw* girls to get me out of L.A. and away from Jim, and I didn't mind a bit. What I thought was going to be a couple of days in Arkansas turned into several weeks of Anna and me staying at Brenda's high-rise condo, "doing" Little Rock, which is almost a contradiction in terms since there wasn't much to do, unless you were into politics, which Brenda was. Certainly, I got to know all the high-ups, including the Clintons, who invited me to perform at the Arkansas State Democratic Convention. But how many functions can a person go to at the Old State House, before it gets a little – pardon the pun – old.

Brenda had a friend in Miami, and thus began what I tagged my "Boys of Summer" period, recalling the Don Henley song, which debuted that fall. There was the bodybuilder in Miami, the surfer dude in Malibu, the politician in Little Rock and the movie star in Hollywood. Except you couldn't really count Leslie Nielsen. Leslie was a movie star, for sure, but hardly a "boy" and certainly not a boyfriend. He was, however, a great pal, and we had a lot in common, because he also had recently split from his spouse. Only a couple of times did we go out in a way that could be termed a "date." More often, Leslie would invite me for lunch at his charming "tree house" on stilts in the Hollywood Hills – chicken soup, bagel and lox—or he'd drop by for an afternoon of conversation at my place, which had changed locations twice during this period.

Upon return from Miami, I made the wise decision to get out of the house that was a constant reminder of my blissful-marriage-turned-agonizing-separation, which coincided with condo-conversion mania in L.A. Michael and his gay pals were especially eager to attend the grand opening of a new conversion on Hayworth Avenue in West Hollywood, where we all went nuts over a unique two-story unit, which had a subterranean courtyard.

"Jim will buy this for me," I said, and so he did. But not for long.

Another feature of my unit was that the glass slider in my den opened onto a patio fifteen feet from the complex's pool. So, one morning, having given up my prescription meds, and unable to sleep, I rose early, deciding what a pleasant idea to have my breakfast tea poolside. Breathing the fragrant steam of Earl Grey from my cup, I headed into the den, reached to open the slider to the patio, and stopped cold, not believing my eyes. Curled into a fetal position on the very edge of the pool was a sleeping man, dressed in filthy rags, clearly homeless. Quite obviously, it was too early in the morning for the condo sales office to have opened, and this poor man had seized the opportunity for a relaxing snooze by the pool.

Odd that none of us had considered the downside of being the first person to buy a unit in a new condo building. No one except Ellen, that is. Another fab feature of my condo was the living-room window-wall overlooking the street. One afternoon, before my draperies were installed, I arrived home to find Ellen on a ladder with an armload of sheets and a mouthful of pins.

"I won't be able to see out," I complained.

"And they won't be able to see in." She pointed at the sidewalk, then she swept her arm around the room indicating the art, antiques and silver on display for any passerby.

Apparently, her makeshift window covering was not soon enough, because a few days later, I returned from a weekend jaunt to find all my fur coats stolen. Nothing else, just the furs. I took it with a shrug. Could have been worse. It wasn't even winter yet, I could get new furs.

Then one night, Neesh woke me from a sound sleep, standing on my stomach, yapping furiously at the sliding glass doors leading to the atrium.

"Shh," I patted Neesh, listening. On the other side of the window, a few feet from my bed, something was making a sound like metal scraping metal. I reached for the phone and dialed 911. "Someone is breaking into my apartment."

Another advantage to this condo, was its location in the middle of the city. Within seconds, blinding lights filled my bedroom and a man's voice yelled, "Hit the ground!"

Burglar caught red-handed. I shuddered to think what might have happened if Neesh hadn't barked. Jim shuddered, too.

"But it's such a trendy area," I explained.

He looked at me like I'd lost my mind. "I wouldn't let you stay here with an armed guard."

"You've already paid for the condo," I reminded him.

"Forget it. We'll find you a better one in a safe neighborhood," he said, and that's how Neesh and I wound up living in a luxury high-rise in Bel Air, which was certainly a safe neighborhood, and seemed to suit Jim quite well, judging by the increased frequency of his visits.

Jim also replaced my fur coats. *Hee Haw's* October taping was coming up, and it would be chilly in Nashville, but a new condo and new furs were not the only surprises in store for me that autumn.

One afternoon, Buck called. "I'm selling Blue Book. Selling Gold Book, too."

"What?" Blue Book and Gold Book were catalogues containing more than two thousand songs, too many mega-hits to list, all of Buck's records,

Buck Owens and Victoria Hallman. (1979) photo courtesy of Becky Scott

like "Act Naturally," "Cryin' Time," Tiger by the Tail," but also hundreds of gold records by other artists, such as "Okie from Muscogee," "Mama Tried" and "Easy Loving."

"Yeah, Buddy Killen, Tree International, bought 'em."

"Well." I laughed, "Knowing you, I bet they paid a pretty penny."

"Yup. Everybody's happy, so we're having a party, which is why I'm calling."

"You want me to sing?"

"No, I want you to go with me. You're still separated, aren't you?"

The party was in Nashville at Tree Publishing's headquarters and everybody was there. Just name somebody, because I wouldn't know where to start naming. If there were any country stars I hadn't already met on the set of *Hee Haw*, I met them that night, but it wasn't the kind of place to make meaningful conversation, so the most remarkable thing about the evening was that I went as Buck's date.

Since my separation from Jim, Buck had been very respectful of my need for time to heal, counseling "Sometimes it's best to let things come apart gradually," and hadn't he been the first to say, "You won't be married long." Over the past seven months, he'd stayed in touch, always making sure I was doing okay, even while asserting that he wasn't one bit worried about me because I was "tough as whit-leather."

Naturally, we worked together on *Hee Haw*, and although this party might count as a professional outing, I had no reason to be there other than as Buck's date, so it was the perfect "toe-in-the-water" of resuming our personal relationship. The next day, we were back at *Hee Haw*, back to work, strictly professional.

Later that day, Producer Sam and Director Bob, called me into Sam's office. Minnie Pearl was there, too.

"Minnie is going to be doing a new spot this time," Sam said.

Miss Minnie beamed, and I congratulated her, happy that she was happy, but confused as to why they were telling me this.

"It's a two-person spot," Bob said.

Minnie clapped her hands together. "You and me."

Then they explained that the spot was called "Grinders Switch Gazette," where Minnie would be the reporter and I her leggy secretary, taking dictation, while sitting on a stool in an extremely skimpy dress. When I saw the costume, I realized that "extremely skimpy" had gone past even *Hee Haw's* extremes, and the huge horn-rimmed glasses they put on my face were a stroke of costuming genius. My alter-ego, Miss Honeydew, was born.

Miss Minnie and I were the latest of *Hee Haw's* magic pairings, like Gunilla and Archie as Nurse Goodbody and Doctor; Misty and Junior in "Samples' Used Cars;" and LuLu and Gailard in "LuLu's Truck Stop." If the chemistry is there, you know it from the first take, and ours was there. Everybody in the studio could feel it, and the place was going crazy. Nobody more so than Miss Minnie. Way back, in a skit for a high-school talent show, she had created the character of Cousin Minnie Pearl as a reporter for the Grinders Switch Gazette, and for many years, she'd been encouraging *Hee Haw's* producers to let her reprise it on the show. Now we'd proven her right.

My reward was to be invited along the following Monday to appear with Grandpa Jones, George Lindsey and Miss Minnie on the *CBS Morning News* with Diane Sawyer. The trip to New York coincided with Jim's visit to Nashville, but more and more, I cared less and less about opportunities to be with Jim.

I was, however, disappointed to miss the cast barbeque to be held Sunday afternoon at Monthaven Plantation, the family home of our newest female cast member, Jackie Waddell. George, Grandpa, Minnie and I would fly into New York City on Sunday morning, giving us time to settle in at the Essex House and get plenty of rest for our very early Monday-morning call-time at CBS. All went well on the show. With the four of us, it wasn't a problem of getting us to talk, but getting us to shut up.

That afternoon, back in my hotel room in Nashville, I had a message to call Linda Thompson.

Victoria as Miss Honeydew with Misty Rowe and Minnie Pearl (1984)

# Chapter 24

"HEY, LITTLE VICTORIA," Linda said in her sweet Memphis drawl, "Something happened while you were gone, and there's a lot of talk going around about it, so I wanted you to hear it from me first."

I was mystified, and even more so when the next thing out of her mouth was, "Yesterday, after you left, I got a call from Diana Goodman."

*Diana Goodman?* What would she be doing calling Linda, and what could it possibly have to do with me?

Linda said, "Diana asked me if you and Jim were *really truly* separated, and when I asked her what she meant by 'really truly,' she said, 'Well, I know they're separated emotionally, but I want to make sure that they are actually living separately because I'm thinking of bringing Jim to the barbecue this afternoon.'"

Linda waited for me to comment, and when I didn't, she continued. "I told her, 'No, Diana, you've got it backwards; Victoria and Jim are living separately but they are definitely not separated emotionally, and under no circumstances should you bring him to that barbecue.'" Linda sighed, "But of course, she did."

"Oh." I thanked Linda for being a good big sister, trying to protect "Little Victoria," as she called me, and I did love her for her concern, although hers seemed greater than mine, and when next day at the studio, the set was a hotbed of gossip about the incident, I just rolled my eyes. Whether or not Diana Goodman was after my husband I didn't know, but I did know she was not someone he would be serious about. I didn't even mention it to him, and when the October taping session ended, he and I set off for our usual stay at Twin Oaks in the Grove, to spend time with my family in Alabama, never giving another thought to Diana Goodman until a while later I heard she was to be released from *Hee Haw,* and that the final straw may have been the rumors about her and my husband. When I told Jim, he gave it the same eye-roll reaction I'd given it in the first place. "Good grief," he said, "that girl didn't have anything to do with anything."

Back in L.A., my friends were beginning to believe Jim's declaration that he had no intention of getting a divorce. After all, we'd been separated for eight months, with things remaining exactly as he'd spelled out in that very first phone conversation when he'd rocked my world by telling me he had moved out. Status quo was Jim having his space, while dating his wife, and whoever else I had no clue, and didn't care to know, because I was free to date whomever I pleased, also.

*What's not to like?* "the girls" said. *He foots the bills for you to live like a queen and you get your choice of toy-boys, in the bargain? Hey, give me that deal.*

I understood their point, but for me, it wasn't about a condo in Bel Air or charge accounts on Rodeo Drive or boys. Part of me still longed for the closeness of our marriage, I hadn't just loved him, I had loved *us.*

*You'll find somebody else,* the girls said, and they set about looking for that somebody. Linda told me Bruce's manager had asked them to introduce us, while confiding that she didn't think I'd go for him, which was correct, so she then suggested our fellow Honey Marianne Gordon Rogers' ex-husband, Michael Trikilis, but he was a buddy of Jim's, so that didn't fly. Then Gunilla's ex-husband Alan Freeman fixed me up with his best friend, Ron, and although I agreed with Alan that Ron made a great pal, that was as far as it went. In a city of three-million people, you'd think the odds of finding one suitable man would be very good, so maybe I just wasn't in the mood.

Then one afternoon Gunilla called. "A friend of Alan's is in town for a golf tournament and needs a date for the dinner-dance awards banquet at Riviera Country Club."

"No."

"It's just one night," she argued, "and Jimmy and I will be there, and Alan and his date. We'll have fun. Besides, Pete's very good-looking. He's also brilliant. I think you'll like each other."

Within five minutes of sitting down to dinner, Pete and I were fighting like cats and dogs. Okay, not exactly fighting, more like "you say po-*tay*to, I say po*tah*to," but we disagreed about so many things that the others began to find it amusing and started laughing at the two of us. Pete laughed, too. I was the only one who didn't see the humor.

"Let's dance," he said, rising to pull out my chair.

Well, if this didn't beat all. He was a better dancer than I was. The entertainment was a big band à la Guy Lombardo. For all I know, it may have been Guy Lombardo, except I think he was dead by then, but this orchestra was a real dance band, meaning they knew the difference between a Rumba and a Cha Cha, and so did Pete. Fox Trot? Here we go. Waltz? That, too.

*Did this guy take a flash course at the Berlitz School of Ballroom Dance the day before he got here?* I had to admit it was fun.

I also had to admit he was good-looking; bright blue eyes, close-cropped brown hair, nice smile, good bone structure, medium build, very fit and trim. Gunilla whispered to me, "Don't fall in love with Pete, he's a notorious heart-breaker."

"You don't need to worry about that," I assured her.

Driving me home, Pete took an unexpected detour into Beverly Hills and parked in front of Tony Roma's restaurant. "Evening's young. Let's have a nightcap."

Tony Roma's was known for their barbecued ribs, but this location also had a lively bar scene. We took a booth in the dimly-lit lounge, and continued the conversational ping pong match we'd been having the whole night.

After an hour or so, and more than one nightcap, Pete narrowed his eyes and said, "I'd love to play Trivial Pursuit with you."

I wagged my finger at him, "Careful what you wish for, I've never been beaten."

He banged his rock-glass onto the tabletop. "Name your time and place."

I leaned in, nose-to-nose. "Anytime, anyplace."

We left Tony Roma's in a light mood, but not light enough for me to invite him in when he walked me to my door. Instead, I offered my cheek for a kiss, and he handed me his business card, saying, "Call me, and we'll set up that Trivial Pursuit game."

Closing the door behind me, I looked at his card. *O International*, it read, presumably for his last name, O'Donnell. The address and phone numbers were Washington, D.C. *Three-thousand miles from here*, I thought, and tossed the card in the wastebasket.

✳   ✳   ✳

With November, came anticipation of the holidays, accompanied by melancholy. After seven years in Los Angeles, I still hadn't adapted to Thanksgiving turkey served poolside and Christmas ornaments hung on palm trees, which was good enough reason for me to head to Alabama for the holidays, and now add to that the idea of my first holiday season post-Jim, and I decided to go earlier rather than later that year.

*Oh, the weather outside is frightful, but the fire is so delightful, and since we've no place to go, let it snow, let it snow, let it snow.* It wasn't snowing in Maplesville, Alabama, but I certainly had no place to go, and sitting in the kitchen at Twin Oaks, keeping a steady rhythm in my Windsor rocking chair, while gazing out the window at the bare trees against the gray sky, I was wondering if coming to Alabama quite so early had been such a good idea, when suddenly the phone rang.

"Hi, Victoria. Peter O'Donnell here."

"Pete? How did you get this number?" Very few people had the phone number for my "place in the country," not even Gunilla.

Pete laughed. "I live in D.C. All my friends work for the CIA."

Now we were both laughing. "No, really," I said, "how did you find me?"

"It took some talking, but I managed to pry your secret location out of your house-sitter."

"Sandy told you?" I was impressed. Sandy was my cousin who frequently stayed at my place when I was out of town, and she was as tight-lipped as they came. Pete must have learned a few interrogation techniques from his CIA buddies.

"I'm calling to set up a time and place for our Trivial Pursuit match. I'm going to Europe in a few weeks, want to come along?"

Glancing through the kitchen doorway into the library, and through the library's French doors into the sixty-foot-long center hall, the house felt awfully big for one tiny woman. "Don't tempt me."

"I wish I thought I could," Pete said. "Don't *tease* me."

"You're right, I was teasing. I'm settled in here for Thanksgiving and Christmas."

\* \* \*

So, I lied. I flew home to L.A. the day after Thanksgiving, but no sooner had I gotten back than I began to second-guess my decision. The giant tinsel snowflakes strung over Wilshire Boulevard were almost more than I could take. *It's eighty degrees. Snowflakes, really?* Thus, Irving Berlin's inspiration for "White Christmas."

I was sitting in the living room of my condo, wondering how the orchid tree on my balcony would look decorated with Christmas balls, when the phone rang.

"Peter O'Donnell here, trying one more time to convince you to come to London – and Paris. How about Morocco?"

The next day, Gunilla and I were keeping up a running chat while trotting alongside each other during our regular power-walk, when I casually dropped into the conversation, "I'm going to London with Pete O'Donnell."

Gunilla stopped dead in her tracks and fell into a hard sit-down on the sidewalk. "What?" She clutched her chest. "I warned you not to get involved with him. The last thing you need is another guy who's going to break your heart."

"Get up, Gunilla," I said, "People in their cars are slowing, wondering what's going on." I reached and pulled her to her feet. "You don't need to worry. Another guy may break my heart, but it won't be Pete O'Donnell."

Gunilla picked up the pace of our jog "We're going back to my house and call Alan right this minute."

Sitting in her cozy breakfast nook, even though she didn't have Alan on speakerphone, I heard him say, "Oh. My. God."

"Talk some sense into her," Gunilla said to him, then handed the phone to me.

Alan said, "Pete's a great guy, one of my best friends, but it's probably not a good idea for you to go to Europe with him."

Then Gunilla's husband, Jimmy, came in, waving his hands in the air, as always. "Vic, don't go."

I went.

The only caveat was that I must have my own room, to which Pete agreed without argument.

I couldn't say no one warned me.

\* \* \*

From the dark green leather chairs in the lounge to the cozy fire on the hearth, I was instantly charmed by Durrants Hotel, most importantly, its location a five-minute walk to the high-end shops of Oxford Street, which was especially appealing since the airline had lost my luggage, ne-

cessitating an immediate round of shopping for items to replace the contents of six suitcases, therefore rendering proximity to Selfridge's the most
charming aspect of all.

If the loss of my luggage had gotten the trip off on the wrong foot, it
careened downhill when the man at the desk handed Pete two keys to our
*room,* singular.

"Excuse me," I stepped forward, "we're supposed to have two
rooms."

The elderly clerk flipped pages in a book, "I do apologize, but we have
nothing available for the time you will be with us."

I gave Pete a dirty look and turned back to the clerk. "All right, then.
Can you give us a room with two beds?"

"Hm," the clerk flipped pages, "We could put you in a room with twin
beds." He looked sorrowful. "I'm afraid that's all we have."

"Perfect," I nodded at Pete with a satisfied smirk. We had yet to begin
our Trivial Pursuit match, and I'd already won the first round.

Pete was gracious in defeat, and our cheerful room, with a classic
English floral chintz draping the windows as well as the *twin* beds, put me
in the holiday spirit for an afternoon of shopping the streets of London,
which were decorated for Christmas, like an illustration from a Dickens
novel. My shopping excursion coincided conveniently with Pete's meeting
with business associates, so we parted with smiles, agreeing to be back for
cocktail hour, then dinner in the hotel dining room.

Safe to say that by dinnertime, we were ready for our cocktails, a
hearty English beefsteak dinner, and each to his own twin bed. Then what
a wonderful surprise, when bright and early the next morning, a knock
came at our door, and in the hallway stood a bellman with my suitcases,
all six of them.

As soon as my luggage was neatly stowed, Pete tipped the bellman,
and closing the door, threw his robe onto the bed, revealing tee shirt
and boxers, and fell face-forward onto the floor, catching himself with
his palms, and counting out one hundred push-ups in half-a-minute, at
which point he leapt to his feet and said, "Let's go for a walk."

Now I knew how he stayed so trim, and I had to admit he looked
rather dishy in his boxers and tee. Great legs. "Don't you want some coffee?" I asked.

"Sure. We'll take a walk and find someplace for breakfast."

Over bacon and eggs in a three-booth café, he asked, "Have you seen
*Evita*?"

"Yes."

"Is it good?"

"It's fabulous."

"Fabulous enough to see twice? I have tickets for tonight."

I welcomed the chance to see *Evita* again, and at the art-deco Prince Edward Theatre, where it premiered, would be a special treat.

Pete and I left the theater that night, humming the tunes from the show. "Have you ever sung any of those songs?" he asked.

"I've sung all of them, at least all of Eva's numbers."

"My favorite is that one, da-da-da-da, da-da-DA-da, he sang."

"'Don't Cry for Me, Argentina,'" I sang.

"Yeah, that's it," He looked at his watch. "I wonder if it's too late for room service." Then he said, "I bet they'd make some sandwiches for us."

"Are you tired?" I asked.

"Not at all, but we've got something to take care of." He smiled. "Have you forgotten why I invited you to come along on this trip?" He lifted his hand, hailing a cab. "Trivial Pursuit."

Room service accommodated with chicken sandwiches and a bottle of white burgundy, to fuel the long hours of heated battle ahead. The match lasted exactly fifteen minutes. That's how long it took him to beat me. I, who had never tasted Trivial-Pursuit defeat. Gunilla hadn't been kidding when she said this guy was brilliant.

Pete grinned like a cat who's just won the cream. "You lost the bet."

"What bet? We didn't make any bet."

"Then we should have."

We were sitting on my bed with the game board between us. He moved the board and scooted closer. "Time to pay up."

I flattened my palms against his chest. "I hope you're joking."

"I am." He raised his eyebrows. "Sort of." He picked up the bottle of burgundy and replenished my glass. "Have some more wine. You need to loosen up. I won fair and square, don't I deserve some sort of prize? A little snuggle, a kiss, something?"

I took a sip of wine, and another. "I guess a little snuggle wouldn't hurt."

Pete was willing to take it slowly. We were going to be in London for two weeks.

\* \* \*

What does one wear to a dinner party at a bona fide English country estate? On my first trip to England, when I was nineteen, I'd gone to some sort of banquet at a medieval castle, but that was a tourist thing, like a Renaissance festival, with actors playing king, queen and so on. According to Pete, our agenda for this evening was to dine at the home of a business acquaintance, who just happened to reside an hour's drive from London on an estate that had once been the family seat of Lord somebody or other. In the U.S. an LBD would surely suffice, but things were a bit more formal here. My grandmother had taken tea with Lord Carnarvon at his estate, so she might know, I checked the time difference, thinking to call her, but Pete waved it away.

"I'm wearing a suit and tie. Anything you put on will be fine. You always look great."

*Men.* I wasn't concerned about looking great, I was concerned about looking appropriate, or more precisely, I was concerned about looking inappropriate.

I wore a waisted black silk taffeta with long sleeves and ruffled hem, and I looked perfect. Although, if I expected an evening with Lord Carnarvon and the like, I couldn't have been further from the mark. As far as I could tell, everyone around this extremely grand table was middle-eastern, or perhaps North African. Pete had mentioned Morocco. If dinner with Lord and Lady Whoever had been beyond my experience, this was more so. The food was delicious, although it might have been sautéed camel brains for all I knew, and the conversation revolved completely around international business and politics, about which I knew nothing. But it hardly mattered that I spoke not a word, because neither did any of the other women present. I occupied myself with taking mental snapshots of my surroundings, which could be described as Highclere Castle decorated by Ali Baba and the Forty Thieves. One thing for certain, my grandmother would have been no help in advising me how to dress for this occasion, and on the ride back to London, I didn't ask any questions of Pete, because I wasn't sure I wanted to know.

The next day, Pete made a tempting offer.

"I'll be going to Morocco tomorrow for a couple of days. If you want to come along, we could make a side trip to Paris."

Although Paris was my other favorite European city, and I'd never been to Morocco, I'd gotten so into the Christmas spirit of merrie olde England, I didn't want to break the magic spell. Strolling the tinsel-trimmed streets during the past week, while enjoying the holiday tableaus of the store windows, I'd spotted oodles of gifts to put under the tree for family and friends, and I was eager to see the festive fabulousness on offer at Harrod's, which would take a whole day by itself, and which I doubted Pete would consider time well spent. Perhaps this short break was a good idea. In his absence, each day, I shopped, till I dropped into the garland and red-ribbon bedecked gilt and marble splendor of the Ritz Hotel's Palm Court for afternoon tea, before heading home to Durrants in the frosty dusk, for a cozy room-service dinner, accompanied by *The Man in the Brown Suit*, one of the few Agatha Christie novels I had yet to read.

By the time Pete returned, I was ready to welcome him with open arms, and for the rest of our stay we were as warm and companionable as a couple who has been together for much longer than we had been.

On our final afternoon in London, Pete put his arms around me and gazed into my eyes. "Wear your sexiest dress tonight. I'm taking you to Les Ambassadeurs."

Les Ambassadeurs, or Les A, as it was called by those in the know, was one of London's most exclusive private clubs, which I had only experienced through scenes of the Beatles' antics on the dance floor in *A Hard Day's Night*, and as the casino in *Dr. No*, where Sean Connery first spoke his signature line, "The name is Bond . . . James Bond."

I smiled at Pete and quoted Nora Charles from *The Thin Man*, "I've got a lulu." It was by Holly Harp, of course, a backless, bias-cut black matte jersey that floated along the curves of my body like a whisper on my bare skin. Nora Charles would be jealous. And so would Pussy Galore.

The movies didn't do justice to Les Ambassadeurs' Mayfair opulence, which began before we entered the building, an edifice to rival any royal palace, continuing into the marble hall and up the sweeping staircase to the library with its paneled walls carved by Florentine master Chevalier Rinaldo Barbetti, then passing James Bond's favorite gaming floor, and on into the dining room, where elegantly attired couples wined, dined and danced to the smooth music of a combo tucked discreetly onto a small corner stage.

The service and food were as impeccable as one would imagine, and not surprisingly, Pete took every opportunity to guide me onto the dance floor. Then between entrée and dessert, he said, "I wonder if the band knows that song from Evita, the one I like so much. What's it called?"

"Don't Cry for Me, Argentina?"

He got up, dropping his napkin in his chair, "I'm going to request it."

Coming back to the table, he nodded – success – and the pianist-band leader played a flourish, then spoke into the microphone, "Ladies and gentlemen please welcome to the stage, direct from *Hollywood*! Miss Victoria Hallman."

My mouth flew open, but Pete and the rest of the room were clapping politely, so there was nothing for me to do but take the bandstand and sing, "It won't be easy, you'll think it strange, if I try to explain how I feel . . . Don't cry for me, Argentina."

Imagine me getting a standing ovation in the same club where Princess Margaret danced the frug with Mick Jagger. It was a grande finale to the trip.

I hadn't been home fifteen minutes when the phone rang.

"Well?" Gunilla said.

"My heart's intact."

"Are you in love?"

"No, I'm just in serious *like*."

"Good," she said, "I've got somebody else I want you to meet."

\* \* \*

I had to admit she was batting a thousand in the looks department. Abe was a slender, handsome, fair-haired fellow, who also happened to be the president of a well-known stock brokerage. He'd chosen the Bistro Garden for our lunch date, which was an excellent choice, if you didn't consider that I was practically one of the family there, and was greeted as such.

When an acquaintance of Abe's stopped by our table, to pay compliments on his choice of lunch companion, Abe told him, "I thought I'd impress her by bringing her to a place where I'm well-known, but she one-upped me."

*So much for this one,* I thought. He didn't seem the kind who would tolerate being one-upped, so I wasn't surprised when, driving me back to my condo, he asked, "Are you also part of Wolfgang Puck's inner circle?"

I laughed. "No, but I did attend his cooking school."

"I guess that means that when you're not dining at the Bistro or Bistro Garden, you're at Spago."

"Surprisingly, I've only been to Spago once," I said.

"Really? Then why don't I make reservations for us tonight?" He picked up his car phone and began pressing numbers.

I shook my head and rubbed my stomach. "I ate too much lunch."

"Hang on," he said into the phone, then asked me, "Tomorrow night?"

"Um." I couldn't think of a reason not to go. I shrugged, "Okay."

He walked me to my door, and when I unlocked it, Neesh was there to greet us. Squatting, Abe ruffled his tiny topknot. "Hi there, little guy." While he continued to pet Neesh, his eyes swept my living room. "Nice place." He stood, gazing toward the glass doors to the balcony. "Bet you can see the Pacific from out there."

"That's what they tell me, but I've never managed to catch a glimpse."

"Too much smog in between," he strolled into the room, and stopped, looking around. "Hallman, hm," he narrowed his eyes, "Are you Jewish?"

"No. Why?"

He spread his arms, encompassing the room. "Not even one poinsettia?"

"Oh," I said, "I've been in London, haven't gotten around to any Christmas decorations, probably won't at this point."

"Yeah, it's a lot of trouble." He leaned and kissed my cheek. "I'll pick you up at seven tomorrow night."

The next afternoon, I was sitting in my doctor's waiting room, prior to a regular checkup, when the receptionist motioned me over, and handed me the phone, "It's your assistant."

Ellen said, "Hope I didn't interrupt, but Flower Fashions called, and they have a delivery for you that can't be left at the door, so if you're going to be held up for a while, I'll go over and take delivery."

"What a nice surprise," I said. "I haven't even seen the doctor yet, so go on over and see what shows up. Thanks."

Harry Findlay's Flower Fashions were Jim's florists, so this delivery would be an early Christmas gift or his way of welcoming me home from London.

Opening the door to my condo, a piney fragrance wafted into the hall, and stepping into the living room, I beheld a full-size Fraser Fir, dripping with crystal ornaments. Upon closer inspection, I saw that the ornaments were Baccarat. I also found an envelope tied to a branch, with red ribbon. The note inside said, *Your home is lovely, but it needed some Christmas cheer.* It was signed, *Abe.*

Impressive, to say the least.

The next week was a flurry of outings with Abe, from dinners at every A-list restaurant I did not frequent, to observing the Christmas Boat Parade at Marina del Rey, from the deck of his yacht. Then one night, driving me home, he grabbed my hand, "I've got a great idea. Don't you think we should take Gunilla and Jimmy to dinner as a way of saying thanks?"

L'Ermitage was the kind of discreet boutique hotel where you might see Elizabeth Taylor and Richard Burton having a romantic dinner *after* they had married others, as I had once seen them. L'Ermitage enjoyed a reputation as the perfect extended-stay luxury hotel for gentlemen who were in the midst of a divorce. Gentlemen such as Abe. On the night we invited Gunilla and Jimmy to join us, Abe had an early-evening business event to attend, and so suggested that for convenience, we meet in the hotel restaurant. I could ride with the McDonoughs and he could take me home afterward. I wasn't sure why he felt the need to make an excuse for dining at L'Ermitage. If it was good enough for Liz and Dick, it was good enough for us.

Even so, Abe arrived making excuses. Indicating his tuxedo, he explained, "Sorry, I didn't have time to change," and about the large sheaf of papers he placed on the table, "Guess I should have dropped these off in my suite."

We all smiled, thinking he might be about to make a quick run to his room to take the papers, which were somewhat in the way of our dining accoutrements, but instead he began to show us the contents of the thick sheaf, which were press clippings, all about him. One after the other, he brought them forth, keeping up a running commentary like a proud grandfather showing off pictures of his first grandchild. Even the waiter taking his cocktail order didn't stop the flow of clippings, and politely, we smiled and nodded as he showed each one, but when the waiter came back for our dinner orders and that didn't stop him, our smiles became raised eyebrows, and exchanged glances. We all breathed sighs of relief when dinner was finally over, only to have Abe suggest brandies in the piano bar, at which time, the McDonoughs made their excuses, and I agreed, saying, "Abe, after two parties in one night, I'm sure you're tired, and I am, too. Why don't I just catch a ride home with Gunilla and Jimmy?"

We beat a hasty retreat, with Gunilla and me falling over each other's apologies, hers for fixing me up with "this nut," and mine for the excruciating "thank you" dinner.

Jimmy laughed, "I've seen guys do just about everything to impress a girl, but that's the first time I've ever seen one bring his PR portfolio to the table."

As much as I liked the Christmas tree, that was it for Abe.

The next day, Jim called and invited me out for New Year's Eve. He suggested we celebrate at Touch, L.A.'s newest private dine-and-dance club, which struck me as a surprising and perhaps significant choice, since it was essentially an exclusive singles bar, where a recently-separated married man wouldn't usually want to be seen with his wife. Come to think of it, I might run into David, or any number of others I'd been avoiding.

As it turned out, although we did exchange New Year's toasts with several friends, nothing occurred to cause any embarrassment or discomfort, and at midnight when they played "Auld Lang Syne," Jim smooched me like a teenager, and came back for more.

He also came back to my place afterward. We began 1985 as every couple should, in bed, lost in love. But when the fireworks were over, instead of cuddling me, as he usually would, Jim sprang from the covers and got dressed. Then he leaned over and gave me a quick kiss, "I'll be back," and with that he was gone.

It happened so fast, I hardly had time to think, but when I finally did, what I thought was that he was not coming back. The evening had been a little too perfect. If this was his way of saying a final goodbye, he'd ended it sweetly. I hadn't shed any tears over our situation for several months, and for longer than that, I'd had no need of medication. I was even beginning to think that perhaps my friends were right, maybe I should relax and enjoy my good fortune, but lying there after he left that night, still wallowing in the holiday sentimentality of "Auld Lang Syne" and all that mush, I felt sad that he had gone.

Then I heard the front door open.

Jim stepped from the foyer into the bedroom, a cigarette dangling from his mouth, a hang-up bag slung over his shoulder and a small carry-on in his other hand. "I'll put these in the guest-room closet for now. I thought I'd start moving some of my things in, a little at a time."

I must have looked puzzled because he said, "Getting back together. Slowly."

"How slow?"

He shrugged. "By March, I'd say."

He went into the guest room, and listening to him hanging things in the closet, I tried to process what he'd said. In March, we would have been apart exactly one year. Apparently, when he'd said the separation would be temporary, he'd meant it. If I had believed him in the beginning, I'd have saved myself a lot of agony. But I hadn't believed him, and pulling myself out of those months of agony had taken more strength and determination than I'd known I had in me. So now, just like that, he was ready to move back in together, and here he came. But I wasn't turning cartwheels, as at one time, I would have thought. I wasn't sure how I felt. Funny that it had been almost exactly five years since he'd asked me to marry him. I smiled now, realizing that I was in a similar situation. Five years ago, when I had said "yes" to his proposal, I knew I had three months to change my mind, which was precisely where things stood now.

# Chapter 25

GEORGE BAUER WAS THE BEST-LOOKING guy in Tracy Roberts' "on-camera" class. In fact, George Bauer was the best-looking guy I'd ever seen. With his darkly wind-burned cheekbones and tawny sun-streaked hair, he looked like he'd just stepped out of a Ralph Lauren magazine spread, because he had. He was also the chiseled face of the new Ray-Ban campaign, but I preferred Jeff, the one paying his class tuition by operating the camera, the one who wore torn jeans and stretched tee-shirts and reminded me of Hugh Grant. Tracy Roberts would have her own ideas about all that.

"Victoria and George," called out Tracy's assistant Alan, and we stepped down from our places among the tiered classroom seats, each of us taking one of the scripts Alan handed us for the scene in which Tracy had paired us that night.

In this cold-reading class, there was no rehearsal. Parts were handed out as class began, and we all looked at our scripts for about five minutes before the camera rolled. Some of the actors would perform solo, some in pairs, in scenes that were snippets of a soap opera or sitcom, sometimes a movie.

When George and I heard our names, we bounded down onto the stage and seated ourselves in front of the camera. "Action," Tracy called, and we read our lines then went back to our seats with the rest of the class to watch our playback.

Murmurs of "wow" began among the class as soon as we came on-screen, and Tracy turned to Alan, stretching her eyes, "Chemistry," she stage-whispered.

Hearing all the hub-bub, George threw back his head, laughing in a way that surprised me because, the few times I'd seen him in class, he'd struck me as somber and serious.

271

Now came the critique. Tracy stood up, raking her fingers through her luxuriant red hair, and chuckling, "Well, well, you two," she opened her palms, "Class?" and our fellow actors began calling out "great," "magic," "chemistry."

Tracy nodded, laughing again, then she looked back and forth between George and me, "Have you two met before tonight?" I had been with Tracy for seven years, but George was new to the class. We both shook our heads.

George Bauer (1984)

"I want you to exchange phone numbers, and put together a scene for the Bernstein Awards."

After class, George and I stopped in the lobby to exchange numbers, then he walked me outside, where we discovered we'd parked next to each other. "Guess somebody's trying to tell us something," he laughed.

"I like your car," I said. It was a silver Audi Quattro sedan. "I once considered getting an Audi Fox." I pointed to his green license plate. "Are you from Colorado?"

"I'm from Philadelphia, but I lived in Aspen for several years, and still have a place there."

"I guess you ski, then."

"Oh, yeah."

"Is that where you get your tan?"

"It's unavoidable. If I'm not skiing, I'm swimming or riding a bike or running."

"I wish I were athletic."

He grinned, "Looks like whatever you're doing is working okay."

"I wasn't fishing," I said, "but thanks." I reached to open my car door. "Will I see you in Scene Study class on Tuesday?"

"Yeah, but you know what, I'm going to a dinner party Saturday night. I'd love to take you if you're not busy."

Busy or not, I was going.

George said the dinner would be "very casual, jeans if you want," but to be on the safe side, I wore navy cotton pants and a cream silk pullover. When he arrived in khakis and a navy pullover, almost a "negative" of my outfit, we looked each other up and down and started laughing. "Somebody is definitely trying to tell us something."

The party was at the condo of his friends, Joni and Jerry, who lived at Marina del Rey. George said he and Jerry were sailing buddies. *This guy didn't just step out of a Ralph Lauren ad*, I thought, *he lives in one*, and as if to prove the point, he then mentioned that he had plans for a heli-skiing trip the following week. When I didn't respond, he glanced at me from the corner of his eye, and said, "But I'm thinking about canceling it."

"What is heli-skiing?" I asked.

"It's off-trail skiing in places you can only get to by helicopter."

"Sounds exciting. And dangerous."

"Do you ski?"

I thought back to the trip to Tahoe, and my experience in the celebrity snow games, when I assumed I could slalom. "No, I do not ski."

"We'll have to do something about that," he said.

I immediately felt comfortable with George's friends, who were a well-heeled, but unpretentious group, and our hosts, bubbly brunette Joni and her husband Jerry, an attractive couple in their mid-forties, who went out of their way to make me welcome, assisted by George's perfect manners, always making sure I was part of the conversation, and never straying far from my side.

At the end of the evening, when he walked me to my door, he deftly spared me the awkward decision of whether to ask him in for a nightcap, by giving me an easy kiss and saying, "We'll talk between now and class on Tuesday."

My phone rang the next afternoon, with George telling me how much he'd enjoyed our evening together. "When I called Joni today to thank her, all she could talk about was how much they liked you, and I said, 'Joni, you know what? I like Victoria, too. I like her more than anybody I've met in a long time.'"

"*How* long?" I asked.

He laughed so hard he had to hold the phone away from his mouth. "Let me put it another way, I can't remember the last time I met anyone I like as much as I like you."

"The feeling is mutual," I agreed.

Class on Tuesday night was a departure from the norm, in that Tracy had gathered a group of directors, from which the Bernstein Awards participants could select, so it was natural that George and I would sit together, touching shoulders to comment quietly after each director gave his presentation.

Leaving class, George said, "Want to go grab a bite and discuss?"

Since he lived in Pacific Palisades and I lived in Bel Air, we met at Old World Restaurant in Westwood Village, which was on the way from Tracy's Beverly Hills Studio to both of our homes.

We slid into a booth against the wall and began a discussion, which came to a quick conclusion when we both expressed a preference for a young director from New York City who had shaggy dark hair, and spoke about how much he genuinely liked actors: *they wear cool old clothes, they drink brown liquor, they smoke unfiltered cigarettes . . .* none of which described George or me, since I had stopped smoking several years before and neither of us drank more than the occasional glass of wine, but while we might not match his actor stereotype, we thought Arthur was the director who best fit us.

Once again, Tracy Roberts would have her own ideas about that.

\* \* \*

"*Hedda Gabler.*"

Seated side-by-side on the studio couch in Arthur's small, dark apartment, we both stared at him, speechless. *Ibsen?*

Arthur pointed at me, "I saw you, Victoria, playing Regina in Lillian Hellman's *Another Part of the Forest*, and I thought; *what is that girl doing on Hee Haw?*" He jumped to his feet and threw his hands in the air. "Let's do something that shows your range."

He paced for a few seconds. "And you!" he whirled and pointed at George. "If you don't stretch, you'll spend the rest of your life doing aftershave commercials."

\* \* \*

"Arthur could not be more wrong!"

Tracy had called George and me into her office for an afternoon conference, but she was too agitated to sit behind her desk. In her fitted jacket with jeans tucked into tall boots, she paced back and forth like a lion tamer ready to crack the whip, while George and I sat on the sofa, watching and waiting for her to strike.

She whirled, extending her hands towards us. "To hide two actors as gorgeous as you, in all that funereal period costume," She pulled at her hair and made an anguished face, "It's just *wrroong!*" Her eyes closed, and her fists clinched, as if trying to regain composure, then she sat down in her desk chair, gazing at us with a mournful look.

George said, "I guess we could do something else."

Tracy clasped her hands on her desk, in a pleading posture. "Anything would be better than *Hedda Gabler.*"

Arthur disagreed. If we didn't want to take his direction, then we could choose another director, he said, and so, the whole thing devolved into a mess, which didn't matter much, because George and I were too giddy with discovering each other to care about anything else, and the actors Arthur ended up directing won the Bernstein Award that year.

Meanwhile, George and I were spending more and more time together and Jim was growing more and more irritated that I was seldom available. Something had to give. Surprisingly, the first something was

Pete O'Donnell, who called one afternoon in late January to say that he was going to be in L.A and wanted to see me. How about if we made a return visit to Tony Roma's and tried the famous ribs this time? After that marvelous treat of a trip to London, how could I refuse?

I wouldn't have believed that George's stone-carved jaw could become any stonier, but it did. "I haven't gone out with anyone else since my first date with you. I even broke several dates that I'd already made."

We were sitting opposite each other in the beige velvet wing chairs in my living room. "I'm sorry you're upset," I said. "We've never discussed being exclusive."

His jaw worked. "Some things don't need to be said. At least that's what I thought. Maybe you don't feel as strongly as I do."

"No," I said, "I do feel the same. I'll tell Pete that tonight, and I'll tell everyone else, too."

He reached and grabbed my hand, squeezing tightly. "From now on, it'll be just us."

I nodded, "Just us."

We went from spending every waking hour together to every hour, waking and sleeping. Some nights I stayed at his place, some nights he stayed at mine. One morning we were in my kitchen, making breakfast, George was leaning against the counter, sipping hot tea. "I feel so weird wearing your husband's robe."

Jim had continued putting things in the closet – as he had said was his intention – and on a chilly morning I saw no reason not to offer his terrycloth bathrobe to George. But suddenly it struck me, "Does it bother you that I'm married?"

He sputtered, choking on his sip of tea. "What would you think?"

"Well, we've been separated for almost a year, and I'm not seeing him anymore, so…"

His amber eyes narrowed.

I shrugged, "I'll get a divorce."

"Good," he said.

I called Jim that afternoon. "We need to talk."

He arrived in the same grumpy mood he'd been in since my relationship with George had made me unavailable. Settling in on the club chair and ottoman that had always been his spot to relax, he scooped Neesh onto his lap, and Neesh snuggled in, like old times.

"I think we should get a divorce," I said.

He lit a cigarette before saying. "I don't want a divorce."

"I do."

He looked at me earnestly, "I love you, Vicki, I've never stopped."

When I didn't reply, he frowned and said, "What made you decide this, all of a sudden?"

"It's not sudden. We've been apart for almost a year."

He stroked Neesh's head, staring into space, thinking. Then he said, "What do you want?"

"A divorce."

"No, I mean money. Stuff."

"The only thing I want is Twin Oaks. I mean, why would you need a house near my family?"

He gave me a hard look. "Because they're my family, too."

That hurt, because I knew it was true. Jim loved me, but he also loved my family, my friends. He loved the whole package.

"Twin Oaks is already yours," he said, "I gifted it to you several years back. Don't you remember? I'll have to pay you some money, too. That's just how it works."

I bit my tongue to keep from saying, *you should know*. Instead, I answered, "Just enough to give me time to get my finances together, figure out some sort of budget. I've become very unaccustomed to that, so it may take a few months."

"Okay," he snuffed out his cigarette, set Neesh on the floor, and got up from his chair, "No need for you to get an attorney. I'll have Bernie draw up the papers," meaning Bernie Silbert, brother of Harvey, both of whom were the trustees Jim's father had left in charge of his fortune. "I'll let you know when everything is ready to sign." He bent down to give me a kiss on the forehead. "Take care of yourself."

Buck was glad to hear it, although he wasn't so sure I didn't need my own attorney. "We'll see how that goes," he said.

The next week, Gunilla called, "Don't you think it's time we met *him*?"

Her brother and sister-in-law, Dick and Sonya McDonough, were visiting from Boston, and Gunilla and Jimmy were having a dinner party that also included Bruce and Linda Thompson Jenner. This would be George's big debut with my "sister" Honeys and their husbands.

As soon as we finished dessert in Gunilla's charming cottagey dining room, Linda pulled me into the powder room. "You have *got* to marry this gorgeous guy and make beautiful babies."

Babies must have been on her mind, because during dinner, Bruce had brought up the subject of having more, and Linda rolled her eyes, "Oh, yes, let's have as many as possible to prove your masculinity."

Linda had a penchant for snarky comments, but it was the first time I'd heard her direct one at Bruce, and it wasn't long after, that she called me one morning, and asked if I'd go to a party with her that night.

*   *   *

It was a beautiful day at the Jenners' rustic Malibu ranch, with the swimming pool sparkling in the sunshine, like a poster for California tourism, but where were the usual kids, dogs, friends and assistants splashing in the water and bronzing on the chaise longues? Linda's white Porsche was the only car parked around back. I pulled up and went in through the side door, expecting two fair-haired boys to come charging down the staircase, but neither Brandon nor Brody appeared.

"I'll be right there, Victoria." Linda called from her bedroom, upstairs.

I sat down at the dining table, thumbing through the latest issue of *People*. Linda was notorious for her tardiness, but once she arrived, her charm made you forget the wait. Dressed in a fluttery silk skirt and top that matched her bronze hair and skin, she floated into the room, stooping to give me a hug. "Hey, honey, you want something to drink?"

"No, thanks," I said, "I'm fine.

Ignoring my answer, she swayed into the kitchen, poured two glasses of ice water and brought them to the table. "Here you go, we're not in a rush to get to the party."

"Where are the boys?" I asked.

She waved a hand. "They'll be back." Linda had a way of replying without answering the question.

"Victoria," she sat down and laced her fingers on top of the table, "we really are going to a party tonight, but before we do, there's something I want to tell you."

Her tone gave me goosebumps.

"Bruce and I are separated, we're divorcing."

# Chapter 26

I DIDN'T REALIZE I was crying until Linda dabbed my cheek with a paper napkin.

"I am so sorry," I said.

"I am, too. Bruce was everything I ever wanted," her voice broke. She took a sip of water. "There are just some things that make it impossible for me to… I wish I could explain, but I can't."

The kitchen phone rang. "Hey, Bruce," Linda gave me a smile, then said to him, "Little Victoria's here. She cried when I told her. Isn't that sweet?"

Allowing her privacy, I walked into the living area and stood in the middle of the room, which was filled with family photos, a gallery of Linda's life, during the time I'd known her. In those six years, we'd both gone from single girls, to women in love, to blissful brides, to happy homemakers. Now here we were single again, and I wasn't sure whether we'd failed or prevailed.

Linda walked into the living room. "Ready to go?"

* * *

Winter turned to spring with George and me planning our future together, and even though Bernie was taking his own sweet time with the divorce papers, we put the cart before the horse, and went on several "honeymoons," first to Catalina Island, whale-watching on the ferry over, then living the life of Edwardian elegance at the Wrigley Mansion, by day, skinny-dipping in the moonlit surf, by night, with beach a recurring theme, whether near, in Malibu, where we had beach picnics and made love in hidden coves, or far, in Cabo San Lucas, for snorkeling and candlelit lobster-shack dinners by the ocean, or the Gulf beach of my childhood memories in the Florida Panhandle, Redneck Riviera, as

Victoria and George Bauer in Cabo San Lucas (1985)

George called it. Then he took me to his other home, Aspen, and I finally learned to snow-ski, taught with loving patience by the "best skier ever to come down the mountain," as the Aspenites made sure to tell me.

With all this "honeymooning," it seemed appropriate that we meet each other's folks, which we accomplished with little effort, since George's beautiful Austrian mother resided in an assisted-living high-rise in Santa Monica, and my annual Easter trip to Alabama was coming up.

My family eyed George with undisguised skepticism. Since Jim and I had continued visiting on holidays, our separation never became reality for them, and George was the "other man" breaking up my marriage, which was hard for me to argue, since technically it was true. Gathered round the table for Easter Sunday dinner at our old-south family home, my grand-mother Sue looked George in the eye and declared, "I still love Jim."

As soon as we returned to L.A., I called Bernie Silbert to find out what was holding up the divorce.

"You and Jim are *divorcing?*" Not only had Jim not mentioned di-vorce to him, he said that Jim behaved as if everything between us was as perfect as the day we married.

My next call was to Buck.

"Yeah, I figured something like that," he said. "Don't worry. I'll get you an attorney, same one who got me out of that mess with Jana Jae."

Let the games begin.

One of the things Jim had told me on that day when he called me at Twin Oaks to tell me he'd moved out was that if I tried to get a divorce, I wouldn't be able to find him to serve him with the papers. Apparently, he'd meant every word he said. We had to hire a detective and a process server, and even then, it took some time. I felt like I needed some of Pete O'Donnell's CIA pals.

One afternoon, George and I decided to go along for the ride with the process server, our mission to corner Jim at the Bistro Garden. We watched from a side street as he entered the restaurant, and the process server got out of the car to follow him in.

Five minutes later, she returned. "He ran out the back door."

This was but one in so many near misses that a lesser woman would have given up, but as Buck said, I was strong as whit-leather, so we kept at it, until finally she trapped him at his mother's house. That night, George and I celebrated with champagne. Yippee, papers served at last!

The next day, Jim cut off all my funds.

"He's trying to starve you into submission," said my attorney, "We'll have to get a court order."

Thank God, my stature at *Hee Haw* was on the rise. The Honeys, glad to see me up from the depths of my separation from Jim, swooned over George when I took him with me to Nashville for the June taping session, and with my Miss Honeydew character gaining a following, there was talk of giving me an additional role on the show. Then one day, back in L.A., Sam called and said, I think it's time you did a solo on *Hee Haw*. Why don't you put together some ideas for a song and come into the office and we'll discuss?

As so often happens, if my career was up, my personal life was down, which, in this case, meant that George's career was down, one of the pitfalls of actors becoming romantically involved. They were casting a new show called L.A Law, and George got one of the lead roles, playing a slick and sleazy lawyer named Arnold Becker. We were over the moon. Then he lost the role to Corbin Bernsen. Depths of despair. Then came a small role on a soap opera that he thought would be enlarged, but instead was phased out, and on and on it went, until one day, he mentioned moving to New York. "Not really moving," he said, "Just going for a while to check out opportunities. I could stay at my family's beach house in Ocean City. You could come."

I understood how he felt. The L.A. vibe was changing. It no longer seemed happy and hopeful, more like the metaphorical Boulevard of Broken Dreams.

*    *    *

The song Sam chose as my *Hee Haw* solo debut was "Close Enough for Me," the ballad that I had produced on myself in that session Jim financed when we became engaged. This was the first time any of the cast or crew had heard me sing anything other than backing vocals for Buck. Their response was gratifying to say the least.

After finishing the song, as I was dressing to leave the studio, one of the office staff knocked on the door, summoning me to the phone. Raves about my solo had reached the producers of *Nashville Now*, the *Tonight Show* of CMT, and they wanted me to do a repeat performance on the show that night.

The *Nashville Now* studio was across the parking lot from the studio where we taped *Hee Haw*, which was convenient since we shared hair and makeup stylists, as well as musicians in our "house" bands, who could finish a day's work on our set, then take the five-minute walk to *Nashville Now's* live nighttime broadcast. So, there was no need to guess how the *Nashville Now* talent coordinator heard about my solo stint only an hour or so after I'd done it, and as soon as I stepped into the makeup room to get a retouch for my second solo of the day, it was obvious who had done most of the bragging about their new talent discovery among the *Hee Haw* Honeys. *Our* hairstylist Gwen and makeup artist Anita were beaming with pride, and began clucking over me like mother hens making sure I'd never looked better in my life.

Come to find out, I would be replacing a "no show" artist, who'd been slated to do three songs. *Three!* No problem, especially since I'd be working with the *Hee Haw* Band musicians, who knew my vocal range almost as well as they knew their own instruments, and picking out a couple more songs was as easy as selecting "When Will I be Loved" and "Crazy" from the set list that I'd been using for seven years opening live shows for Buck. To add even more family atmosphere, *Nashville Now's* host, Ralph Emery, was a former Disc Jockey who frequently hung out backstage at *Hee Haw*, shooting the breeze with his longtime music-biz buddies, and

Victoria Hallman's *Hee Haw* performance of her record "Next Time I Marry," with the Nashville Edition. L-R: Wendy Suits, Joe Babcock, Dolores Edgins, Hurshel Wiginton, and Victoria's sister Robin Hallman Broadhead in background (1987)

to top it off, the other guest star on the *Nashville Now* conversation sofa that night, would be Hervé Villechaize, Tattoo from *Fantasy Island*, who had also done a guest-star stint on *Hee Haw* earlier that day. So much switching and sharing might have been head-spinning, had I not been used to it, and had it not been for another piece of sage advice from Jack McFadden when I first came to Music City.

"Jesse Rose," he'd said, "while you're in Nashville, don't do anything that you don't want everybody in town to know, because country music is an incestuous little family."

My first of many appearances on *Nashville Now* was an example of country-music nepotism at its best.

Towards the end of each show, Ralph Emery always took a few live phone calls from viewers, and that night one of them said that he thought my version of "Crazy" was the best he'd ever heard. I wasn't so sure I agreed with him, considering the original by Patsy Cline, but his compliment would be one I'd never forget.

Next morning, the *Hee Haw* set was abuzz with word of my "overnight" success, and almost as soon as I stepped into the dressing room, there was a knock at the door, with an important call for me in the Green Room.

When I picked up the phone, Jack McFadden said, "Why didn't you tell me you were doing *Nashville Now* last night?"

"I didn't know it myself. I was a last-minute replacement."

"Okay, well. I want you to sit still and listen carefully, because I've got something important to tell you."

"I'm sitting still, and I'm listening," I promised.

"I watch every episode of *Nashville Now*," he said, "and I always tape it, just in case I don't get to watch. Last night, was one of those times, but right about what must have been midway through your first song, I got a phone call from a record producer named Larry Rogers.

"Larry said, 'Jack, I don't know who this girl is that's singing on Nashville Now tonight. but I do know she's a star, and Ralph Emery said something about her being on *Hee Haw*, so I thought you might be able to help me find her, because if she's not signed, I want to produce her.'"

Jack paused to let the importance of what he'd said travel from my ear to my brain then he continued, "So I told him, 'Larry, my man, I'm pretty sure I know who that girl is, and I'll have her in your studio tomorrow afternoon.'"

"Wow."

"Yes. Larry is a very good producer. Unfortunately, I've got to leave for California in a few minutes, so I can't go with you, but I'll have a car there to pick you up when you get through taping today, and you'll go straight to Larry's studio on Music Row."

*  *  *

The driver took a circuitous route that I had never traveled. Or had I? Some landmark or other must have reminded me of my first trip to Nashville, when I was six-years-old and Kenneth Shackleford brought me to the Disc Jockey Convention to promote the little Christmas record I'd cut. Suddenly, everything seemed eerily familiar.

Studio 19 was a square, beige brick building on 19th Avenue. A stunning black-eyed brunette greeted me at the reception desk. "Hi, Victoria, I'm Marilyn, Larry's wife." She got up from her chair, and motioned, "Follow me."

Larry Rogers was a cute young guy with spiky blond hair, dressed in a tee shirt and jeans a bit more faded and not nearly as tight as the ones I had on. Behind his desk, the wall was covered with awards and gold records. I particularly noticed, "Who's Cheatin' Who" and "Men," by Charly McClain, and "Louisiana Saturday Night," by Mel McDaniel, because those were recent hits, which answered the all-important question: *What have you done lately?*

Marilyn smiled and exited, closing the door, and Larry came around his desk to shake my hand. "Have a seat."

Once I'd made myself comfortable on the sofa, he went and settled into his desk chair with his hands behind his head. "I can't believe you're not already signed with somebody," he said.

I laughed, "Neither can I," although I was already thinking this meeting was meant to be.

Larry and I talked as easily as old friends catching up after a long time apart, comparing notes about our escapades in the "biz", how and why we wound up where we were, and what we hoped to accomplish in the future, which included a hit record for me, neither of us doubting that we'd achieve it, as ultimately, we did.

Leaving the studio that night, beyond the car window, dusk was falling, the skyline twinkling like a city lit with magic, and it struck me that while Nashville's star was rising, L.A. was losing its luster. Never had I thought of moving here, now suddenly, the possibility seemed real.

The thought left me breathless; there was much to consider.

Or was there? Hadn't George recently mentioned moving to New York, and hadn't Buck all but retired? This was not about Buck or George or Jim, or anyone else at all. This was about me, and wasn't it about time?

Gazing at the Nashville skyline, I knew I had come full circle.

# Victoria Hallman
## Writer/Co-author

BY THE TIME she joined Buck Owens' Buckaroos and landed a ten-year stint as *Hee Haw's* Miss Honeydew, Victoria Hallman was a show-biz veteran, whose career began at age six in recording and TV studios with grown-ups like Roy Orbison, Merv Griffin and Steve Allen, before continuing into her teens as the opening act for a list of legends from Jerry Lee Lewis to Bob Hope, leading to a successful career as a recording artist, with two records in the national charts, and performances for presidents Richard Nixon and Bill Clinton.

In 1999, Victoria began a career as a freelance writer-editor, becoming contributing editor for the national publication *flower magazine* (2008-2013), and in January 2016, as Nashville Editor for the Alabama Music Office, with her blog "The Alabama-Nashville Connection" featured on their website. She is a member of The Authors Guild and Screen Actors Guild.

DIANA GOODMAN

# Diana Goodman
## Co-author

**BEFORE SIGNING** a five-year contract with *Hee Haw*, Diana Goodman gained fame as Miss Georgia USA, an NFL Cheerleader for the Atlanta Falcons, and the celebrity girlfriend of Elvis Presley.

Having lost her beloved husband, Roger McDaniel, in February 2017, Diana finds fulfillment in her role as mother and grandmother to the family they created together.

Made in the USA
Columbia, SC
20 May 2020